IMMIGRATION

Opposing Viewpoints®

Other Books of Related Interest in the Opposing Viewpoints Series:

American Values
America's Future
Central America
The Environmental Crisis
The Homeless
Latin America and U.S. Foreign Policy
Poverty
Social Justice
The Third World
The Vietnam War

Additional Books in the Opposing Viewpoints Series:

Abortion
AIDS
American Foreign Policy
American Government
America's Elections
America's Prisons
Animal Rights
Biomedical Ethics
Censorship
Chemical Dependency
China
Civil Liberties
Constructing a Life Philosophy
Crime and Criminals
Criminal Justice
Death and Dying
The Death Penalty
Drug Abuse
Eastern Europe
Economics in America
The Elderly
Euthanasia
Genetic Engineering
The Health Crisis
Israel
Japan
Male/Female Roles
The Mass Media
The Middle East
Nuclear War
The Political Spectrum
Problems of Africa
Religion in America
Science & Religion
Sexual Values
The Soviet Union
The Superpowers: A New Detente
Teenage Sexuality
Terrorism
Violence in America
War and Human Nature
War on Drugs

IMMIGRATION

Opposing Viewpoints®

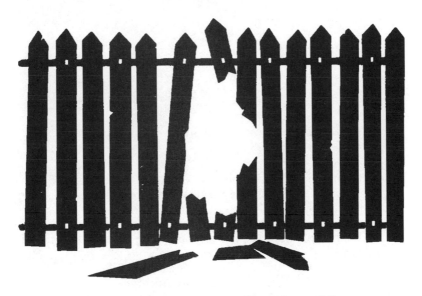

David L. Bender & Bruno Leone, *Series Editors*

William Dudley, *Book Editor*

OPPOSING VIEWPOINTS SERIES ®

Greenhaven Press, Inc.   PO Box 289009   San Diego, CA 92198-0009

Library of Congress Cataloging-in-Publication Data

Immigration : opposing viewpoints / William Dudley, book editor.
 p. cm. — (Opposing viewpoints series)
 Includes bibliographical references and index.
 Summary: Prominent observers offer differing views on the so-cial, political, and legal impact of continuing immigration to the United States.
 ISBN 0-89908-485-0 (lib.). — ISBN 0-89908-460-5 (pap.)
 1. United States—Emigration and immigration. 2. United States—Emigration and immigration—Government policy.
[1. United States—Emigration and immigration.] I. Dudley, William, 1964–   .   II. Series : Opposing viewpoints series (Unnumbered)
JV6455.5.I66   1990
325.73—dc20
                                                         90-13854

"Congress shall make no law . . .
abridging the freedom of speech,
or of the press."

First Amendment to the U.S. Constitution

The basic foundation of our democracy is the first amendment guarantee of freedom of expression. The Opposing Viewpoints Series is dedicated to the concept of this basic freedom and the idea that it is more important to practice it than to enshrine it.

Contents

Page

Why Consider Opposing Viewpoints?   9
Introduction   13

Chapter 1: Historical Debate: Should Immigration
          Be Restricted?
  Chapter Preface   16
  1. America Should Welcome Immigration (1845)   17
     Thomas L. Nichols
  2. America Should Discourage Immigration (1849)   25
     Garrett Davis
  3. Restrictions on Immigration Are Necessary (1913) 31
     Frank Julian Warne
  4. Restrictions on Immigration Are Unnecessary (1912) 39
     Peter Roberts
  5. National Origins Quotas Should Be Abolished (1963) 47
     John F. Kennedy
  6. National Origins Quotas Should Be Retained (1964) 54
     Marion Moncure Duncan
  A Critical Thinking Activity: 62
     Evaluating Sources of Information

Chapter 2: How Do Immigrants Affect America?
  Chapter Preface   65
  1. Immigrants Threaten American Culture   66
     Thomas Fleming
  2. Immigrants Do Not Threaten American Culture   74
     James Fallows
  3. Immigrants Help the U.S. Economy   80
     Julian L. Simon
  4. Immigrants Harm the U.S. Economy   85
     Garrett Hardin
  5. Illegal Immigrants Cause Crime   90
     Palmer Stacy & Wayne Lutton
  6. Illegal Immigrants Are Victims of Crime   96
     Roberto Martínez
  A Critical Thinking Activity: 100
     Recognizing Stereotypes

Periodical Bibliography 102

Chapter 3: How Should U.S. Immigration Policy Be Reformed?

Chapter Preface 104

1. The U.S. Should Limit Immigration 105
   Richard D. Lamm

2. The U.S. Should Encourage Immigration 113
   Ben J. Wattenberg & Karl Zinsmeister

3. The U.S. Should Admit Immigrants on the Basis 121
   of Job Skills
   Barry R. Chiswick

4. The U.S. Should Admit Immigrants on the Basis 129
   of Family Ties
   Arthur C. Helton

5. The U.S. Should Accept More Refugees 137
   Stephen Moore

6. The U.S. Should Not Accept More Refugees 145
   Gerda Bikales

A Critical Thinking Activity: 152
   Distinguishing Between Fact and Opinion

Periodical Bibliography 154

Chapter 4: How Should the U.S. Respond to Illegal Immigration?

Chapter Preface 156

1. Illegal Immigration Is a Crisis 157
   William F. Jasper

2. Illegal Immigration Is Not a Crisis 165
   Pete Hamill

3. Illegal Immigration Should Be Stopped 171
   Edward Abbey

4. Illegal Immigration Should Be Legalized 176
   Alan W. Bock

5. Employers Who Hire Illegal Immigrants Should 182
   Be Punished
   Daniel A. Stein

6. Punishing Employers of Illegal Immigrants Is 188
   Counterproductive
   Aurora Camacho de Schmidt

A Critical Thinking Activity: 194
   Recognizing Statements That Are Provable

Periodical Bibliography   196

Chapter 5: What Policies Would Help Immigrants Adapt to the U.S.?

Chapter Preface   198
1. Bilingual Education Helps Immigrants   199
   National Coalition of Advocates for Students
2. Bilingual Education Hurts Immigrants   207
   Rosalie Pedalino Porter
3. Making English the Official Language Would   214
   Help Immigrants
   S.I. Hayakawa
4. Making English the Official Language Would   221
   Hurt Immigrants
   Arturo Madrid
5. Third World Immigrants Are Adapting to the U.S.   226
   National Council of La Raza
6. Third World Immigrants Cannot Adapt to the U.S.   234
   Robert N. Hopkins
A Critical Thinking Activity: 242
   Understanding Words in Context
Periodical Bibliography   244

Chronology of Immigration   245
Organizations to Contact   250
Bibliography of Books   255
Index   258

Why Consider Opposing Viewpoints?

"It is better to debate a question without settling it than to settle a question without debating it."

Joseph Joubert (1754-1824)

The Importance of Examining Opposing Viewpoints

The purpose of the Opposing Viewpoints Series, and this book in particular, is to present balanced, and often difficult to find, opposing points of view on complex and sensitive issues.

Probably the best way to become informed is to analyze the positions of those who are regarded as experts and well studied on issues. It is important to consider every variety of opinion in an attempt to determine the truth. Opinions from the mainstream of society should be examined. But also important are opinions that are considered radical, reactionary, or minority as well as those stigmatized by some other uncomplimentary label. An important lesson of history is the eventual acceptance of many unpopular and even despised opinions. The ideas of Socrates, Jesus, and Galileo are good examples of this.

Readers will approach this book with their own opinions on the issues debated within it. However, to have a good grasp of one's own viewpoint, it is necessary to understand the arguments of those with whom one disagrees. It can be said that those who do not completely understand their adversary's point of view do not fully understand their own.

A persuasive case for considering opposing viewpoints has been presented by John Stuart Mill in his work *On Liberty*. When examining controversial issues it may be helpful to reflect on this suggestion:

The only way in which a human being can make some approach to knowing the whole of a subject, is by hearing what can be said about it by persons of every variety of opinion, and studying all modes in which it can be looked at by every character of mind. No wise man ever acquired his wisdom in any mode but this.

Analyzing Sources of Information

The Opposing Viewpoints Series includes diverse materials taken from magazines, journals, books, and newspapers, as well as statements and position papers from a wide range of individuals, organizations, and governments. This broad spectrum of sources helps to develop patterns of thinking which are open to the consideration of a variety of opinions.

Pitfalls to Avoid

A pitfall to avoid in considering opposing points of view is that of regarding one's own opinion as being common sense and the most rational stance, and the point of view of others as being only opinion and naturally wrong. It may be that another's opinion is correct and one's own is in error.

Another pitfall to avoid is that of closing one's mind to the opinions of those with whom one disagrees. The best way to approach a dialogue is to make one's primary purpose that of understanding the mind and arguments of the other person and not that of enlightening him or her with one's own solutions. More can be learned by listening than speaking.

It is my hope that after reading this book the reader will have a deeper understanding of the issues debated and will appreciate the complexity of even seemingly simple issues on which good and honest people disagree. This awareness is particularly important in a democratic society such as ours where people enter into public debate to determine the common good. Those with whom one disagrees should not necessarily be regarded as enemies, but perhaps simply as people who suggest different paths to a common goal.

Developing Basic Reading and Thinking Skills

In this book, carefully edited opposing viewpoints are purposely placed back to back to create a running debate; each viewpoint is preceded by a short quotation that best expresses the author's main argument. This format instantly plunges the reader into the midst of a controversial issue and greatly aids that reader in mastering the basic skill of recognizing an author's point of view.

A number of basic skills for critical thinking are practiced in the activities that appear throughout the books in the series. Some of the skills are:

Evaluating Sources of Information. The ability to choose from among alternative sources the most reliable and accurate source in relation to a given subject.

Separating Fact from Opinion. The ability to make the basic distinction between factual statements (those that can be demonstrated or verified empirically) and statements of opinion (those that are beliefs or attitudes that cannot be proved).

Identifying Stereotypes. The ability to identify oversimplified, exaggerated descriptions (favorable or unfavorable) about people and insulting statements about racial, religious, or national groups, based upon misinformation or lack of information.

Recognizing Ethnocentrism. The ability to recognize attitudes or opinions that express the view that one's own race, culture, or group is inherently superior, or those attitudes that judge another culture or group in terms of one's own.

It is important to consider opposing viewpoints and equally important to be able to critically analyze those viewpoints. The activities in this book are designed to help the reader master these thinking skills. Statements are taken from the book's viewpoints and the reader is asked to analyze them. This technique aids the reader in developing skills that not only can be applied to the viewpoints in this book, but also to situations where opinionated spokespersons comment on controversial issues. Although the activities are helpful to the solitary reader, they are most useful when the reader can benefit from the interaction of group discussion.

Using this book and others in the series should help readers develop basic reading and thinking skills. These skills should improve the reader's ability to understand what is read. Readers should be better able to separate fact from opinion, substance from rhetoric, and become better consumers of information in our media-centered culture.

This volume of the Opposing Viewpoints Series does not advocate a particular point of view. Quite the contrary! The very nature of the book leaves it to the reader to formulate the opinions he or she finds most suitable. My purpose as publisher is to see that this is made possible by offering a wide range of viewpoints that are fairly presented.

David L. Bender
Publisher

Introduction

"America is a nation of immigrants, but Americans have never really liked immigration."

Chuck Lane, *The New Republic*,
April 1, 1985.

Between 1820, when the U.S. began keeping count, and 1987, over fifty-four million people left their former homes and migrated to the U.S. With the arguable exception of Native Americans and African-American descendants of slaves, everyone in the U.S. today is an immigrant or is descended from immigrants. Today the United States takes in more immigrants than all of the other world's nations combined.

Despite these facts, Americans have both celebrated and feared immigration. On the one hand, many Americans can recall with pride their immigrant forebears. Many others bear a profound respect for the Statue of Liberty's famous lines, "Give me your tired, your poor, your huddled masses yearning to breathe free." On the other hand, many Americans have a nagging fear of the world's huddled masses, now billions strong, many of whom are jostling to become American residents. Immigration analyst Chuck Lane writes, "While there were many Americans who wanted to heed the Statue of Liberty's poetic injunction to open a 'Golden Door' to immigrants, there were even more who wanted to lock the 'Golden Door' and throw away the key."

For supporters, immigration is nothing less than the continuing reenactment of the American dream. "For each new immigrant," writes journalist William Broyles Jr., "the dream is born again, fresh and powerful. 'Come,' it says, 'no matter who you are, and be one of us. Come and be free.'" The American dream, in this view, is the vision all immigrants share of a better life in the U.S. John F. Kennedy argued that immigration thus becomes essential to defining what America is:

> This was the secret of America: a nation of people with the fresh memory of old traditions who dared to explore new frontiers, people eager to build lives for themselves in a spacious society that did not restrict their freedom of choice and action.

Yet for some people immigration is an American nightmare.

13

Many Americans past and present have reacted to immigrants with fear: fear of unemployment and lower standards of living, fear of different religions and races, fear that immigration was spoiling the U.S. for those already here. People who oppose immigration often believe that it threatens the very survival of America as we know it. For example, *The Immigration Time Bomb* is the title of not one but two recent books on immigration. Newspaper headlines warn of an "alien invasion." To some Americans, immigration took on the airs of a national security crisis in 1983 when President Ronald Reagan said, "This country has lost control of its own borders, and no country can sustain that kind of position."

While most Americans hold opinions somewhere between these two extremes, immigration remains a controversial and profound issue that deserves careful thought. *Immigration: Opposing Viewpoints* probes the following questions: Historical Debate: Should Immigration Be Restricted? How Do Immigrants Affect America? How Should U.S. Immigration Policy Be Reformed? How Should the U.S. Respond to Illegal Immigration? What Policies Would Help Immigrants Adapt to the U.S.? The viewpoints in this volume highlight America's continuing ambivalence about American immigration and reveal deeper debates about America's past, future, and vision of itself.

Historical Debate: Should Immigration Be Restricted?

Chapter Preface

The debate over immigration is as old as the United States itself. "Despite the fact that almost all of us are immigrants or descendants of immigrants," writes immigration scholar George J. Borjas, "American history is characterized by a never-ending debate over when to pull the ladder in." Each of the waves of new immigrants—Irish in the 1840s, Chinese in the 1870s, Italians at the turn of the century, Cubans in the 1960s, Southeast Asians in the 1970s, and others—have had to live with the controversy they sparked among Americans whose immigrant forebears arrived earlier.

Many of the historical complaints about immigration are similar to those voiced today. The People's Party platform of 1882 proclaimed, "We condemn . . . the present system, which opens up our ports to the pauper and criminal classes of the world, and crowds out our wage earners." Borjas comments, "It seems that little has changed in the past hundred years. Today the same accusations are hurled at illegal aliens, at boat people originating in Southeast Asia and Cuba, and at other unskilled immigrants."

A prevalent theme in the immigration debate is racism. Many people persist in believing that the latest immigrants to arrive in the U.S. are racially inferior to those who have dominated previous immigration waves. Around the turn of the century, for example, Francis Walker, president of the Massachusetts Institute of Technology, expressed the opinion of many people when he described the incoming Italians, Greeks, Poles, and Russians as "beaten men from beaten races, representing the worst failures in the struggle for existence." Racism also played a major role in the immigration laws passed in the 1920s. These laws severely limited immigration from Asia, Latin America, and southern and Eastern Europe. Their passage—the first time the U.S. had harshly restricted immigration—and eventual repeal in 1965 are major turning points in the history of U.S. immigration.

Examining past debates on immigration can shed light on present-day controversies. The viewpoints in this chapter present arguments on immigration at three different periods in American history.

16

"The emigration of foreigners to this country is not only defensible on grounds of abstract justice . . . [but] it has been in various ways highly beneficial to this country."

America Should Welcome Immigration (1845)

Thomas L. Nichols

Thomas L. Nichols (1815-1901) was a doctor, dietician, social historian, and journalist. In the following viewpoint, written in 1845, he criticizes movements in the U.S. to restrict immigration. He argues that prejudices against immigrants are unfounded and that immigration has been beneficial to the U.S.

As you read, consider the following questions:

1. What racial beliefs does Nichols express concerning immigration?
2. How does the author characterize American immigrants?
3. According to Nichols, what is the worse thing that can be said about immigrants?

Thomas L. Nichols, "Lecture on Immigration and Right of Naturalization," in *Historical Aspects of the Immigration Problem*, Edith Abbott, ed. New York: Arno Press, 1969.

The questions connected with emigration from Europe to America are interesting to both the old world and the new—are of importance to the present and future generations. They have more consequence than a charter or a state election; they involve the destinies of millions; they are connected with the progress of civilization, the rights of man, and providence of God!

Examining Prejudices

I have examined this subject the more carefully, and speak upon it the more earnestly, because I have been to some extent, in former years, a partaker of the prejudices I have since learned to pity. A native of New England and a descendant of the puritans, I early imbibed, and to some extent promulgated, opinions of which reflection and experience have made me ashamed. . . .

But while I would speak of the motives of men with charity, I claim the right to combat their opinions with earnestness. Believing that the principles and practices of Native Americanism are wrong in themselves, and are doing wrong to those who are the objects of their persecution, justice and humanity require that their fallacy should be exposed, and their iniquity condemned. It may be unfortunate that the cause of the oppressed and persecuted, in opinion if not in action, has not fallen into other hands; yet, let me trust that the truth, even in mine, will prove mighty, prevailing from its own inherent power!

The right of man to emigrate from one country to another, is one which belongs to him by his own constitution and by every principle of justice. It is one which no law can alter, and no authority destroy. "Life, liberty, and the pursuit of happiness" are set down, in our Declaration of Independence, as among the self-evident, unalienable rights of man. If I have a right to live, I have also a right to what will support existence—food, clothing, and shelter. If then the country in which I reside, from a superabundant population, or any other cause, does not afford me these, my right to go from it to some other is self-evident and unquestionable. The *right to live*, then, supposes the right of emigration. . . .

I proceed, therefore, to show that the emigration of foreigners to this country is not only defensible on grounds of abstract justice—what we have no possible right to prevent, but that it has been in various ways highly beneficial to this country.

Emigration first peopled this hemisphere with civilized men. The first settlers of this continent had the same right to come here that belongs to the emigrant of yesterday—no better and no other. They came to improve their condition, to escape from

18

oppression, to enjoy freedom—for the same, or similar, reasons as now prevail. And so far as they violated no private rights, so long as they obtained their lands by fair purchase, or took possession of those which were unclaimed and uncultivated, the highly respectable natives whom the first settlers found here had no right to make any objections. The peopling of this continent with civilized men, the cultivation of the earth, the various processes of productive labor, for the happiness of man, all tend to "the greatest good of the greatest number," and carry out the evident design of Nature or Providence in the formation of the earth and its inhabitants.

Let Them Come

The poor flock to our shores to escape from a state of penury, which cannot be relieved by toil in their own native land. The man of enterprise comes, to avail himself of the advantages afforded by a wider and more varied field for the exercise of his industry and talents; and the oppressed of every land, thirsting for deliverance from the paralyzing effects of unjust institutions, come to enjoy the blessings of a government which secures life, liberty, and the pursuit of happiness to all its constituents. Let them come. They will convert our waste lands into fruitful fields, vineyards, and gardens; construct works of public improvement; build up and establish manufactures; and open our rich mines of coal, of iron, of lead, and of copper. And more than all, they will be the means of augmenting our commerce, and aiding us in extending the influence of our political, social, and religious institutions throughout the earth.

Western Journal, vol. 6, 1851.

Emigration from various countries in Europe to America, producing a mixture of races, has had, and is still having, the most important influence upon the destinies of the human race. It is a principle, laid down by every physiologist, and proved by abundant observation, that man, like other animals, is improved and brought to its highest perfection by an intermingling of the blood and qualities of various races. That nations and families deteriorate from an opposite course has been observed in all ages. The great physiological reason why Americans are superior to other nations in freedom, intelligence, and enterprise, is because that they are the offspring of the greatest intermingling of races. The mingled blood of England has given her predominance over several nations of Europe in these very qualities, and a newer infusion, with favorable circumstances of climate, position, and institutions, has rendered Americans still superior. The Yankees of New England would never have shown those qualities for which they have been distinguished in war and peace throughout the world had there not been mingled with the puritan English, the calculating Scotch, the warm hearted Irish, the gay and chivalric French, the steady persevering Dutch, and the transcendental Germans, for all these nations contributed to make up the New England character, before the Revolution, and ever since to influence that of the whole American people.

It is not too much to assert that in the order of Providence this vast and fertile continent was reserved for this great destiny; to be the scene of this mingling of the finest European races, and consequently of the highest condition of human intelligence, freedom, and happiness; for I look upon this mixture of the blood and qualities of various nations, and its continual infusion, as absolutely requisite to the perfection of humanity. . . . Continual emigration, and a constant mixing of the blood of different races, is highly conducive to physical and mental superiority.

Economic Benefits

This country has been continually benefited by the immense amount of capital brought hither by emigrants. There are very few who arrive upon our shores without some little store of wealth, the hoard of years of industry. Small as these means may be in each case, they amount to millions in the aggregate, and every dollar is so much added to the wealth of the country, to be reckoned at compound interest from the time of its arrival, nor are these sums like our European loans, which we must pay back, both principal and interest. Within a few years, especially, and more or less at all periods, men of great wealth have been among the emigrants driven from Europe, by religious oppression or political revolutions. Vast sums have also fallen to emigrants and their descendants by inheritance, for every few days we read in the papers of some poor foreigner, or descendant of foreigners, as are we all, becoming the heir of a princely fortune, which in most cases, is added to the wealth of his adopted country. Besides this, capital naturally follows labor, and it flows upon this country in a constant current, by the laws of trade.

But it is not money alone that adds to the wealth of a country but every day's productive labor is to be added to its accumulating capital. Every house built, every canal dug, every railroad graded, has added so much to the actual wealth of society; and who have built more houses, dug more canals, or graded more railroads, than the hardy Irishmen? I hardly know how our great national works could have been carried on without them then; while every pair of sturdy arms has added to our national wealth, every hungry mouth has been a home market for our agriculture, and every broad shoulder has been clothed with our manufactures.

Receive Them as Friends

Let us by no means join in the popular outcry against foreigners coming to our country, and partaking of its privileges. They will come, whether we will or no; and is it wise to meet them with inhospitality, and thus turn their hearts against us? Let us rather receive them as friends, and give them welcome to our country. Let us rather say, "The harvest before us is indeed great, and the laborers are few: come, go with us, and we will do thee good." Our hills, and valleys, and rivers, stretch from ocean to ocean, belting the entire continent of the New World; and over this rich and boundless domain, Providence has poured the atmosphere of liberty. Let these poor sufferers come and breathe it freely. Let our country be the asylum of the oppressed of all lands. Let those who come bent down with the weight of European tithes and taxation, here throw off the load, and stand erect in freedom.

Samuel Griswold Goodrich, *Ireland and the Irish*, 1841.

From the very nature of the case, America gets from Europe the most valuable of her population. Generally, those who come here are the very ones whom a sensible man would select. Those who are attached to monarchical and aristocratic institutions stay at home where they can enjoy them. Those who lack energy and enterprise can never make up their minds to leave their native land. It is the strong minded, the brave hearted, the free and self-respecting, the enterprising and the intelligent, who break away from all the ties of country and of home, and brave the dangers of the ocean, in search of liberty and independence, for themselves and for their children, on a distant continent; and it is from this, among other causes, that the great mass of the people of this country are distinguished for the very qualities we should look for in emigrants. The same spirit which sent our fathers across the ocean impels us over the Alleghenies, to the valley of the Mississippi, and thence over the Rocky mountains into Oregon.

Indebted to Immigrants

For what are we not indebted to foreign emigration, since we are all Europeans or their descendants? We cannot travel on one of our steamboats without remembering that Robert Fulton was the son of an Irishman. We cannot walk by St. Paul's churchyard without seeing the monuments which admiration and gratitude have erected to Emmet, and Montgomery. Who of the thousands who every summer pass up and down our great thoroughfare, the North River, fails to catch at least a passing glimpse of the column erected to the memory of Thaddeus Kosciusko? I cannot forget that only last night a portion of our citizens celebrated with joyous festivities the birthday of the son of Irish emigrants, I mean the Hero of New Orleans!

Who speaks contemptuously of Alexander Hamilton as a foreigner, because he was born in one of the West India Islands? Who at this day will question the worth or patriotism of Albert Gallatin, because he first opened his eyes among the Alps of Switzerland—though, in fact, this was brought up and urged against him, when he was appointed special minister to Russia by James Madison. What New Yorker applies the epithet of "degraded foreigner" to the German immigrant, John Jacob Astor, a man who has spread his canvas on every sea, drawn to his adopted land the wealth of every clime, and given us, it may be, our best claim to vast territories!

Who would have banished the Frenchman, Stephen Girard, who, after accumulating vast wealth from foreign commerce, endowed with it magnificent institutions for education in his adopted land? So might I go on for hours, citing individual examples of benefits derived by this country from foreign immigration. . . .

The "Harms" of Immigration

I have enumerated some of the advantages which such emigration has given to America. Let us now very carefully inquire, whether there is danger of any injury arising from these causes, at all proportionable to the palpable good.

"Our country is in danger," is the cry of Nativism. During my brief existence I have seen this country on the very verge of ruin a considerable number of times. It is always in the most imminent peril every four years; but, hitherto, the efforts of one party or the other have proved sufficient to rescue it, just in the latest gasp of its expiring agonies, and we have breathed more freely, when we have been assured that "the country's safe." Let us look steadily in the face of this new danger.

Are foreigners coming here to overturn our government? Those who came before the Revolution appear to have been generally favorable to Republican institutions. Those who have come here since have left friends, home, country, all that man naturally holds dearest, that they might live under a free government—they and their children. Is there common sense in the supposition that men would voluntarily set about destroying the very liberties they came so far to enjoy?

"But they lack intelligence," it is said. Are the immigrants of today less intelligent than those of fifty or a hundred years ago? Has Europe and the human race stood still all this time? . . . The facts of men preferring this country to any other, of their desire to live under its institutions, of their migration hither, indicate to my mind anything but a lack of proper intelligence and enterprise. It has been charged against foreigners, by a portion of the whig press, that they generally vote with the democratic party. Allowing this to be so, I think that those who reflect upon the policy of the two parties, from the time of John Adams down to that of Mayor Harper, will scarcely bring this up as the proof of a lack of intelligence!

The truth is, a foreigner who emigrates to this country comes here saying, "Where Liberty dwells, there is my country." He sees our free institutions in the strong light of contrast. The sun seems brighter, because he has come out of darkness. What we know by hearsay only of the superiority of our institutions, he knows by actual observation and experience. Hence it is that America has had no truer patriots—freedom no more enthusiastic admirers—the cause of liberty no more heroic defenders, than have been found among our adopted citizens. . . .

But if naturalized citizens of foreign birth had the disposition, they have not the power, to endanger our liberties, on account of their comparatively small and decreasing numbers. There appears to be a most extraordinary misapprehension upon this subject. To read one of our "Native" papers one might suppose that our country was becoming overrun by foreigners, and that there was real danger of their having a majority of votes. . . .

Immigration Is Insignificant

There is a point beyond which immigration cannot be carried. It must be limited by the capacity of the vessels employed in bringing passengers, while our entire population goes on increasing in geometrical progression, so that in one century from now, we shall have a population of one hundred and sixty millions, but a few hundred thousands of whom at the utmost can be citizens of foreign birth. Thus it may be seen that foreign immigration is of very little account, beyond a certain period, in the population of a country, and at all times is an insignificant item. . . .

In the infancy of this country the firstborn native found himself among a whole colony of foreigners. Now, the foreigner finds himself surrounded by as great a disproportion of natives, and the native babe and newly landed foreigner have about the same amount, of either power or disposition, to endanger the country in which they have arrived; one, because he chose to

23

come—the other because he could not help it.

I said the power or the disposition, for I have yet to learn that foreigners, whether German or Irish, English or French, are at all disposed to do an injury to the asylum which wisdom has prepared and valor won for the oppressed of all nations and religions. I appeal to the observation of every man in this community, whether the Germans and the Irish here, and throughout the country, are not as orderly, as industrious, as quiet, and in the habit of performing as well the common duties of citizens as the great mass of natives among us.

The worst thing that can be brought against any portion of our foreign population is that in many cases they are poor, and when they sink under labor and privation, they have no resources but the almshouse. Alas! shall the rich, for whom they have labored, the owners of the houses they have helped to build, refuse to treat them as kindly as they would their horses when incapable of further toil? Can they grudge them shelter from the storm, and a place where they may die in peace?

"The mighty tides of immigration . . . bring to us not only different languages, opinions, customs, and principles, but hostile races, religions, and interests."

America Should Discourage Immigration (1849)

Garrett Davis

In the 1820s and 1830s the rate of immigration to the United States increased dramatically, with Ireland and Germany replacing Great Britain as the main source of immigrants. Many of these new immigrants faced prejudice in the U.S. The following viewpoint is taken from an 1849 speech by Garrett Davis (1801-1872) in which he argues that immigrants endanger America. He contends that the U.S. should discourage immigration and should restrict the immigrants' right to vote. Davis served as a U.S. senator and congressman for the state of Kentucky.

As you read, consider the following questions:

1. How does Davis describe America's newest immigrants?
2. What predictions does Davis make concerning Europe and the U.S.?
3. What connection does the author make concerning immigration and slavery?

Garrett Davis, speech delivered to the Convention to Revise the Constitution of Kentucky, December 15, 1849, in *Historical Aspects of the Immigration Problem*, Edith Abbott, ed. New York: Arno press, 1969.

Why am I opposed to the encouragement of foreign immigration into our country, and disposed to apply any proper checks to it? Why do I propose to suspend to the foreigner, for twenty-one years after he shall have signified formally his intention to become a citizen of the United States, the right of suffrage, the birthright of no man but one native-born? It is because the mighty tides of immigration, each succeeding one increasing in volume, bring to us not only different languages, opinions, customs, and principles, but hostile races, religions, and interests, and the traditionary prejudices of generations with a large amount of the turbulence, disorganizing theories, pauperism, and demoralization of Europe in her redundant population thrown upon us. This multiform and dangerous evil exists and will continue, for "the cry is, Still they come!". . .

The most of those European immigrants, having been born and having lived in the ignorance and degradation of despotisms, without mental or moral culture, with but a vague consciousness of human rights, and no knowledge whatever of the principles of popular constitutional government, their interference in the political administration of our affairs, even when honestly intended, would be about as successful as that of the Indian in the arts and business of civilized private life; and when misdirected, as it would generally be, by bad and designing men, could be productive only of mischief, and from their numbers, of mighty mischief. The system inevitably and in the end will fatally depreciate, degrade, and demoralize the power which governs and rules our destinies.

Most Immigrants Unfit

I freely acknowledge that among such masses of immigrants there are men of noble intellect, of high cultivation, and of great moral worth; men every way adequate to the difficult task of free, popular, and constitutional government. But the number is lamentably small. There can be no contradistinction between them and the incompetent and vicious; and their admission would give no proper compensation, no adequate security against the latter if they, too, were allowed to share political sovereignty. The country could be governed just as wisely and as well by the native-born citizens alone, by which this baleful infusion would be wholly excluded. . . .

The Situation in Europe

This view of the subject is powerfully corroborated by a glance at the state of things in Europe. The aggregate population of that continent in 1807 was 183,000,000. Some years since it was reported to be 260,000,000 and now it is reasonably but little short of 283,000,000; showing an increase within a period of

Imminent Peril

It is an incontrovertible truth that the civil institutions of the United States of America have been seriously affected, and that they now stand in imminent peril from the rapid and enormous increase of the body of residents of foreign birth, imbued with foreign feelings, and of an ignorant and immoral character, who receive, under the present lax and unreasonable laws of naturalization, the elective franchise and the right of eligibility to political office.

Declaration of the Native American National Convention, July 4, 1845.

about forty years of 100,000,000. The area of Europe is but little more than that of the United States, and from its higher northern positions and greater proportion of sterile lands, has a less natural capability of sustaining population. All her western, southern, and middle states labor under one of the heaviest afflictions of nations—they have a redundant population. The German states have upward of 70,000,000, and Ireland 8,000,000; all Germany being not larger than three of our largest states, and Ireland being about the size of Kentucky. Daniel O'Connell, in 1843 reported 2,385,000 of the Irish people in a state of destitution. The annual increase of population in Germany and Ireland is in the aggregate near 2,000,000; and in all Europe it is near 7,000,000. Large masses of these people, in many countries, not only want the comforts of life, but its subsistence, its necessaries, and are literally starving. England, many of the German powers, Switzerland, and other governments, have put into operation extensive and well-arranged systems of emigrating and transporting to America their excess of population, and particularly the refuse, the pauper, the demoralized, and the criminal. Very many who come are stout and industrious, and go to labor steadily and thriftily. They send their friends in the old country true and glowing accounts of ours, and with it the means which they have garnered here to bring, too, those friends. Thus, immigration itself increases its means, and constantly adds to its swelling tides. Suppose some mighty convulsion of nature should loosen Europe, the smaller country, from her ocean-deep foundations, and drift her to our coast, would we be ready to take her teeming myriads to our fraternal embrace and give them equally our political sovereignty? If we did, in a few fleeting years where would be the noble Anglo-American race, where their priceless heritage of liberty, where their free constitution, where the best and brightest hopes of man? All would have perished! It is true all Europe is not coming to the United States, but much, too much of it, is; and a

27

dangerous disproportion of the most ignorant and worst of it, without bringing us any territory for them; enough, if they go on increasing and to increase, and are to share with us our power, to bring about such a deplorable result. The question is, Shall they come and take possession of our country and our government, and rule us, or will we, who have the right, rule them and ourselves? I go openly, manfully, and perseveringly for the latter rule, and if it cannot be successfully asserted in all the United States, I am for taking measures to maintain it in Kentucky, and while we can. Now is the time—prevention is easier than cure.

A Surplus Population

The governments of Europe know better than we do that they have a great excess of population. They feel more intensely its great and manifold evils, and for years they have been devising and applying correctives, which have all been mainly resolved into one—to drain off into America their surplus, and especially their destitute, demoralized, and vicious population. By doing so, they not only make more room and comfort for the residue, but they think—and with some truth—that they provide for their own security, and do something to avert explosions which might hurl kings from their thrones. . . .

We have a country of vast extent, with a great variety of climate, soil, production, industry, and pursuit. Competing interests and sectional questions are a natural and fruitful source of jealousies, discords, and factions. We have about four millions of slaves, and the slaveholding and free states are nearly equally divided in number, but the population of the latter greatly preponderating, and every portion of it deeply imbued with inflexible hostility to slavery as an institution. Even now conflict of opinion and passion of the two great sections of the Union upon the subject of slavery is threatening to rend this Union, and change confederated states and one people into hostile and warring powers. Cession has recently given to us considerable numbers of the Spanish race, and a greatly increasing immigration is constantly pouring in upon us the hordes of Europe, with their hereditary national animosities, their discordant races, languages, and religious faiths, their ignorance and their pauperism, mixed up with a large amount of idleness, moral degradation, and crime; and all this "heterogeneous, discordant, distracted mass," to use Mr. Jefferson's language, "sharing with us the legislation" and the entire political sovereignty. . . .

Washington and Jefferson and their associates, though among the wisest and most far-seeing of mankind, could not but descry in the future many formidable difficulties and dangers, and thus be premonished to provide against them in fashioning our institutions. If they had foreseen the vast, the appalling in-

The Dangers of Foreigners

The rapid increase of any nation, by means of an influx of foreigners, is dangerous to the repose of that nation; especially if the number of emigrants bears any considerable proportion to the old inhabitants. Even if that proportion is very small, the tendency of the thing is injurious, unless the newcomers are more civilized and more virtuous, and have at the same time, the same ideas and feeling about government. But if they are more vicious, they will corrupt; if less industrious, they will promote idleness; if they have different ideas of government, they will contend; if the same, they will intrigue and interfere.

Samuel Whelpley, *A Compend of History from the Earliest Times, Comprehending a General View of the Present State of the World*, 1825.

---

crease of immigration upon us at the present, there can be no reasonable doubt that laws to naturalize the foreigners and to give up to them the country, its liberties, its destiny, would not have been authorized by the constitution. The danger, though great, is not wholly without remedy. We can do something if we do it quickly. The German and Slavonic races are combining in the state of New York to elect candidates of their own blood to Congress. This is the beginning of the conflict of races on a large scale, and it must, in the nature of things, continue and increase. It must be universal and severe in all the field of labor, between the native and the stranger, and from the myriads of foreign laborers coming to us, if it does not become a contest for bread and subsistence, wages will at least be brought down so low as to hold our native laborers and their families in hopeless poverty. They cannot adopt the habits of life and live upon the stinted meager supplies to which the foreigner will restrict himself, and which is bounteous plenty to what he has been accustomed in the old country. Already these results are taking place in many of the mechanic arts. Duty, patriotism, and wisdom all require us to protect the labor, and to keep up to a fair scale the wages of our native-born people as far as by laws and measures of public policy it can be done. The foreigner, too, is the natural foe of the slavery of our state. He is opposed to it by all his past associations, and when he comes to our state he sees 200,000 laborers of a totally different race to himself excluding him measurably from employment and wages. He hears a measure agitated to send these 200,000 competitors away. Their exodus will make room for him, his kindred and race, and create such a demand for labor, as he will reason it, to give him high wages. He goes naturally for the measure, and becomes an emancipationist. While the slave is with us, the foreigner will not crowd us, which will postpone to a long day the affliction of nations, an excess of population; the slaves away, the great tide of immigration will set in upon us, and precipitate upon our happy land this, the chief misery of most of the countries of Europe. Look at the myriads who are perpetually pouring into the northwestern states from the German hives—making large and exclusive settlements for themselves, which in a few years will number their thousands and tens of thousands, living in isolation; speaking a strange language, having alien manners, habits, opinions, and religious faiths, and a total ignorance of our political institutions; all handed down with German phlegm and inflexibility to their children through generations. In less than fifty years, northern Illinois, parts of Ohio, and Michigan, Wisconsin, Iowa, and Minnesota will be literally possessed by them; they will number millions and millions, and they will be essentially a distinct people, a nation within a nation, a new Germany. We can't keep these people wholly out, and ought not if we could; but we are getting more than our share of them. I wish they would turn their direction to South America, quite as good a portion of the world as our share of the hemisphere. They could there aid in bringing up the slothful and degenerate Spanish race; here their deplorable office is to pull us down. Our proud boast is that the Anglo-Saxon race is the first among all the world of man, and that we are a shoot from this noble stock; but how long will we be as things are progressing? In a few years, as a distinctive race, the Anglo-Americans will be as much lost to the world and its future history as the lost tribes of Israel. . . .

No well-informed and observant man can look abroad over this widespread and blessed country without feeling deep anxiety for the future. Some elements of discord and disunion are even now in fearful action. Spread out to such a vast extent, filling up almost in geometrical progression with communities and colonies from many lands, various as Europe in personal and national characteristics, in opinions, in manners and customs, in tongues and religious faiths, in the traditions of the past, and the objects and the hopes of the future, the United States can, no more than Europe, become one homogeneous mass—one peaceful, united, harmonizing, all self-adhering people. When the country shall begin to teem with people, these jarring elements being brought into proximity, their repellant and explosive properties will begin to act with greater intensity; and then, if not before, will come the war of geographical sections, the war of races, and the most relentless of all wars, of hostile religions. This mournful catastrophe will have been greatly hastened by our immense expansion and our proclamation to all mankind to become a part of us.

"By restricting immigration we . . . will give to a large body of citizens a decent and comfortable standard of living."

Restrictions on Immigration Are Necessary (1913)

Frank Julian Warne

The late 1800s and early 1900s were peak years for immigration to the U.S. Many of these immigrants came from southern and eastern Europe, and their arrival rekindled debates over immigration. Some people argued that these new arrivals were racially inferior, while others said immigrants took away jobs and depressed wages. The following viewpoint is excerpted from the book *The Immigrant Invasion* by Frank Julian Warne (1874-1948). Focusing on economics instead of race, Warne states that too many immigrants are creating a lower standard of living for all Americans, and argues that the U.S. needs national legislation restricting immigration. Warne was an economist and author, and served as a special expert on immigrants for the 1910 United States Census.

As you read, consider the following questions:

1. What is the central issue of immigration, according to Warne?
2. How does the author respond to the argument that immigrants take jobs other people do not want?
3. What kinds of new laws on immigration does Warne propose?

Excerpted from *The Immigration Invasion* by Frank Julian Warne. New York: Dodd, Mead and Company, 1913.

Different people studying and observing the immigration phenomenon do not always see the same thing—they receive different impressions from it. Sometimes the other view is apparent to their consciousness but usually their mind is so taken up with their own view that the other is of lesser significance.

Two Views

One view of immigration is that which is conspicuous to the worker who has been and is being driven out of his position by the immigrant; to members of the labour union struggling to control this competition and to maintain their standard of living; to those who see the socially injurious and individually disastrous effects upon the American worker of this foreign stream of cheap labour; to those who know the pauperising effects of a low wage, long hours of work, and harsh conditions of employment; to those personally familiar with the poverty in many of our foreign "colonies"; to those acquainted with the congested slum districts in our large industrial centres and cities and the innumerable problems which they present; to those who long and strive for an early realisation of Industrial Democracy. . . .

The other view is seen, however, by those who believe that the immigrant is escaping from intolerable religious, racial, and political persecution and oppression; whose sympathies have been aroused by a knowledge of the adverse economic conditions of the masses of Europe; by those immigrants and their children already here who desire to have their loved ones join them; by producers and manufacturers seeking cheap labour; by those holding bonds and stocks in steamship companies receiving large revenues from the transportation of the immigrant; by those who see subjects of European despotism transformed into naturalised citizens of the American republic, with all that this implies for them and for their children.

The so-called good side of immigration is seen primarily from the viewpoint of the immigrant himself. Any perspective of immigration through the eyes of the alien must necessarily, as a rule, be an optimistic one. Although some of them are possibly worse off in the United States than if they had remained in their European home, at the same time the larger number improve their condition by coming to America. Let us admit, then, that immigration benefits the immigrant.

Thus are indicated two views of immigration. These opposite views are very rapidly dividing the American people into two camps or parties—those who favour a continuance of our present liberal policy and those who are striving to have laws passed that will further restrict immigration. The different groups are made up for the most part of well-intentioned people looking at identically the same national problem but who see entirely different aspects or effects. . . .

The Real Issue

Those who are desirous of settling the immigration question solely from the point of view of the best interests of the country are quite frequently sidetracked from the only real and fundamental argument into the discussion of relatively unimportant phases of it. The real objection to immigration at the present time lies not in the fact that Slavs and Italians and Greeks and Syrians instead of Irish and Germans and English are coming to the United States. Nor does it lie in the fact that the immigrants are or become paupers and criminals. The real objection has nothing to do with the composition of our immigration stream, nor with the characteristics of the individuals or races composing it. It is more than likely that the evils so prominent today would still exist if we had received the Slavs and Italians fifty years ago and were receiving the English and Irish and Germans at the present day.

Reprinted by permission of the State Historical Society of Missouri, Columbia.

The real objection to immigration lies in the changed conditions that have come about in the United States themselves. These conditions now dominate and control the tendencies that immigration manifests. At the present time they are giving to the country a surplus of cheap labour—a greater supply than our industries and manufacturing enterprises need. In consequence this over-supply has brought into play among our industrial toilers the great law of competition. This economic law is controlled by the more recent immigrant because of his immediate necessity to secure employment and his ability to sell his labour at a low price—to work for a low wage. Against the operation of this law the native worker and the earlier immigrant are unable to defend themselves. It is affecting detrimentally the standard of living of hundreds of thousands of workers—workers, too, who are also citizens, fathers, husbands.

Immigrants and Machines

But who will do the rough work that must be done if we cannot get the immigrant? asks the liberal immigrationist. And to clinch his argument he goes into raptures over the industrial characteristics of the immigrant and points out enthusiastically the important part the alien has played in America's material upbuilding.

Immigration tends to retard the invention and introduction of machinery which otherwise would do this rough work for us. It has prevented capital in our industries from giving the proper amount of attention to the increase and use of machines, says Professor John R. Commons in "Races and Immigrants in America." "The cigar-making machine cannot extensively be introduced on the Pacific coast because Chinese cheap labour makes the same cigars at less cost than the machines. High wages stimulate the invention and use of machinery and scientific processes, and it is machinery and science, more than mere hand labour, on which reliance must be placed to develop the natural resources of a country. But machinery and science cannot be as quickly introduced as cheap immigrant labour. . . . In the haste to get profits the immigrant is more desired than machinery."

As long as cheap labour is available this tendency will continue. Even in spite of the large supply of immigrants who work for a low wage, what has already been accomplished along the line of adapting machinery to do the rough work is but indicative of what would be done in this direction if immigration were restricted. . . .

U.S. Immigration Hurts Other Countries

When anyone suggests the restriction of immigration to those who believe in throwing open wide our gates to all the races of the world, the conclusion is immediately arrived at that the proposer has some personal feeling in the matter and that he is not in sympathy with the immigrant. As a matter of fact the restriction of immigration is herein suggested not alone from the point of view of the future political development of the United States, but also from that of the interest and welfare of the immigrant himself and his descendants. It is made in order to prevent them from becoming in the future an industrial slave class in America and to assist them in throwing off in their European homes the shackles which now bind them and are the primary cause of their securing there so little from an abundant world.

Unite to Reduce Immigration

It is the duty of all Americans from Maine to Texas and from Washington to Florida to forget the dissensions of the past and unite in an effort to reduce immigration to the lowest possible point or stop it altogether, and to compel the foreigners now here either to accept our traditions and ideals or else to return to the land from which they came, by deportation or otherwise.

Madison Grant, *The Alien in Our Midst*, 1930.

One of the strongest arguments in the past of the liberal immigrationist is that the downtrodden and oppressed of Europe are fleeing from intolerable economic, political, and religious conditions into a land of liberty and freedom which offers opportunities to all. It may be very much questioned if these immigrants are finding here the hoped-for escape from oppression and servitude and exploitation, for since the newer immigration began in the eighties there has come to dwell in America a horrible modern Frankenstein in the shape of the depressing conditions surrounding a vast majority of our industrial toilers. But even granting that the immigrants coming to us do better their condition, a very pertinent question is as to the effect the prevention of this immigration would have upon the countries from which it comes. If we grant that the immigrants are able-bodied, disposed to resent oppression and are striving to better their condition, are they not the very ones that should remain in their European homes and there through growing restlessness and increasing power change for the better the conditions from which they are fleeing? As it is now, instead of an improvement in those conditions the stronger and more able-bodied—the ones better able to cope with them and improve them—are running away and leaving behind the less able and weaker members, who continue to live under the intolerable conditions.

If immigration to the United States were stopped one would not likely be far wrong in prophesying that either one of two things would happen in these European countries: Either a voluntary remedying by the European Governments themselves of political, religious, and economic evils, or else those countries would soon be confronted by revolutions springing from this unrest of the people which now finds an escape through emigration to the United States. . . . Pent up discontent, unrelieved by emigration, would burst its bounds to the betterment of the general social conditions of the European masses.

Another phase of this same aspect of immigration is the fact that indirectly the United States which, if it stands for anything, stands in opposition to nearly all that is represented by the European form of government—this country, to a considerable extent, helps to keep in power these very governments against which it is a living protest. This is done in one way through the enormous sums of money that immigrants in the United States send each year to the European countries.

It is estimated that from two hundred to two hundred and fifty million dollars are sent abroad annually to the more important European countries by the foreign born in the United States. Part of this enormous sum finds its way by direct and indirect taxation into the coffers of the Government and the Bureaucracy and thus tends to support and continue them in power. When this fact is kept in mind—the fact that nearly two hundred and fifty million dollars are sent abroad each year by immigrants in the United States—it is an argument that answers thoroughly the claim of large employers of labour that immigration is an advantage to the country in that it brings to us annually through the immigrant nearly $25,000,000. The fact is that an amount nine times greater than that brought in is sent out of the country each year by the immigrant. . . .

Needed: More Restrictions

Virtually all objection or opposition to any suggestion as to immigration restriction comes from the immigrant races themselves. As for the attitude of the native, he seems for the greater part to be apathetic when it comes to taking some practical action to remedy conditions, although his grumbling and open opposition is becoming louder than ever before.

Our present statutes, except as they relate to labourers brought in under contract, exclude only such manifestly undesirable persons as idiots, the insane, paupers, immigrants likely to become a public charge, those with loathsome or dangerous contagious diseases, persons whose physical or mental defects prevent them from earning a living, convicted criminals, prostitutes, and the like. Even a strict enforcement of these laws makes it possible to keep out only the poorest and worst elements in these groups who come here.

Referring to the fact that certain undesirable immigrants are not being reached by the present laws the Commissioner of Immigration at Ellis Island, Mr. William Williams, says:

> We have no statutes excluding those whose economic condition is so low that their competition tends to reduce the standard of our wage worker, nor those who flock to the congested districts of our large cities where their presence may not be needed, in place of going to the country districts where immigrants of the right type are needed. As far back as 1901 reference was made by President Roosevelt in his annual message to Congress to those foreign labourers who 'represent a standard of living so depressed that they can undersell our men in the labour market and drag them to a lower level,' and it was recommended that 'all persons should be excluded who are below a certain standard of economic fitness to enter our industrial fields as competitors with American labourers.' There are no laws under which aliens of the class described can be kept out unless they happen to fall within one of the classes now excluded by statutes (as they sometimes do); and yet organised forces are at work, principally on the other side of the ocean, to induce many to come here whose standards of living are so low that it is detrimental to the best interests of the country that the American labourers should be compelled to compete with them.

To regulate, and this means to restrict immigration so that we may continue to receive its benefits while at the same time the welfare of the country is safeguarded against its evils, is the issue. . . .

Immigration Should Cease

I have become convinced that the safety of our institutions, the continuity of our prosperity, the preservation of our standards of living, and the maintaining of a decent level of morals among us depends upon a most rigid limitation of immigration and the maintaining of a rigid standard as to even those few who may be admitted.

Albert Johnson, *The Alien in Our Midst*, 1930.

It is a curious fact, but none the less a fact, that too much, even of something that in moderate amounts is good for us, may become very injurious—so injurious as to necessitate the regulation of the quantity we should have. The quantity of present immigration is no bugaboo but a real danger threatening most seriously the success of "The American Experiment" in government and social organisation. It is such as to over-tax our wonderful powers of assimilation. . . .

In the case of the immigration stream now pouring in huge

volume into the United States, have we, through our public schools and like safeguards, erected a sufficiently strong dam to protect our institutions? Our forefathers bequeathed to us an educational system that was designed and which was supposed to be strong enough to withstand any flood of ignorance that might beat against our institutions. But this system was not devised in any of its particulars to care for the great volume of ignorance which is now washing into the United States with tremendous force from out of eastern and southern Europe. In many respects it is even now too late to strengthen this educational system. What effect is this volume of ignorance, which is breaking in and overflowing our safeguards, to have on political and religious structures and our social and national life?. . .

The American Republic, with its valuable institutions, approaches the parting of the ways. Fortunately the writing on the signboards is plain. The choice the people are to make as to which way they shall go will determine the kind of civilisation that is to have its home in the United States for coming generations. This choice has to be made—there is no way out of it. It will be made even if no political or governmental action is taken. In this case the choice will be to continue our present policy of unrestricted immigration in cheap labour. This will mean a continuance of the development in feverish haste of the country's material resources by an inpouring of labourers with low standards of living and the perpetuation of a debased citizenship among both the exploited and the exploiters.

The alternative is to restrict immigration so that we can catch our breath and take an inventory of what we already have among us that must imperatively be raised to a higher standard of living and a safer citizenship.

America's Choice

Our decision means a choice between two conditions. By continuing our present policy we choose that which is producing a plutocratic caste class of idle nobodies resting upon the industrial slavery of a great mass of ignorant and low standard of living toilers. By restricting immigration we influence the bringing about of a condition that will give to a large body of citizens a decent and comfortable standard of living. This desired result is to be obtained by a more just distribution of wealth through wages and prices and dividends.

"Immigration to the United States suffers from too much legislation."

Restrictions on Immigration Are Unnecessary (1912)

Peter Roberts

Peter Roberts (1859-1932) was a Congregationalist pastor and author of several books on immigrants. The following viewpoint is excerpted from *The New Immigration*, a study of immigrants from southern and eastern Europe first published in 1912. Roberts argues that these immigrants have been beneficial to the U.S. He maintains that more legislation restricting immigration is unnecessary, and calls for Americans to accept these new immigrants.

As you read, consider the following questions:

1. Why does the author reject commonly accepted stereotypes of immigrants?
2. According to the author, how do immigrants affect jobs and wages?
3. Why does Roberts argue against new immigration legislation?

Excerpted from *The New Immigration* by Peter Roberts. New York: Arno Press, 1970.

All students of immigration should try to do two things: first, get the facts, argue from them, and discard popular prejudices and antipathies—we want to know conditions as they are and not as the biased imagine them to be; second, not to lay at the door of the foreigners evils and conditions which are due to the cupidity, short-sightedness, and inefficiency of the native-born.

Scum of the Earth

The statements that the millions of "the distressed and unfortunate of other lands and climes," "the scum of Europe," "the beaten men of beaten races," "the inefficient, impoverished, and diseased," seek American shores, are untrue, uncharitable, and malicious. Emigration from any land, taken as a whole, is made up of the most vigorous, enterprising, and strongest members of the race. No one denies this when the character of the immigrants who came to America in 1820-1880 is discussed. Censors and prophets of evil proclaimed the stereotyped catalogue of calamities when they came, but their fears were not realized; the men made good and their children are an honor to the nation. The men of the new immigration are now under the eye of the censor, and the prophets of calamities are not wanting, but those who know the newer immigrants intimately believe that they, as their predecessors, will make good and that their children will be an honor to us, if the same opportunities are given these men and thirty years of American influences are allowed to shape and mold their lives. In the winning of the West, the Atlantic states lost much of its best blood by migration, and the same may be said of the exodus of young men from southeastern European countries to America. Every European government, losing its workers by emigration, bemoans the fact and is looking around for some means to check the outflow of strong manhood: would any of them do this if the "scum," "the unfortunate," "the beaten" emigrated?. . .

The slums of Europe are not sent here. The facts and figures of immigration to the United States clearly show that the men of the new immigration come from the farm, and they compare favorably in bodily form and strength with men raised in agricultural communities elsewhere. In the stream, undesirables are found, but the percentage is low. Taken as a whole, they do not show moral turpitude above the average of civilized men. Although transplanted into a new environment, living under abnormal conditions in industrial centers, and meeting more temptations in a week than they would in a lifetime in rural communities in the homeland, yet when their criminal record is compared with that of the native-born males, it comes out

40

better than even.

All the immigrants landed do not stay here. In the decade 1900-1910, 8,795,386 arrived, but the last census enumerators only found 13,343,583 foreign-born in the United States, as against 10,213,817, in 1900. These figures clearly indicate that little more than 60 per cent of the total arrivals of that decade were in the country in 1910. A large percentage of this returning stream represents men and women who could not stand the stress and strain of American life; or, in other words, the unfit were more carefully weeded out by industrial competition than by the laws regulating immigration. This again works in favor of virile accretions to the population of the United States.

Composition of Immigrants by Decades

	From Northwest Europe	From Southeast Europe	All Others
	Per Cent	Per Cent	Per Cent
1821-1830	76.5	8.0	15.5
1831-1840	84.3	10.0	5.7
1841-1850	93.4	5.1	1.5
1851-1860	93.3	4.3	2.4
1861-1870	85.5	10.9	3.6
1871-1880	72.0	16.5	11.5
1881-1890	68.0	18.9	12.1
1891-1900	48.2	51.0	2.8
1901-1910	26.1	65.9	8.0

Peter Roberts, *The New Immigration*, 1970.

We constantly hear about the stream of gold going to Europe, which reached high-water mark in 1907, the year when immigration exceeded a million and a quarter, and the industrial boom was at its height. In that year, the Immigration Commission estimated the amount of money sent back to Europe at $275,000,000. America is a great country, and this sum should be compared with our industrial and commercial importance. The value of the coal mined that year was nearly two and a half times larger than the sum sent to Europe; the products of our mines were eight times as valuable; our commerce with foreign countries aggregated a sum more than eleven times as great; the value of the produce of the farms of the United States was twenty-one times as great; the value of the products of our manufacturing was fifty times larger; and if we compare the sum sent by immigrants to Europe during this year of prosperity with the total estimated wealth of the nation in 1907, it is about two-tenths of one per cent. Can the economists and statesmen, who, in this great country of ours, become excited over this item, as if the welfare of America depended upon its retention on this side of the water, be taken seriously? We don't think they take themselves seriously. . . .

But we are told that "the immigrants most dangerous are those who come . . . to earn the *higher wages* offered in the United States, with the fixed intention of returning to their families in the home country to spend those wages." The fact is, that the immigrants earn the *lower wages* offered in the United States, suffer most from intermittent and seasonal labor, and, being largely employed in hazardous industries, pay the major part of the loss of life and limb incident to these operations. The country owes a debt to every immigrant who returns having spent many years of his life in our industrial army. . . .

Bad Effects

We are also told that the foreigners have reduced wages and affected the American standard of living. On the first point, the Department of Commerce and Labor, after long and patient investigation, has failed to find a reduction in wage in the industries largely manned by immigrants.

Is it not a fact that wages were never as high in the industries of the United States as in 1907, the year when immigration touched high-water mark and 1,285,349 came to America? The immigrants from southeastern Europe, when they understand what the standard wage is, will fight for it with far greater solidarity than the Anglo-Saxon or the Teuton. The most stubborn strikes in recent years have been the anthracite coal strike, the McKees Rocks, the Westmoreland, etc., in each of which the men of the new immigration were in the majority. It would be difficult to give concrete instances of foreigners actually reducing wages, but many instances may be given where they have stubbornly resisted a reduction and bravely fought for an increased wage. As to the second point, the American standard of living is a shifting one. In the mill towns and mine patches of West Virginia, North Carolina, and Alabama, the foreigners would have to come down many degrees in order to conform with the standard of living of Americans of purest blood. In a town in New England, a banker said that the New England Yankee was in his capacity to save money a close second to the Magyar, who led the foreigners in this respect. Put the native-born on $450 a year—the average wage of foreigners—and will he be able to build a home, raise a family, and push the children several degrees up in the economic scale? The immigrants are doing this. Suppose the new immigration had kept away, would the wages of unskilled labor be higher? This leads us to the region of conjecture. One thing we know, that the wage has steadily advanced notwithstanding the unprecedented inflow of the last decade. . . .

The Declaration of Independence

A little attention to the principles involved would have convinced us long ago that an American citizen who preaches wholesale restriction of immigration is guilty of political heresy. The Declaration of Independence accords to *all* men an equal share in the inherent rights of humanity. When we go contrary to that principle, we are not acting as Americans; for, by definition, an American is one who lives by the principles of the Declaration. And we surely violate the Declaration when we attempt to exclude aliens on account of race, nationality, or economic status. "All men" means yellow men as well as white men, men from the South of Europe as well as men from the North of Europe, men who hold kingdoms in pawn, and men who owe for their dinner. We shall have to recall officially the Declaration of Independence before we can lawfully limit the application of its principles to this or that group of men.

Mary Antin, *They Who Knock at Our Gates*, 1914.

We are further told that "the immigrants are not *additional* inhabitants," but that "their coming displaces the native stock"; "that the racial suicide is closely connected with the problem of immigration." If "racial suicide" were a phenomenon peculiar to the United States, there would be force in the argument. There is no immigration into France, and yet sterility and a low birth rate have been the concern of statesmen and moralists in that country for the last quarter of a century. The same phenomenon is observed among the middle classes in England and the Scandinavian peninsula. Artificial restriction on natality is practiced in every industrial country by men and women whose income is such that they must choose between raising a family or maintaining their social status. One or the other of these two institutions must suffer and it is generally the family. This is the case in America. The native-born clerk, tradesman, machinist, professional man, etc., whose income ranges between $800 and $1200 a year, can hardly risk matrimony in an urban community. If he does take a wife, they can hardly afford to raise one child, while two cause great anxiety. A low birth rate is a condition that is superinduced by industrial development. The opportunity for advancement, social prestige, love of power and its retention in the family, etc., these are some of the causes of a low birth rate. "But greater than any other cause is 'the deliberate and voluntary avoidance of child-

43

bearing on the part of a steadily increasing number of married people, who not only prefer to have but few children, but who know how to obtain their wish,'" [according to W.B. Bailey]. Immigration is no more the cause of racial suicide than the countryside superstition that a plentiful crop of nuts is the cause of fecundity. . . .

Immigrants Do Needed Work

The foreigners are despised for the work they do. Must this work be done? Can America get along without sewer digging, construction work, tunnel driving, coal mining, meat packing, hide tanning, etc.—disagreeable work, which the English-speaking shun? This labor is necessary and the foreigners do it uncomplainingly. Should they be contemned, despised, and dubbed "the scum of the earth" for doing basic work which we all know is a necessity, but which we ourselves will not perform? A percentage of foreigners is illiterate, and a still larger percentage is unskilled, but every one who has studied these men knows that they have common sense, meekness, patience, submission, docility, and gratitude—qualities which have made them admirably suited for the coarse work America needs done. The accident of birth accounts largely for skill in reading and writing as well as for a knowledge of the trades: we cannot choose the country of our birth any more than hereditary tendencies; why, then, should we blame men for the consequence of these accidents? The best judges of America's need of unskilled labor are employers, men of affairs, and leaders in the industrial development of the nation, and these without exception say that the foreigner has been a blessing and not a curse. In 1910, the National Board of Trade received letters from ninety-three such men, residing in thirty-five states, expressing their views as to the effect of immigration on labor and the industries, and the following is the summary of their answers:—

1. That the general effect of immigration to this country has been beneficial.

2. That immigration so far has not constituted a menace to American labor.

3. That it is still needed for our industrial and commercial development.

In view of these conclusions, the right of the foreigner to respect and honorable treatment from Americans ought to be acknowledged; the credit due him for the part he has played in the industrial development of America should be freely given; his right to the free enjoyment of the fruit of his labor wherever he chooses to spend his money should be conceded; but unfortunately none of these rights is recognized by a vast number of native-born men in the immigration zone. . . .

Immigrants and Prosperity

The economic supremacy of the United States was attained during the very period when large numbers of immigrants were coming into the country. . . .

Immigrants have contributed greatly to the industrial development of this country; contributed not alone by their numbers but also by their age, sex and training.

Constantine Panunzio, *Immigration Crossroads*, 1927.

We have reason to believe that immigration to the United States suffers from too much legislation. Multiplicity of laws will not secure to the United States immunity from the evils of immigration. Each new barrier erected invites the cunning and duplicity of shrewd foreigners to overcome it and affords an opportunity to exploit the ignorant. It is the duty of the government to guard the gates against the diseased, the insane, and the criminal, and our present laws, in the hands of competent men, do this. The immigrant has a right to look for transportation conveniences on steamships and accommodations in detention stations, which comply with the demands of sanitary science and personal hygiene. Every important distributing center should have detention halls, where the immigrants could be kept until called for by friends or guided by responsible parties to their destination. America collects $4 per head from all immigrants coming to the country. Canada spends that amount per head to give the newcomers the necessary information as to agricultural opportunities and economic conditions, so that the men may exercise their judgement as to place to locate and employment to seek. The immigrants will never be distributed in the states and the communities where their labor would count for most, as long as the hands of the division of information of the Bureau of Immigration are tied by the want of funds to fulfill the purpose for which it was created. The attempt to regulate the inflow of immigrants by legislation according to the labor supply of this country is impracticable and will inevitably lead to political skirmishing. Who is to decide the condition of the labor market, the operators or the trades-union? Economic law will regulate this far more effectually and promptly. While the recommendations of the Immigration Commission wait the action of Congress, industrial depression has driven 2,000,000 workers out of the country. If the "Conclusions and Recommendations" of the Commission were written in 1907 instead of 1910, their tone would be very different. A few efficient laws left alone and well executed are better than many statutes, continuous legislative tinkering, and inefficiency.

The assimilation of the immigrants must depend more upon private effort than upon legislation. No action of either Federal or state government can do half as much for aliens wishing to join the family as the conduct of Americans in the immigration zone, who can help this cause more by throwing open the school building than by urging the enactment of state laws concerning the illiteracy of foreigners. Centers opened in every public school in foreign colonies, where immigrants could be taught, would do more for foreigners in one year, than ten years of legislative inhibition as to what the foreigners should or should not do. . . .

Personal Contact

Legislative action and private organizations can do much for immigrants, but the most effective of all remedies is personal contact. We can legislate as we have a mind to, but unless the native-born is ready to take the foreign-born in confidence and sympathy into the family, there will be no assimilation. Of the 13,500,000 foreign-born in the country at present, about half of them are from southeastern Europe: in other words in a population of 90,000,000 whites, just one out of every fifteen is a child of the backward races of Europe, and we all stand in awe of him and say he is a menace. Would it not be better to trust the brother, believe that he is capable of infinite good, give him a fair chance in the race, secure to him all freedom of opportunity, and treat him at all times as a responsible moral being with rights and duties as other men? If this personal touch is secured, righteous treatment given, and broad sympathetic interest shown, the immigration problem will be solved in the light of the brotherhood of man and the spirit of our democracy.

"The use of a national origins system is without basis in either logic or reason."

National Origins Quotas Should Be Abolished (1963)

John F. Kennedy

In 1921 and 1924, Congress passed laws which sharply limited immigration. These laws awarded each foreign country immigration quotas based on the ethnic composition of the U.S. The effect of the laws, revised but not changed significantly in 1952, was to sharply limit immigration from southern and eastern Europe, as well as Africa and Asia. Many people over time criticized this quota system as racist and a betrayal of American values. In the following viewpoint, John F. Kennedy (1917-1963) argues that this system of national origins quotas is embarrassing to the U.S. and should be eliminated. Kennedy, a great-grandson of Irish immigrants, was elected President of the United States in 1960. Many of the ideas Kennedy states in this viewpoint were enacted into law in 1965, two years after he was assassinated.

As you read, consider the following questions:

1. What were the motivations behind the immigration laws of 1921 and 1924, according to Kennedy?
2. Why are national origins quotas racist, according to the author?
3. What reforms to U.S. immigration law does Kennedy propose?

Excerpts from A NATION OF IMMIGRANTS by John F. Kennedy. Copyright © 1964 by Anti-Defamation League of B'nai B'rith. Reprinted by permission of HarperCollins Publishers.

From the start, immigration policy has been a prominent subject of discussion in America. This is as it must be in a democracy, where every issue should be freely considered and debated.

Ambiguous Attitudes

Immigration, or rather the British policy of clamping down on immigration, was one of the factors behind the colonial desire for independence. Restrictive immigration policies constituted one of the charges against King George III expressed in the Declaration of Independence. And in the Constitutional Convention James Madison noted, "That part of America which has encouraged them [the immigrants] has advanced most rapidly in population, agriculture and the arts." So, too, Washington in his Thanksgiving Day Proclamation of 1795 asked all Americans "humbly and fervently to beseech the kind Author of these blessings . . . to render this country more and more a safe and propitious asylum for the unfortunate of other countries."

Yet there was the basic ambiguity which older Americans have often shown toward newcomers. In 1797 a member of Congress argued that, while a liberal immigration policy was fine when the country was new and unsettled, now that America had reached its maturity and was fully populated, immigration should stop an argument which has been repeated at regular intervals throughout American history. . . .

By the turn of the century the opinion was becoming widespread that the numbers of new immigrants should be limited. Those who were opposed to all immigration and all "foreigners" were now joined by those who believed sincerely, and with some basis in fact, that America's capacity to absorb immigration was limited. This movement toward restricting immigration represented a social and economic reaction, not only to the tremendous increase in immigration after 1880, but also to the shift in its main sources, to Southern, Eastern and Southeastern Europe.

The Quota System

Anti-immigration sentiment was heightened by World War I, and the disillusionment and strong wave of isolationism that marked its aftermath. It was in this climate, in 1921, that Congress passed and the President signed the first major law in our country's history severely limiting new immigration by establishing an emergency quota system. An era in American history had ended; we were committed to a radically new policy toward the peopling of the nation.

The Act of 1921 was an early version of the so-called "na-

"What Happened To The One We Used To Have?"

From *The Herblock Book* (Beacon Press, 1952).

tional origins" system. Its provisions limited immigration of numbers of each nationality to a certain percentage of the number of foreign-born individuals of that nationality resident in the United States according to the 1910 census. Nationality meant country of birth. The total number of immigrants permitted to enter under this system each year was 357,000.

In 1924 the Act was revised, creating a temporary arrangement for the years 1924 to 1929, under which the national quotas for 1924 were equal to 2 percent of the number of foreign-born persons of a given nationality living in the United States in 1890, or about 164,000 people. The permanent system, which went into force in 1929, includes essentially all the elements of immigration policy that are in our law today. The immigration statutes now establish a system of annual quotas to govern immigration from each country. Under this system 156,987 quota immigrants are permitted to enter the United States each year. The quotas from each country are based upon the national origins of the population of the United States in 1920.

The use of the year 1920 is arbitrary. It rests upon the fact that this system was introduced in 1924 and the last prior census was in 1920. The use of a national origins system is without basis in either logic or reason. It neither satisfies a national need nor accomplishes an international purpose. In an age of interdependence among nations such a system is an anachronism, for it discriminates among applicants for admission into the United States on the basis of accident of birth.

Favors Northern Europe

Because of the composition of our population in 1920, the system is heavily weighted in favor of immigration from Northern Europe and severely limits immigration from Southern and Eastern Europe and from other parts of the world.

To cite some examples: Great Britain has an annual quota of 65,361 immigration visas and used 28,291 of them. Germany has a quota of 25,814 and used 26,533 (of this number, about one third are wives of servicemen who could enter on a non-quota basis). Ireland's quota is 17,756 and only 6,054 Irish availed themselves of it. On the other hand, Poland is permitted 6,488, and there is a backlog of 61,293 Poles wishing to enter the United States. Italy is permitted 5,666 and has a backlog of 132,435. Greece's quota is 308; her backlog is 96,538. Thus a Greek citizen desiring to emigrate to this country has little chance of coming here. And an American citizen with a Greek father or mother must wait at least eighteen months to bring his parents here to join him. A citizen whose married son or daughter, or brother or sister, is Italian cannot obtain a quota number for them for two years or more. Meanwhile, many thousands of quota numbers are wasted because they are not wanted or needed by nationals of the countries to which they are assigned.

In short, a qualified person born in England or Ireland who wants to emigrate to the United States can do so at any time. A person born in Italy, Hungary, Poland or the Baltic States may

50

have to wait many years before his turn is reached. This system is based upon the assumption that there is some reason for keeping the origins of our population in exactly the same proportions as they existed in 1920. Such an idea is at complete variance with the American traditions and principles that the qualification of an immigrant do not depend upon his country of birth, and violates the spirit expressed in the Declaration of Independence that "all men are created equal."

Immigrants' Contributions

One can go on and on pointing out the contributions made by immigrants to our arts, economic growth, health, and culture in general. . . . We should continue by all means to receive these people and facilitate their entry into the United States by doing away with the inequities of the national origins quota system.

America is based upon equality and fair play but our present immigration laws are contrary to the basic principles of this democracy.

A change in our immigration laws is long overdue.

John Papandreas, testimony before Congress, August 7, 1964.

One writer has listed six motives behind the Act of 1924. They were: (1) postwar isolationism; (2) the doctrine of the alleged superiority of Anglo-Saxon and Teutonic "races"; (3) the fear that "pauper labor" would lower wage levels; (4) the belief that people of certain nations were less law-abiding than others; (5) the fear of foreign ideologies and subversion; (6) the fear that entrance of too many people with different customs and habits would undermine our national and social unity and order. All of these arguments can be found in Congressional debates on the subject and may be heard today in discussions over a new national policy toward immigration. Thus far, they have prevailed. The policy of 1924 was continued in all its essentials by the Immigration and Nationality Act of 1952. . . .

1952 Revisions

The Immigration and Nationality Act of 1952 undertook to codify all our national laws on immigration. This was a proper and long overdue task. But it was not just housekeeping chore. In the course of the deliberation over the Act, many basic decisions about our immigration policy were made. The total racial bar against the naturalization of Japanese, Koreans and other East Asians was removed, and a minimum annual quota of one hundred was provided for each of these countries. Provision

51

was also made to make it easier to reunite husbands and wives. Most important of all was the decision to do nothing about the national origins system.

The famous words of Emma Lazarus on the pedestal of the Statue of Liberty read: "Give me your tired, your poor, your huddled masses yearning to breathe free." Until 1921 this was an accurate picture of our society. Under present law it would be appropriate to add: "as long as they come from Northern Europe, are not too tired or too poor or slightly ill, never stole a loaf of bread, never joined any questionable organization, and can document their activities for the past two years."

Indefensible Racial Preference

Furthermore, the national origins quota system has strong overtones of an indefensible racial preference. It is strongly weighted toward so-called Anglo-Saxons, a phrase which one writer calls "a term of art" encompassing almost anyone from Northern and Western Europe. Sinclair Lewis described his hero, Martin Arrowsmith, this way: "a typical pure-bred-Anglo-Saxon American—which means that he was a union of German, French, Scotch-Irish, perhaps a little Spanish, conceivably of the strains lumped together as 'Jewish,' and a great deal of English, which is itself a combination of primitive Britain, Celt, Phoenician, Roman, German, Dane and Swede."

Yet, however much our present policy may be deplored, it still remains our national policy. As President Truman said when he vetoed the Immigration and Nationality Act (only to have that veto overridden): "The idea behind this discriminatory policy was, to put it boldly, that Americans with English or Irish names were better people and better citizens than Americans with Italian or Greek or Polish names. . . . Such a concept is utterly unworthy of our traditions and our ideals.". . .

A Legitimate Argument

There is, of course, a legitimate argument for some limitation upon immigration. We no longer need settlers for virgin lands, and our economy is expanding more slowly than in the nineteenth and early twentieth centuries. . . .

The clash of opinion arises not over the number of immigrants to be admitted, but over the test for admission—the national origins quota system. Instead of using the discriminatory test of where the immigrant was born, the reform proposals would base admission on the immigrant's possession of skills our country needs and on the humanitarian ground of reuniting families. Such legislation does not seek to make over the face of America. Immigrants would still be given tests for health, intelligence, morality and security. . . .

Religious and civic organizations, ethnic associations and newspaper editorials, citizens from every walk of life and groups of every description have expressed their support for a more rational and less prejudiced immigration law. Congressional leaders of both parties have urged the adoption of new legislation that would eliminate the most objectionable features of the McCarran-Walter Act and the nationalities quota system. . . .

A Formula for Immigration

The Presidential message to Congress of July 23, 1963, recommended that the national origins system be replaced by a formula governing immigration to the United States which takes into account: (1) the skills of the immigrant and their relationships to our needs; (2) the family relationship between immigrants and persons already here, so that the reuniting of families is encouraged; and (3) the priority of registration. Present law grants a preference to immigrants with special skills, education or training. It also grants a preference to various relatives of the United States' citizens and lawfully resident aliens. But it does so only within a national origins quota. It should be modified so that those with the greatest ability to add to the national welfare, no matter where they are born, are granted the highest priority. The next priority should go to those who seek to be reunited with their relatives. For applicants with equal claims, the earliest registrant should be the first admitted. . . .

These changes will not solve all the problems of immigration. But they will insure that progress will continue to be made toward our ideals and toward the realization of humanitarian objectives.

We must avoid what the Irish poet John Boyle O'Reilly once called

> Organized charity, scrimped and iced,
> In the name of a cautious, statistical Christ.

Immigration policy should be generous; it should be fair; it should be flexible. With such a policy we can turn to the world, and to our own past, with clean hands and a clear conscience. Such a policy would be but a reaffirmation of old principles. It would be an expression of our agreement with George Washington that "The bosom of America is open to receive not only the opulent and respectable stranger, but the oppressed and persecuted of all nations and religions; whom we shall welcome to a participation of all our rights and privileges, if by decency and propriety of conduct they appear to merit the enjoyment."

"Without the quota system, it is doubtful whether or not America could indefinitely maintain its traditional heritage."

National Origins Quotas Should Be Retained (1964)

Marion Moncure Duncan

Marion Moncure Duncan (1912-1978) was president general of the Daughters of the American Revolution from 1962 to 1965. DAR is a patriotic and social organization composed of women descendants of Revolutionary War veterans. The following viewpoint is taken from 1964 testimony before Congress in which Duncan argues against revising immigration law. Duncan specifically states that national origins quotas, which since 1921 had limited immigration from places other than northern Europe, should be retained in order to maintain ethnic unity in the U.S.

As you read, consider the following questions:

1. What should be the goals of immigration law, according to Duncan?
2. How are contemporary immigrants different from past immigrants, according to the author?
3. Why does Duncan believe national origins quotas are necessary?

Marion Moncure Duncan, statement before the U.S. House of Representatives Committee on the Judiciary, August 10, 1964.

I speak in support of maintaining the existing provisions of the Immigration and Nationality Act of 1952, especially the national origins quota system. . . .

I speak not as a specialist or authority in a particular field. Rather, the focus is that of attempting to present to you and ask your consideration of the conscientious convictions of an organization keenly and, more importantly, actively interested in this subject almost since its own inception nearly three-quarters of a century ago. . . .

The DAR is not taking a stand against immigration per se. Any inference in that direction is in error and completely false. DAR, as a national organization, is among the foremost "to extend a helping hand" to immigrants admitted on an intelligent, orderly, equitable basis such as is allowed under the current Immigration and Nationality Act of 1952. If, from time to time, there be need for change or adjustment, it should be provided through logical, deliberate amendment, still retaining the national origins quota system and other vitally basic, protective features of the law. These constitute a first line of defense in perpetuating and maintaining our institutions of freedom and the American way of life. To discard them would endanger both.

From the point that immigration is definitely a matter of national welfare and security, it is imperative that a logical and rational method of governing and administering same be maintained. The [1952] Walter-McCarran Act has done and will continue equitably to accomplish just this. It denies no nation a quota, but it does provide a reasonable, orderly, mathematical formula (based, of course, upon the 1920 census figures) which is devoid of the political pressure which could inevitably be expected to beset any commission authorized to reapportion unused quotas as proposed in the legislation before you.

The 1952 Immigration Act

By way of background: What prompted passage of the Immigration-Nationality Act of 1952? It will be recalled that this was the product of a tedious, comprehensive study of nearly 5 years' duration, covering some 200 laws on selective immigration, special orders and exclusions, and spanned the period from passage of the first quota law by Congress in 1924. This law codified and coordinated all existing immigration, nationality, and deportation laws.

Despite repeated efforts to weaken, circumvent and bypass this protective legislation, its soundness has been demonstrated over the period it has been in operation.

It embodies the following important features—all in the best interest of our constitutional republic:

(a) Recognizing the cultural identity and historic population basis of this Nation, it officially preserved the national origin quota system as the basis for immigration, wisely giving preference to those nations whose composite culture—Anglo-Saxon from northern and western European countries—has been responsible for and actually produced the American heritage as we know it today.

(b) It abolished certain discriminatory provisions in our immigration laws—those against sexes and persons of Asiatic origin.

(c) "Quality versus quantity" preference for skilled aliens was provided, as well as broadened classifications for nonquota immigrants. No nation or race is listed ineligible for immigration and naturalization, although the acknowledged purpose is to preserve this country's culture, free institutions, free enterprise economy and racial complex, yes, and likely even language. Ready assimilability of the majority of immigrants is a prime factor.

(d) It provides the U.S. Immigration Department with needed authority to cope with subversive aliens by strengthening security provisions.

U.S. Must Be Selective

We will gain neither respect, gratitude, nor love from other nations by making our homes their doormat. Nations, like men, must be reasonably selective about whom they adopt into the bosom of their family. . . .

We cannot maintain our priceless heritage of individual liberty as outlined in the three classic cornerstones of our Republic; in the Declaration of Independence, our Federal and State Constitutions, and our Bill of Rights, if we permit our already overpacked "melting pot" to be inundated from the world's most deprived areas; or if we break down those barriers which now permit us to screen out those who neither know, nor appreciate, the value of American institutions or the aims of our great country.

Myra C. Hacker, statement before Congress, August 11, 1964.

Perhaps the sentiment and deep concern of the DAR relative to the matter of immigration and its appeal for retention of the present law is best expressed by excerpting salient points from recent resolutions on the subject:

(1) For building unity and cohesiveness among American citizens, whose social, economic and spiritual mind has been and is under increasing pressures and conflicts, wise and comprehensive steps must be taken.

(2) For the protection and interest of all citizens from foreign elements imbued with ideologies wholly at variance with our republican form of government should be excluded.

On basis of FBI [Federal Bureau of Investigation] analysis statistics and information available through investigation by the House Un-American Activities Committee, loopholes through which thousands of criminal aliens may enter this country constitute a continuing threat for the safety of American institutions.

(3) Since it is a recognized fact that free migration allowing unhampered movement of agents is necessary for triumph of either a world socialist state or international communism as a world conspiracy, this would explain the motivation on the part of enemies of this country for concentrated effort to undermine the existing immigration law.

(4) Admittedly, major problems confronting the Nation and threatening its national economy are unemployment, housing, education, security, population explosion, and other domestic problems such as juvenile delinquency, crime, and racial tensions. This is borne out by numerous statistics and the current Federal war on poverty effort. In view of this, revisions as per proposed new quotas to greatly increase the number of immigrants would be a threat to the security and well-being of this Nation, especially in face of the cold war inasmuch as it would be impossible to obtain adequate security checks on immigrants from satellite Communist-controlled countries.

In summation: A comparative study would indicate increased aggravation of existing problems and unfavorable repercussions on all facets of our economy such as employment, housing, education, welfare, health, and national security, offering additional threat to the American heritage—cultural, social, and ethnic traditions. . . .

The Difference Between Then and Now

While DAR would be the first to admit the importance of immigrants to America, its membership ties linking directly with the first waves of immigrants to these shores, it would seem well, however, to point out a "then and now" difference factor currently exists attributable to time and circumstance—no uncomplimentary inference therein. A common desire shared by immigrants of all time to America has been the seeking of freedom or the escape from tyranny. But in the early days, say the first 150 years, it is noteworthy that those who came shared common Anglo-Saxon bonds and arrived with the full knowledge and intent of founders or pioneers who knew there was a wilderness to conquer and a nation to build. Their coming indicated a willingness to make a contribution and assume such a role. In the intervening years, many fine, high-caliber immigrants, and I know some at personal sacrifice, following ideals in which they believed, have likewise come to America imbued with a constructive desire to produce and add to the glory of their new homeland. They, however, have come to a nation already established with cultural patterns set and traditions already rooted.

Further, in recent years, en masse refugee movements, though responding to the very same ideal which is America, have been motivated primarily by escape. This has had a tendency possibly to dim individual purpose and dedication and possibly project beyond other considerations, the available benefits to be secured as an American citizen.

Quota System Is Fair

The fact is that the national origins quota system does not predicate the quotas upon the race, culture, morality, intelligence, health, physical attributes, or any other characteristics of the people in any foreign country.

The quotas are based upon our own people. The national origins system is like a mirror held up before the American people and reflecting the proportions of their various foreign national origins.

Assertions by critics that the national origins system is in some way discriminatory or establishes the principle that some foreign nations or ethnic groups are defined as "superior" or "inferior" are entirely without foundation.

National origins simply attempts to have immigration into the United States conform in composition to our own people.

John B. Trevor Jr., testimony before Congress, May 20, 1965.

Abandonment of the national origins system would drastically alter the source of our immigration. Any change would not take into consideration that those whose background and heritage most closely resemble our own are most readily assimilable.

In testimony before you, this point was touched upon by a high official when he said, "To apply the new principle rigidly would result, after a few years, in eliminating immigration from these countries almost entirely." Admittedly such a situation would be undesirable. A strict first-come, first-served basis of allocating visa quotas as proposed would create certain problems in countries of northern and western Europe, and could ultimately dry up influx from that area.

Going a step further, would not the abolishment of the national origin quota system work a hardship and possibly result in actual discrimination against the very nations who supplied the people who now comprises the majority of our historic population mixture? Further, such a change in our existing laws would appear to be an outright accommodation to the heaviest population explosions throughout the world—India, Asia, and Africa. Certainly these countries could naturally be expected to take full advantage of such an increased quota opportunity.

Is it, therefore, desirable or in the best interest to assign possible 10-percent quotas to say proliferating African nations to the end that our own internal problems become manifold? America, as all other nations, is concerned over rapid population growth of this era. Staggering statistics are readily available on every hand.

Immigration Is a Privilege

Attention is called to the fact that immigration is not an alien's right; it is a privilege. With privilege comes its handmaiden responsibility. Before tampering with the present immigration law, much less destroying its basic principles, due regard must also be given to our own unemployment situation. No less an authority than the late President John F. Kennedy, who was for this bill, stated on March 3, 1963, that we had 5 million unemployed and 2 million people displaced each year by advancing technology and automation.

Irrespective of recent and reoccurring reports on unemployment showing temporary increases or decreases, the fact is, it remains a matter of economic concern. Latest figures available as of June 1964 indicate 4.7 million or 5.3 percent.

In view of this, it would seem highly incongruent if not outright incredible to find ourselves in a situation, on the one hand, waging war on poverty and unemployment at home, while on the other hand, simultaneously and indiscriminately letting down immigration bars to those abroad. Not only employment alone but mental health and retardation problems could greatly increase. Another source of concern to the heavy laden taxpayer to whom already the national debt figure is astronomical.

It is asserted that our economy will get three consumers for every worker admitted and that our economy generates jobs at a rate better than one for every three consumers. Why, then, are we presently plagued with unemployment? And how is it possible to guarantee that these new immigrants will "fill jobs that are going begging because there are not enough skilled workers in our economy who have the needed skills?" Are there enough such jobs going begging to justify destroying an immigration law which has been described as our first line of defense?

Rightly, it would seem U.S. citizens should have first claim on jobs and housing in this country. With manpower available and the recent emphasis on expanded educational facilities, why is not definite concentrated effort made to provide and accelerate vocational and special skill training for the many who either through disinclination, native inability or otherwise are not qualified potentials for schooling in the field of science, medicine, law, or other such professions?

The Need for National Quotas

Without the quota system, it is doubtful whether or not America could indefinitely maintain its traditional heritage: Economic, cultural, social, ethnic, or even language.

Free institutions as we have known them would stand to undergo radical change if the proposal to permit reapportionment of unused quotas is also adopted. It is felt reassignment of unused quotas would be as damaging to the basic principles of the Immigration and Nationality Act as repeal of the national origins system itself. . . .

The National Society, Daughters of the American Revolution, which initially supported the Walter-McCarran bill when it was introduced and has continuously done so since, wishes again to officially reaffirm its support of the existing law, firmly believing that the present Immigration and Nationality Act of 1952 not only safeguards our constitutional Republic and perpetuates our American heritage, but by maintaining its established standards, that it actually protects the naturalized American on a par with the native born, and as well offers encouragement to desirable immigrants to become future American citizens. Any breakdown in this system would be an open invitation to Communist infiltration. Likewise, a poor law, newly enacted, and improperly administered, could provide the same opportunity to the detriment, if not the actual downfall, of our country.

The well-intentioned, humanitarian plea that America's unrestricted assumption of the overpopulous, troubled, ailing people of the world within our own borders is unrealistic, impractical, and if done in excess could spell economic bankruptcy for our people from point of both employment and overladen taxes to say nothing of a collapse of morale and spiritual values if nonassimilable aliens of dissimilar ethnic background and culture by wholesale and indiscriminate transporting en masse overturn the balance of our national character.

In connection with the liberalization proposals, it would seem timely to refer to the words of Senator Patrick McCarran, who, when he presented the bill, warned:

If the enemies of this legislation succeed in riddling it to pieces, or in amending it beyond recognition, they will have contributed more to promote this Nation's downfall than any other group since we achieved our independence as a nation.

Somewhat the same sentiment was expressed by Abraham Lincoln, who admonished:

You cannot strengthen the weak by weakening the strong; and you cannot help men permanently by doing for them what they could and should do for themselves.

Many inspiring words have been written of America. I would conclude with those of the late historian, James Truslow Adams:

America's greatest contribution to the world has been that of the American dream, the dream of a land where life shall be richer, fuller, and better, with opportunity for every person according to his ability and achievement.

The question is: Can it continue so if, through reckless abandon, the United States becomes mired, causing the country to lose its image as the land of opportunity, the home of the free? Ours is the responsibility to maintain and preserve it for the future.

Evaluating Sources of Information

When historians study and interpret past events, they use two kinds of sources: primary and secondary. Primary sources are eyewitness accounts. For example, letters written in 1900 by an immigrant describing his voyage to America and his experiences would be a primary source. A book about U.S. immigration at the turn of the century by an author who used these letters would be a secondary source. Primary and secondary sources may be decades or even hundreds of years old, and often historians find that the sources offer conflicting and contradictory information. To fully evaluate documents and assess their accuracy, historians analyze the credibility of the documents' authors and, in the case of secondary sources, analyze the credibility of the information the authors used.

Historians are not the only people who encounter conflicting information, however. Anyone who reads a daily newspaper, watches television, or just talks to different people will encounter many different views. Writers and speakers use sources of information to support their own statements. Thus, critical thinkers, just like historians, must question the writer's or speaker's sources of information as well as the writer or speaker.

While there are many criteria that can be applied to assess the accuracy of a primary or secondary source, for this activity you will be asked to apply three. For each source listed on the following page, ask yourself the following questions: First, did the person actually see or participate in the event he or she is reporting? This will help you determine the credibility of the information—an eyewitness to an event is an extremely valuable source. Second, does the person have a vested interest in the report? Assessing the person's social status, professional affiliations, nationality, and religious or political beliefs will be helpful in considering this question. By evaluating this you will be able to determine how objective the person's report may be. Third, how qualified is the author to be making the statements he or she is making? Consider what the person's profession is and how he or she might know about the event. Someone who has spent years being involved with or studying the issue may be able to offer more information than someone who simply is offering an uneducated opinion; for example, a politician or layperson.

Keeping the above criteria in mind, imagine you are writing a paper on immigration to the U.S. between 1880 and 1930. You decide to cite an equal number of primary and secondary sources. Listed below are several sources which may be useful for your research. *Place a P next to those descriptions you believe are primary sources. Place an S next to those descriptions you believe are secondary sources.* Next, based on the above criteria, *rank the primary sources assigning the number (1) to what appears to be the most valuable, (2) to the source likely to be the second-most valuable, and so on, until all the primary sources are ranked. Then rank the secondary sources, again using the above criteria.*

		Rank in
P or S		*Importance*
_____	1. Information from the 1900 census describing the foreign-born population of the U.S.	_____
_____	2. Records from Ellis Island documenting the entry of immigrants who were processed there.	_____
_____	3. An editorial in *The Nation* opposing the 1924 Immigration Act.	_____
_____	4. A pamphlet by the Immigration Restriction League in 1894 calling for restrictive immigration laws.	_____
_____	5. Speeches in the U.S. Senate supporting the Chinese Exclusion Act of 1882.	_____
_____	6. An autobiography published in 1971 of a Polish woman who moved to Chicago in 1909 at the age of eight.	_____
_____	7. Viewpoint 3 in this chapter.	_____
_____	8. Viewpoint 4 in this chapter.	_____
_____	9. The text of the 1924 Immigration Act which created national origins quotas on immigration.	_____
_____	10. A Chinese historian's book examining the racist attitudes that led to the passage of the Chinese Exclusion Act.	_____
_____	11. An editorial in *The New York Times* advocating restrictions on immigration.	_____
_____	12. A book by a Catholic priest examining the lives of immigrant members of his parish.	_____

How Do Immigrants Affect America?

Chapter Preface

The U.S. is in the midst of an immigration wave. Each year more than 600,000 legal immigrants and refugees—more than 1,600 a day—enter the U.S. In fact, more immigrants came to the U.S. in the 1980s than in any previous decade.

Today's immigrants are geographically and culturally diverse. The 600,000 people who legally immigrated in 1985, for instance, included 60,000 Mexicans, 48,000 Filipinos, 35,000 Koreans, 24,000 Dominicans, 20,000 Cubans, 19,000 Jamaicans, 16,000 Iranians, 15,000 Taiwanese, and 13,000 British.

How has the United States been changed by this continuing influx of people? The viewpoints in the following chapter examine this question.

"A United States dominated by Third World immigrants will be a very different nation in its cultural and its economic life."

Immigrants Threaten American Culture

Thomas Fleming

Since settlers came from England in 1607, the majority of immigrants to America have come from Europe. After restrictions against non-European immigrants were removed in 1965, however, about 80 percent of all American immigrants have since come from Asia and Latin America. Some studies have estimated that by the year 2080, as much as 37 percent of Americans will be descendants of immigrants arriving after 1980. In the following viewpoint, Thomas Fleming argues that American values and culture could be harmed by the influx of these new immigrants, and maintains that the U.S. can no longer afford massive immigration. Fleming is editor of *Chronicles*, a magazine on American culture published by the Rockford Institute in Rockford, Illinois.

As you read, consider the following questions:

1. How does Fleming respond to the statement that America is a nation of immigrants?
2. What possible future scenarios does Fleming foresee resulting from uncontrolled immigration?
3. What revisions in immigration policy does the author recommend?

Thomas Fleming, "The Real American Dilemma," *Chronicles*, vol. 13, no. 3, March 1989. Reprinted with permission.

America is a nation of immigrants. How often is that declaration trotted out to explain why it would be immoral to do something about controlling immigration, as if every country were not a nation of immigrants. If Britain ever had an indigenous population, it was overrun by Celts, Germans, Danes, and Normans—to say nothing of the Hollanders brought over and ennobled when Dutch William drove his father-in-law from the throne. Almost any country, excepting the poor benighted Scandinavians, could tell a similar story, and the present condition of Sweden is as good an argument as I can think of against a restricted gene pool. (It is also a total refutation of the hilarious idea of Nordic supremacy.)

It is conventional to speak of the great contributions made by immigrants and at the same time to deplore the unpleasant reception they were given by the WASP population. No one ever seems to carry the argument back to the reception the Indians usually tried to arrange for European settlers pushing into their territories. We are all, even the Indians, descended from immigrants, and it is hard to pick which group has contributed most to the fabric of our civilization. . . .

In recent years, however, while the main focus in the polite media has remained on the contributions and sufferings of hyphenated Americans, ordinary Americans are more concerned with the problems caused by the virtual flood of arrivals from the Third World. For some years now, legal immigration has been at an average rate of over 600,000 per year, while the number of illegals in this country is anybody's guess. In 1985 Richard Lamm and Gary Imhoff (*The Immigration Time Bomb: The Fragmenting of America*) estimated eight and a half to eleven million, mostly from Latin America.

The Need for Reform

Immigration reform was the great issue of the Reagan years that never really took shape, and it will be up to Mr. Bush, the Congress, and above all to the opinion industry to settle the future of the United States. There was a debate, of course, and one celebrated bill that didn't make it (Simpson-Mazzoli) as well as the version that did, but most of the discussion was safely trivial: whether or not to tighten up the border controls and send back (temporarily) a certain number of illegals, and how merciful to be in granting amnesty. Ultimately—and this is a sign of how low we have fallen—most of the conversation was about money. Think of the jobs that need to be done, the fruit that needs to be picked, the houses cleaned. Think of the contributions to science and industry made by talented immigrants.

67

After we've done thinking about what's in it for agribusiness and electronics, we just might begin to wonder what is in store for the American people. Not too long ago, I had a chance to go over the whole ground with one of the brightest defenders of free trade and open borders in the country. He waxed eloquent over the family values of the Mexicans and the high intelligence of the Orientals. Finally, I asked him: suppose we could set off neutron bombs all over the United States, wipe out the current citizen population and replace them with brilliant and hardworking Chinese. From his perspective, wouldn't that be a plus? I'm still waiting for an answer.

American Intangibles

Those who believe a deeper American culture still exists and ought to be conserved (they used to be called "conservatives") have good reason to worry that the new throngs of foreigners among us will not assimilate to it in any enduring way. Not simply language and clothing, but also less tangible qualities, such as the unspoken assumptions of political culture, art and literature, entertainment and religion, education, morals, the family, and concepts of work and property together create the set of common norms by which Americans know themselves to be different from Canadians, Mexicans, Europeans, and other cultures. But the process of becoming a real member of a living society is somewhat more complicated than translating advertising slogans into Japanese or Swahili.

Samuel T. Francis, *Chronicles*, March 1990.

The trouble began with treating the nation as an abstraction: the land of the free and the home of the brave was turned into the land of opportunity for what the Statue of Liberty's plaque so quaintly calls "the wretched refuse" of the world. A real country, with its own history, its own particular set of virtues and vices, its own special institutions, was reduced to cheap slogans and loyalty oaths.

The truth is, we have to confine our discussion to abstractions, including that abstraction that serves as a metaphor for an entire way of life—money, because what some Americans worry about cannot be spoken to the network reporters doing on-the-street interviews for the evening news. Despite the risks, some people are incautious enough to sign letters to the editor or call in to the radio talk shows that are increasingly the only form for free expression. What these simple folk are saying is that they do not care how smart the Chinese are or how religious the Mexicans are. If they're so smart, virtuous, and diligent, how come the countries they are leaving are in such a god-awful mess? The old question, "If you so smart, why ain't you rich?" applies to nations as well as individuals.

American Civilization

In his essay "Immigration and Liberal Taboos" (in *One Life at a Time, Please*), Edward Abbey sums up the situation with his customary restraint and discretion: "They come to stay and they stay to multiply. What of it? say the documented liberals; ours is a rich and generous nation, we have room for all, let them come. And let them stay, say the conservatives; a large, cheap, frightened, docile, surplus labor force is exactly what the economy needs. Put some fear into the unions: tighten discipline, spur productivity, whip up the competition for jobs. The conservatives love their cheap labor; the liberals love their cheap cause."

Abbey concludes by asking, "How many of us, truthfully, would prefer to be submerged in the Caribbean-Latin version of civilization?" Stripped of its anger, Abbey's question is worth asking. If we can judge from his novels, Abbey actually likes Mexico and its people. But for better or worse, he likes his own country more, and not necessarily because it is better (although he obviously thinks, as I do, that it is). But a nation, as the word implies (from *nascor*, be born) is a fictional extended family. Like members of a family, the citizens of a nation prefer each other's company and will sacrifice for the common good, not because they think their family or nation is superior to every other, but simply because it is theirs. The Germans may have better music, the English a clearer prose, the Russians a deeper spirituality, but Americans have, on occasion, been willing to shoot any of them in the defense or even the interest of the United States. And, it goes without saying, that all of these European people have displayed a marked capacity for becoming Americans.

There's the rub. Do Abbey's liberals and conservatives believe that there is anything particular about the American identity? After all, most of us don't blame the French for wanting to be French, and we all profess to sympathize with the desire of black Africans to rule their own countries and develop their own traditions without interference from white Europeans. Why is it only America that is denied an identity?

There is, after all, an American story that is primarily a saga of enterprising men and women who came here from Europe. The language and culture, as well as the legal and political systems, were derived from Britain. This way of life of ours is not the result of any general principle; it is the legacy of our forebears and a civilization that goes back to Greece and Rome. It is vastly creative and has shown an enormous capacity for transforming immigrants from somewhat differing cultures. This capacity is not infinite, and a United States dominated by Third World immigrants will be a very different nation in its cultural and its economic life.

A Question of Numbers

Part of the problem is a question of numbers. Talented immigrants are, for the most part, highly assimilable, but mass migrations are disruptive and threaten social cohesion. Between 1976 and 1986, the number of immigrants from Africa doubled, while the numbers from Asia, Mexico, and Haiti all quadrupled. (Haiti, by the way, was on the low side for the Caribbean: Jamaica was up 700 percent). The big winner, however, was India, whose stock rose an impressive 2,000 percent.

The Dangers of Immigration

Let me say it directly: massive immigration involves serious and profound social and cultural dangers. The United States is not immune to the trends that have affected and altered all other human societies. Civilizations rise and civilizations fall—and there are certain universal pathologies that characterized the fall of history's civilizations. Ethnic, racial, and religious differences can become such a pathology; they can grow, fester, and eventually splinter a society. The "melting pot" society is clearly an exception to history's lesson, and we make a serious mistake if we think that all our differences can and will harmonize (or homogenize) without our work and care.

I believe that America's culture and national identity are threatened by massive levels of legal and illegal immigration.

Richard D. Lamm and Gary Imhoff, *The Fragmenting of America*, 1985.

Like most Americans since, Thomas Jefferson firmly believed that this country should provide a haven for talented and freedom-loving people. He was also aware of the risks. In his *Notes on the State of Virginia*, Jefferson pointed out that the American form of government was derived from "the freest principles of the English Constitution." It was diametrically opposed to the absolutisms that ruled over most of Europe. Emigrants from such countries, he warned, "will bring with them the principles of the governments they leave . . . or, if able to throw them off, it will be in exchange for an unbounded licentiousness, passing, as is usual, from one extreme to another."

What would have especially aroused Jefferson's fears is the current reigning assumption that special arrangements have to be made for "refugees" from political oppression. Conservatives want to open the door to Cubans and Nicaraguans, while leftists give shelter to Salvadorans and South African blacks. What both groups are saying, in essence, is that they would like the United States to turn into Nicaragua or Haiti. Of course, all humane people sympathize with the victims of political oppression; wherever possible we would like to do something for them. But we must never forget that immigration policy is the most significant means of determining the future of our nation, and we owe it to our children not to squander their birthright in spasms of imprudent charity. . . .

If we refuse to control immigration, our options are severely limited. The least unattractive solution would be to implement the federal principle on a state and regional level, recognizing Hispanics and Orientals, in states where they form a majority, as the dominant group—much as the French are given special status in Quebec. (We must not imitate the disastrous Canadian policy of nationwide bilingualism.) Descendants of the old settlers that fought and won the land from Mexico will be quite rightly indignant with what many Mexicans are already calling the Reconquest, and we shall probably have far more trouble than Canada in adjusting to a multicultural situation. Perhaps after a century or two we can evolve into a safely neutered society of consumers—like Switzerland. It is just as likely to be a bloodbath.

A far less attractive scenario than either Switzerland or tribal civil war Nigerian style would be a forced Americanization on the grand scale. It didn't work all that well the last time we tried it, when Catholics were hectored and bullied out of the officially Protestant public schools, and considering the sort of people who run the federal bureaucracy today, we will in effect be writing the death sentence on republican self-government. Only an empire, with a vast machinery of manipulation (including some form of state religion) could succeed in creating order out of such a Babel, and the best we could hope for would be either a military *junta* or a fascist welfare state—Sweden with a führer.

What Should Be Done?

What then, if anything, can be done? There are several obvious changes in immigration policy that need to be made. First of all, we need to put an end to the mass migrations to the US. It was the *Völkerwanderungen* of the Germans and Huns that brought the Roman Empire down, and we shall be in even worse straits if we fail to control our Southern border and do not adopt a more hard-nosed approach to refugees fleeing the political turmoil, high population growth, and economic chaos of the Third World.

We also need to reexamine our priorities. From the 20's to the 50's, American immigration law made it very clear that we intended to be what we had always been: a European nation. The quota that took effect in 1929 was based on the ethnic background of the existing population of the US and allotted 85 percent of the total to northern and western Europe and 12 percent to the rest of Europe.

Preserving National Quotas

The Immigration Act of 1952 did preserve the national origins quota (not abolished until 1965), but within the system a separate set of ordered priorities were established. Preference was given first to immigrants with desirable (i.e. marketable) skills, second to relatives of citizens and resident aliens. Along with the abolition of national quotas in 1965 came changes in the preference system. Now unmarried children of citizens come first, spouses of resident aliens second, and exceptional and talented immigrants third. Other relatives of citizens and resident aliens come fourth and fifth, while workers with needed skills come sixth.

The result is the all-too-familiar scams by which undesired aliens contrive to give birth on US soil or arrange marriages of convenience. In either event, one unskilled alien can end up bringing "all his sisters and his cousins (whom he reckons up by dozens) and his aunts." The figures tell the story. Despite a total quota of only 270,000, the special categories have accelerated the rate of legal immigration to almost three times that. Ted Kennedy, by the way, is primarily responsible for the difference. In 1965, he served as floor manager of the legislation in the Senate, and in 1980 he sponsored amendments that removed the ceiling on admission, promising no more than 50,000 additional immigrants as a consequence.

What should come first is not the interest of the alien or even of US businesses, but the interest of the historical population of the country. Family members must, as Lamm and Imhoff among others insist, be included under a comprehensive total. We should continue, as Jefferson wished, to open our doors to talented emigrants not because they will make money for IBM, but because bright and able people are a precious and scarce commodity. More fruitpickers we do not need. Cut off the welfare payments and we shall be surprised at how many agricultural workers are living right now in Chicago and New York. The most pressing need, however, is the reestablishment of national quotas. These need not be based on the formulas of the 1920's; but nonetheless should give first priority to the population base of the nation.

One doesn't wish to be unkind, but cultural pluralism is not the most attractive legacy we can leave to our children. As a nation, we have barely survived the existence of two separate populations, black and white, and we have a long way to go in working out better relations between those two groups. What shall we do when the whole of America becomes a multiracial Alexandria? As the Romans realized, citizenship implies certain very concrete rights and duties: the right to trade and make contracts, the obligation to serve in the army, the right to inter-marry. While it is true that there are no laws restricting marriage between the races, such unions are very uncommon. According to census figures, less than two percent of existing marriages are of mixed race, and even projecting a modest rate of increase over the next few decades, it is highly unlikely that we shall realize anything approaching a homogeneous population in the near future.

Class Stratification

The problem, if it is a problem, is not simply one more case of white intolerance. The pressures against mixed-race dating and marriage are every bit as strong in the black and Oriental communities. This is not a question of *ought*, but a case of *is*, and the result will be a nation no longer stratified simply by class but by race as well. Europeans and Orientals will com-pete, as groups, for the top positions, while the other groups will nurse their resentment on the weekly welfare checks they receive from the other half. Perhaps such an arrangement can be worked out, but whatever emerges will not be a nation, cer-tainly not the United States.

The situation is quite as serious as even the most frightened alarmists have suggested, but we cannot begin even to speak seriously about changes in the law until we are willing to vio-late the code of silence that the left has imposed upon the topic. There is a pressing need for plain speech and open dis-cussion in which those who happen to agree with the over-whelming majority of Americans throughout our history are not stigmatized as xenophobes and racists. If the notion of aliens' rights really takes hold, we are in danger of losing the entire concept of American citizenship. Above all, we have to quit lying to ourselves about who we are and what we face. If sober and sensible people cannot solve the immigration prob-lem through an orderly process of debate and legislation, then there are genuine crazies out there only waiting for the chance to use such an issue as a springboard to power.

"America . . . faced the challenge of immigration in much more intense form a century ago; and instead of being weakened, it was enriched."

Immigrants Do Not Threaten American Culture

James Fallows

James Fallows is Washington editor of *The Atlantic Monthly*. He has written numerous articles on Asia, where he lived for several years, and on American society and social policy. In the following viewpoint, taken from his book *More Like Us*, he argues that U.S. culture thrives on the continuing influx of new immigrants from different countries. Fallows believes that fears of the U.S. becoming a culturally divided nation are unfounded.

As you read, consider the following questions:

1. What fundamental difference does Fallows describe between America and Japan?
2. Why should Americans not be too concerned about the assimilation of immigrants into U.S. society, according to the author?
3. Why does Fallows oppose totally uncontrolled immigration?

Excerpted, with permission, from *More Like Us: Making America Great Again* by James Fallows. New York: Houghton Mifflin Company, 1989. Copyright © 1989 by James Fallows.

That immigration is "good" is a quaint American belief that, to most people, seems no more than quaint. "Immigrants" were the doughty grandparents and great-grandparents who came to America eighty years ago; what happened to them doesn't seem too urgent or instructive anymore.

The Importance of Immigration

But of course immigration is still going on, and it is important to America in both a practical and a symbolic way. In practical terms, it continues to be America's major advantage over other countries, especially Japan. A disproportionate share of the ambitious people of the world are fighting for a chance to use their ambitions in the United States. Most other countries, with the exception of Australia and Canada, can't use these foreigners' talents. America can. On the symbolic level, America, by remaining open to immigrants, shows that it understands what kind of country it is. It is not a particular ethnic group or the result of a particular tradition; it is an arena, in which new people can try their best.

The economic evidence about immigration is open and shut. Immigrants are disproportionately entrepreneurial, determined, and adaptable, and through history they have strengthened the economy of whatever society they join. John Higham, of Johns Hopkins University, probably the leading historian of American immigration, has argued that immigrants strengthened American capitalism during its rocky periods at the turn of the century, and that they add crucial flexibility today. "At the simplest level one notes the prominence of the foreign-born among American inventors and also entrepreneurs and technicians in new, high-risk industries such as textile manufacturing in the early nineteenth century, investment banking in mid-century, and movie-making in the early twentieth century," Higham told a congressional committee in 1986. "Migration looses and sometimes breaks the bonds of tradition. It creates needs that cannot be met in customary ways, while throwing together people with rich, unsuspected potentialities.". . .

America's long-term strategic secret is that it can get the most out of people by putting them in surprising situations. Competition from other Americans is the source of most of this ultimately healthful disruption, but a continual supply of new competition is invigorating too.

Fear of the Other

The main resistance to immigration at the moment is not economic but cultural. The strain on the social fabric may seem too great. For each group of Nguyens starting new businesses and working round the clock, there may well be a group of

Latin Americans refusing to learn English, or Haitians practicing voodoo, or Iranians preaching Shi'ite fundamentalism—or, more generally, *outsiders* diluting the sense of Americanness.

Language is the easiest aspect of this problem to discuss. About half of today's immigrants, legal and illegal, are thought to be Spanish-speaking. (They are "thought" rather than "known" to be because estimates of illegal immigration are so imprecise.) That is a higher proportion of people in this country from one non-English-language group than ever before. The previous high was Germans, who made up about a third of all immigrants in the mid-nineteenth century. In addition, there are now Spanish-language TV stations and bilingual schools, which some see as slowing an immigrant's progression to English; and many of the immigrants are really "sojourners," who travel back and forth to Mexico, with little incentive to learn English.

American Culture Needs New Ideas

It's true that if a lot of new people come here with a lot of new customs, languages, and ideas, America will look different. So what? . . .

It might make sense to protect "recognizable" national characteristics in a society where national identity is fundamentally associated with a single religion, or language, or set of folkways. Thus the French might well worry about the effect of immigration on their national culture. They have one—including everything from Catholicism to a taste for fine Beaujolais. But because we are a nation of immigrants, such things are much less important in defining our national identity. Our culture is an amalgam of many. Was the old Yiddish-language *Jewish Daily Forward* an American newspaper or an Eastern European one? Is Taco Bell American or Mexican? Is gospel music American or African?

Chuck Lane, *The New Republic*, April 1, 1985.

These omens seem threatening, but in fact there is no evidence that Spanish-speaking immigrants are behaving differently from the way Italian, Polish, or German immigrants behaved several generations earlier. In retrospect it may look as if their transition to English went quickly and easily, but many dragged their feet just as some Spanish speakers do today. According to most studies by linguists, first-generation immigrants typically were not very comfortable in English. The transition came with their American-born children, and much the same pattern seems to hold today. Los Angeles, Houston, and Miami are full of Spanish-language billboards and graffiti, but those are indications of the large number of immigrants who have arrived relatively recently. The people who speak only Spanish are nearly all foreign-born. Their American-born children may speak Spanish as well as English, but that's an advantage, not a problem.

At Miami Senior High School, I talked with a hulking Puerto Rican football player who said he hoped to join the navy after he graduated. I heard his story and then I asked him his name. He told me, and I wrote "Ramon." He came around behind me and looked at my pad. "No, no!" he shouted, making me fear for my safety. "You should have put R-A-Y-M-O-N-D."

Emotional Concerns

The concern that lurks behind language is ethnic, racial, and emotional. America may be a multiracial country, but it has been mainly white and of European origin. Until the immigration laws were made "color blind" in 1965, European countries accounted for more than four fifths of all legal immigration to the United States. In the last twenty years the proportion has switched; Latin America and Asia now account for more than 80 percent of the legal total, split equally between the two areas. That may be economically efficient, because of people like the Nguyens, but is it wise to dilute the country's major cultural identity so rapidly?

Early in 1988, I got a letter expressing these fears from an American friend who had lived for many years in Japan and felt unsettled by what he saw when he went "home." I quote from it because even though I think my friend is wrong, I know that he's not the only one to feel as he does.

> None of the great outpourings of human civilization was, so far as I know, prompted by immigration. In fact, Attic Greece, Imperial Rome, Han China, Renaissance Italy, Bourbon France, Imperial England all were products of a racially and culturally homogeneous people. . . . With the most depressing regularity, it seems that great cultures have been the products of single peoples. . . . I think that part of the horror of New York City is due to its ethnic heterogeneity. It is very, very hard to develop a sense of kinship or commonality with people who look, act, and sound so different from oneself. Where there is no sense of commonality, there's not even the semblance of order, and where there is greatness there is always a strong sense of commonality. . . .
>
> Just ask the Tamils, the Karens, the Ibos, the Kurds, the Armenians, the Palestinians, the Assamese, the Khmers Rouges, the Afghans, the Acholi and the Baganda, the Hutu and the Tutsi, the Kosovo Albanians and the Sikhs what they think with. They think with their blood and with little else. That's why they are so ready to spill it.

As a description of what the rest of the world does, "thinking

77

with blood" may be correct. Certainly there is little evidence in Asia or Africa that people can rise above racial, ethnic, or tribal divisions. But, . . . America *is* abnormal. It faced the challenge of immigration in much more intense form a century ago; and instead of being weakened, it was enriched. By all accounts, the immigrants from Eastern and Southern Europe seemed more threatening and alien to the Americans of the late nineteenth century than Mexicans, Vietnamese, and Ethiopians do to the white and black Americans of today. No president of a major university would say today what Francis Walker, the president of MIT, said at the turn of the century: the Italians, Greeks, Poles, and Russian immigrants were "beaten men from beaten races, representing the worst failures in the struggle for existence." No one has contended, as the scientific experts of the day did then, that the new arrivals were inherently less intelligent than the native-born. Many of those now considered to be part of "mainstream" white American culture are descended from people seen as totally alien when they poured in. Was there less "real" difference between those Greek, Italian, and Russian immigrants and the native stock at the start of the century than there is between today's Americans and the Hmong? Maybe, but it doesn't matter: racial difference is in the eye of the beholder. (To outsiders, the Ashanti and Ewe tribes of Ghana look very similar. To each other, they are hostile foreigners, for all practical purposes different "races.")

Cultures Need Change

Cultures and societies, like living organisms, need food from outside in order to grow and to survive. And, like every living organism, the moment they cease changing they begin to die.

Justo L. González, *Basta !*, February 1990.

That is, America has been through worse racial disruption than any risk posed by today's immigration, and it emerged as the strongest, most dynamic, and most open society in the world. The disruption was worse then because the newcomers seemed more foreign and because the flow was proportionately much greater than it is today. (At the turn of the century, the annual influx of immigrants was as high as 1 percent of the existing population. During the 1980s, the peak has been less than a third of 1 percent, and the average has been about a fifth of 1 percent.) We've already proven that we are the great exception and can withstand strains that other societies could not tolerate. The racial problem that afflicts America has nothing to do with immigrants, whatever their color or origin. Indeed, it arises from the one great exception to voluntary immigration in the peopling of America.

Completely open immigration would be too great a strain even for American society. At the beginning of the twentieth century, when the relative flow was three to five times greater than it is now, the backlash was widespread and severe. It led to the "national origins" laws, which essentially restricted immigration to people from Western Europe. These laws, together with the Depression and World War II, dramatically slowed the influx for the next thirty years. The backlash that would result from extreme, rapid change is the main argument for limiting immigration at all. Like totally open capitalism, without safety standards or child-labor laws, totally uncontrolled immigration is too raw for modern societies to accept. But short of open immigration, the United States should keep taking at least as many people as it does now—somewhere between 600,000 and 800,000 per year, depending on surges of refugees and other factors—and should feel grateful for the new blood, rather than resentful of it.

"Talented young immigrants . . . make us richer and not poorer."

Immigrants Help the U.S. Economy

Julian L. Simon

Some people argue that immigrants increase the unemployment rate and rely excessively on welfare. In the following viewpoint, Julian L. Simon argues that these and other ideas are false. He argues that most immigrants are young, talented, hard-working, and in general contribute much to the U.S. economy. He concludes that the U.S. should allow more immigrants into the country. Simon is a professor of business administration at the University of Maryland in College Park. His books include *The Ultimate Resource* and *The Economic Consequences of Immigration.*

As you read, consider the following questions:

1. Why does Simon contend that immigrants do not drain welfare services?
2. In the author's opinion, why do many people oppose immigration?
3. How many immigrants should the U.S. let in annually, according to Simon?

There was once little factual information available about the effects of immigration. Primitive "common sense" arguments were therefore accorded respect. . . .

Social scientists have now gathered an impressive body of knowledge about immigration. This research, which contradicts the popular wisdom on most matters, points us toward sound national choices. The main findings are as follows:

• *Immigrants do not cause native unemployment, even among low-paid and minority groups.* A spate of recent studies, using a variety of methods, have shown that the bogey of "displacement" of natives does not exist. New entrants take jobs, but they also make jobs. And the jobs they create with their purchasing power, and with the new businesses which they start up, are at least as numerous as the jobs which immigrants fill.

• *Immigrants do not rip off natives by over-using welfare services.* Immigrants typically arrive when they are young and healthy. Hence new immigrant families use fewer welfare services than do average native families because immigrants do not receive expensive Social Security and other aid to the aged. And immigrant families pay more taxes than do native families. Therefore, immigrants contribute more to the public coffers in taxes than they draw out in welfare services. Every year, an average immigrant family puts about $2,500 into the pockets of natives from this excess of taxes over public costs.

• *Immigrants are typically as well-educated and occupationally skilled as natives.* (This was true even a century ago.) New arrivals bring valuable technical knowledge with them, and the proportion with post-graduate education is far higher than the average of the native labor force. Immigrants who arrived between 1970 and 1980 were 50% more likely than natives to have post-graduate education; immigrants from Asia were 2½ times more likely to have post-graduate education than natives.

Of course, people at all levels of skill and education benefit the economy. And the total number of immigrants is the most important issue. An overall increase in immigration is the best way to boost the crucial stock of talented scientists, inventors, engineers, and managers who will improve U.S. competitiveness.

Nobel Winners

• *Immigrants demonstrate desirable economic traits.* Compared to natives, immigrants save more, apply more effort during working hours, have twice as great a propensity to be self-employed (according to Teresa Sullivan of the University of Texas), have higher rates of participation in the labor force and are unusually self-reliant and innovative. Immigrants contribute important new productivity-enhancing ideas to industry and sci-

81

ence, and they win Nobel prizes.

First- and second-generation children do astonishingly well in school—at Boston's 17 public high schools, 13 of the 1989 valedictorians were immigrants or the children of immigrants. They win an astonishing proportion of scholastic prizes—22 of 40 Westinghouse Science Talent Search finalists in [a] recent contest, according to the American Enterprise Institute's Karl Zinsmeister and Ben Wattenberg.

How Many Immigrants?

Arrivals as a percentage of population

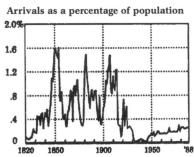

Number of arrivals, in thousands

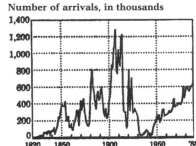

Bureau of the Census

• *Immigration as a proportion of population is less than a fifth of what it was at the turn of the century.* (See the charts nearby.) Even in absolute numbers, total immigration is nowhere near its volume in those years when U.S. population was less than half of what it now is.

The foreign-born population is only about 6% now—less than the proportion in such countries as Britain, France, and West Germany, and vastly lower than in Australia and Canada. The U.S. is not at present a "country of immigrants"—it is a country of the descendants of immigrants.

• *Admissions policy is nepotistic.* More than three-quarters of all immigrants obtain visas through family connections here in the U.S.; less than one-quarter are admitted on the basis of their skills and economic productivity.

• *Natural resources and the environment are not at risk from immigration.* The long-term trends reveal that our air and water are getting cleaner rather than dirtier, and our supplies of natural resources are becoming more available rather than exhausted, contrary to common belief. Immigration increases the technical knowledge to speed these benign trends.

• *Immigrants of all origins assimilate quickly.* In every decade, the "new" immigrants are thought difficult to assimilate, unlike the "old" immigrants. But in each decade—including the 1970s and 1980s—the "new" immigrants have adjusted quickly both economically and culturally. Within a decade or two, immigrants come to earn more than natives with similar educational characteristics.

• *Immigrants increase the flexibility of the economy.* Newcomers are unusually mobile both geographically and occupationally even after they arrive. Hence they mitigate the tight labor markets that the U.S. is beginning to experience.

• *Immigration reduces the uncuttable social costs of the elderly.* More and more of the U.S. population is retired, with a smaller proportion of adults in the labor force. New immigrants typically are just entering the prime of their work lives and tax-paying years. Immigration is the best way to lighten the Social Security burden of the aging U.S.population. It also reduces the federal deficit, which would not exist if people still lived the short lives, and had the large number of children, that they did early in the century.

An Overblown Scare

Illegal immigration is an overblown scare. Fantastic guesses about the number of illegal aliens in the U.S., based on little except the desire to create public fear, were passed off as fact in the 1970s and early 1980s. The head of the Immigration and Naturalization Service told Congress in 1976 that there were between 4 million and 12 million illegal aliens.

A solid body of research has now shown that the actual number of illegals at its peak in the early 1980s was perhaps 3 million, many of whom were only transitory workers. The million-plus number of persons who registered for the amnesty of 1987-88 verifies that the total was and is nowhere near the huge numbers that were bandied about when the 1986 Simpson-Mazzoli law was passed.

Public opinion has always opposed immigration, and for the same reasons it does now. Magazine articles in earlier decades, and public-opinion polls more recently, show bigotry to have been the main driving force, according to research by Rita Simon of American University. Nowadays it is no longer acceptable to publicly state crude racist arguments about color, ethnicity and religion. "Cultural homogeneity" is the contemporary codeword for racist opposition to immigration. Supposed dangers from terrorism, crime, disease and social disorganization also are used to arouse antagonism against immigrants.

The Kennedy-Simpson legislation before the Congress will allow no more immigrants than previously, and maybe fewer, even though our population and economy are growing. According to the General Accounting Office, the bill probably would result in a quota increase of between 20,000 and 60,000 new arrivals a year, but would close some loopholes. Net, the bill would essentially freeze legal immigration at present levels. This is restrictiveness, no matter how it is dressed up.

Behind the law is some combination of economic ignorance and plain racism. The nativism is as clearly at work here as it is in Britain, where Margaret Thatcher makes no bones about restricting immigration so as to "keep Britain British." In order to raise immigration from some preferred countries, immigration from China, the Dominican Republic, Britain (many of whose emigrants are non-white), India, Mexico, the Philippines, South Korea and Hong Kong would be reduced. That is, the law would offer entry to fewer Asians and Hispanics.

Immigration Is Necessary

Immigration is not a benefit to be doled out by a generous nation. It is instead a fundamental life force for capitalist expansion. . . .

The older the country's population and social order, the more it needs these periodic transfusions and inspirations of human capital. Our best imports are just-liberated people.

Warren T. Brookes, *Conservative Chronicle*, January 17, 1990.

It is in the nature of interest-group scuffling in Washington that many conflicts attract attention—family immigration vs. merit-based immigration; agricultural workers vs. others; this ethnic quota versus that one, and so on. But one issue vastly overwhelms all the others: the total number of immigrants that will be allowed in. That total dominates the effect of immigration on national welfare. Focusing on the zero-sum trade-offs will best serve the purpose of those who wish to restrict total immigration, just as the illegal immigration issue was used for so long to divert attention from the key issue of total legal immigration.

The nub of the policy issue is as follows: Talented young immigrants help us advance every one of our national goals. They make us richer and not poorer, stronger and not weaker.

I suggest that during a study period of perhaps three years, total immigration be boosted by a million per year, to a level still well within the range of prior absorption experience. If there are no unexpected problems, the total could again be raised for a study period, and so on until unexpected problems are encountered.

"Free immigration can be the death of free enterprise."

Immigrants Harm the U.S. Economy

Garrett Hardin

Garrett Hardin is a professor of biology and human ecology at the University of California at Santa Barbara. His books include *Exploring New Ethics for Survival* and *Population, Evolution, and Birth Control.* In the following viewpoint, he argues that immigrants harm the U.S. economy by using and depleting the nation's natural resources and by taking jobs away from American citizens.

As you read, consider the following questions:

1. How much immigration does Hardin believe the U.S. should have?
2. How does immigration undermine the free enterprise system, according to Hardin?
3. What point does the author make by examining the shortage of trained nurses?

Garrett Hardin, a paper presented to the Conference on the Purpose of Legal Immigration in the 1990s and Beyond, sponsored by the Federation for American Immigration Reform, June 10, 1988. Reprinted with permission.

Immigrants are welcomed by many different power groups: by merchants, who see immigrants as consumers; by employers, who look for subservient labor; by ethnic units, who seek more political power; and by traditionalists, because "we are a nation of immigrants." (But so are all nations!)

Zero Immigration

I oppose all four groups. I argue that we should, as rapidly as possible, reduce net immigration into the United States (immigration minus emigration) to zero.

This is not put forward as a bargaining position. However, I recognize that it cannot be achieved overnight. But I maintain that the quality of our immigration program is best measured by the paucity with which zero net immigration is achieved.

The world is moving ever more deeply into the realm of shortages. Every increase in population brings an increase in the per capita cost of reducing pollution. Congestion grows. Traffic gridlocks become the norm as more valuable time is lost to commuting. Costs increase, tempers are frayed.

Perhaps the most effective political agents working to increase population through the importation of immigrants are employers. Tragically, many businessmen fail to realize that a free immigration policy undermines the economic system they praise.

The Free Enterprise System

The ideal free enterprise system is a procedure in which work is matched to workers by open bidding. Business enterprisers announce what they are willing to pay, and workers either accept the bid or make a counter-offer. It's a good system. We should not undermine it.

When practiced faithfully it is a self-adjusting system. That does not mean that adjustments come without pain. An increase in the cost of labor must be paid for out of an increase in the price of the product. That may mean lower sales or lower profits. Or the enterpriser may find a new way to increase production without increasing the price.

The life of free enterprisers is not a bed of roses, but that is why the monetary rewards are so high. Society pays businessmen to solve problems, not to evade them. Subsidies are an evasion of the free enterprise system. So also is reaching outside the national community for cheaper, more subservient labor in the form of immigrants. Every evasion of a self-adjusting system stores up trouble for the future.

If there were a shortage of labor there might be an excuse for immigration. But there isn't. Except in war time there has been no shortage of labor in America for more than a century. We are afflicted with an excess of labor: we call it "unemployment."

During the past 15 years the army of unemployed Americans has fluctuated between 4 and 10 million. That's the officially unemployed. The true numbers may be as much as 50 percent higher. There is no present reason to think that it will ever sink lower.

A Resource Issue

At the most basic and fundamental level, immigration is an environmental and resource issue. Each additional immigrant, regardless of his or her personal qualifications and merits, swells our numbers and further increases the already dangerous level of environmental pollution.

Each additional immigrant (plus his or her descendants) further depletes our increasingly scarce reserves of natural resources, thus rendering the U.S. more and more dependent on imports for essential supplies of energy and materials.

Negative Population Growth, Inc., *Zero Net Migration*, 1986.

There are plenty of people to fill all the employment slots. Of course, many of the unemployed cannot fill particular slots, but the employment game is a game of musical chairs. Those who are better prepared and already employed can move on to higher jobs, while their old positions are occupied by others whose skills are, perhaps, poorer to begin with.

Given the apparently perpetual existence of a surplus of labor how are we to interpret an outcry of "labor shortage"? Only one way makes sense: "labor shortage" is a warning signal that someone is seeking a labor subsidy from outside the national system. How should rational men and women react to such warnings?

The Warning Whistle

I remind you that it is dangerous to ignore warning signals. Remember the railroad wreck near Baltimore on 4 January, 1987? Sixteen lives were lost, 170 people were injured, and property damages amounted to $15 million. Why did the accident occur? Because the warning whistle, installed for safety's sake, annoyed the crew, and one of them taped it shut. That's no way to run a railroad.

In the economic system "labor shortage!" is the shriek of a warning whistle. . . .

As concerns particular professions, a persistent shortage means

87

that there is something wrong with the way our schools, and society at large, educate the young and reward those who work.

We can understand the meaning of "labor shortage!" better if we examine one situation in detail. I propose to look at the nursing profession.

Issues of Work

Every few years there is an outcry about a shortage of trained nurses. Yet at every moment there are thousands of trained nurses who have left the profession to take other jobs. Why did they switch? Because nursing is not attractive enough, relative to other work. The pay may be too low; the hours may be too long; the assignments may be too unpredictable; or there may be too little autonomy for a competent, self-respecting nurse. (Doctors and head nurses can be pretty overbearing.)

The warning whistle, "shortage of nurses!" tells us to address the issues of work and its rewards. Medical administrators ignore the warning as they try to import more subservient women from poor countries. A hospital administrator who calls for immigrant labor is trying to tape the warning whistle shut.

He ignores the need to improve the working conditions of nurses, and hence the quality of nursing. Patients suffer. America suffers.

A similar analysis applies to every so-called "labor shortage." Periodic complaints of shortages of engineers, teachers, farm workers, and unskilled labor yield to this analysis. In every case those who want to import immigrants want to tape the warning whistle shut. The whistle is attached to the American free enterprise system, to which most businessmen pay lip service, but which all too many try to escape when it is applied to their own affairs.

The businessman who imports labor from less developed countries is plugging shut the warning whistle. Each immigrant who comes in becomes the instant heir of all the expensive infrastructure accumulated by generations of Americans. This structure includes public highways, the services of private enterprises, and the welfare functions of the state.

Costs of Immigration

In all fairness, the immigrant should "buy into the firm." He doesn't; nor does his employer buy in for him. Without paying a cent the immigrant can instantly draw on the resources of public hospitals and schools which have been paid for over many years by tax-paying Americans. More, the immigrant's demands are often increased by his family, generally large, which he imports or generates on the spot.

It is true that immigrants also create jobs—but not as many as the workers they displace. (If they created more, Americans could become rich instantly by importing all the rest of the world's people. But no apologist for immigration has the gall to suggest that!)

Immigration makes the unemployment problem worse than it would otherwise be. Unemployment is worst among the young. As an incidental consequence of this fact, those who have never held a job are most easily recruited into the well-paying illegal drug trade. Should we blame the recruits? Or society for tolerating immigration and other practices that increase the need for employment of some kind?

Immigrants and the Labor Force

America presently can too easily get its labor force from legal and illegal immigrants. This is not an irrational act: immigrants are hard workers and often work for low wages and no benefits. Illegal immigrants will come to America and live in appalling conditions, accept payment in cash, do without any benefits and, if they complain, an employer can turn them in to the Immigration Service. It is a functional source of labor to many Americans.

But it is too often dysfunctional to America. What America does *not* need in the 1990's is ten million unskilled immigrants to move in and take our low-skill jobs. America should turn from the Cold War to a domestic crusade to solve our problem of the dysfunctional poor. We must start our own poor up the ladder of success, and thus a tight labor market is needed.

Richard D. Lamm, *Chronicles*, July 1990.

Is immigration to blame for the evils of society? Not solely. Is overpopulation to blame? Again, not solely. Overpopulation by itself (whatever that means) may not actually cause anything. But it sure as hell exaggerates the evils caused by other forces.

So long as we cannot reduce unemployment to zero we should reduce immigration to zero. We must escape the mental habits of the past, adopted when times were different. We must build the world of the future on the free enterprise system, toward which even centrally directed economies like China and Russia are now moving. The free enterprise system is a pretty good system. The world is crowded with many desperately poor countries looking for an outlet for their people. Free immigration can be the death of free enterprise. When that goes not much will remain of other freedoms.

"There is scarcely a community in America that has gone untouched by alien-related crime."

Illegal Immigrants Cause Crime

Palmer Stacy and Wayne Lutton

Much of the controversy over immigration stems from fears that immigrants contribute to America's crime problem. In the following viewpoint, Palmer Stacy and Wayne Lutton argue that the United States is suffering a crime wave brought on by immigrants. They assert that many illegal immigrants have little respect for U.S. laws. Stacy is president of Americans for Immigration Control, a lobbying organization which seeks to restrict immigration. Lutton has lectured and written extensively on immigration issues. He has coauthored two books and his articles have appeared in *National Review* and *Strategic Review*.

As you read, consider the following questions:

1. Why has the U.S. admitted so many immigrant criminals, according to Stacy and Lutton?
2. What crimes do immigrants commit, according to the authors?
3. What actions do Stacy and Lutton recommend?

Palmer Stacy and Wayne Lutton, *The Immigration Time Bomb.* Revised edition. Monterey, VA: The American Immigration Control Foundation, 1988. Excerpted with permission.

One of the consequences of ceasing to enforce sensible immigration controls has been the wave of alien-related crime that has struck our nation from coast to coast. Our immigration laws prohibit the entry of criminals and ex-convicts, the mentally ill, persons likely to become welfare charges, prostitutes and procurers and other undesirable individuals. Despite the intent of these laws, politicians have allowed thousands of dangerous criminals and perverts to enter our country.

The Cuban Invasion

The 1980 Cuban and Haitian invasion of southern Florida turned what was an alien crime *problem* into an alien crime *crisis*. After the Carter Administration made it clear that no action would be taken to halt the illegal flood of "refugees" from Mariel Harbor, Castro seized the opportunity to rid his island of some of the dregs of the Cuban population and proceeded to empty his prisons and insane asylums. As many as 40,000 hardcore criminals and sex deviates were welcomed by Jimmy Carter with "an open heart and open arms."

Bullets and knives were soon entering the hearts of other Americans, such as Lieutenant Jan Brinkers of the New York City Housing Police, murdered May 4, 1981, by Cuban "boat people." According to a shocking *New York* magazine article entitled "Los Bandidos Take the Town: Castro's Outcasts Shoot Up New York," some 2,000 Cuban gunmen prowl New York City, where they commit "thousands of shootings, robberies, and rapes."

"They seem to be the dregs of Cuban society, the sweepings of jails and streets," reports Lt. James McGowan of the New York Police Department. Most of the *bandidos* are followers of an African-derived cult and worship a "thunder god" named Chango; many are homosexuals. Their witches conduct a ceremony in which the blood of decapitated animals is dripped in front of images of their pagan gods. The carcasses are then burned and the ashes sprinkled on the *bandidos* to protect them from the police.

These Cuban *bandidos* specialize in armed robbery. If the victims show any sign of resistance, they are murdered. Among the thousands of crimes committed in the New York City area by these thugs have been:

• The murder of a rent collector in the Bronx by a *bandido* named Camacho, who strangled the man by tightening an electrical cord around his neck until he choked to death. Camacho was also responsible for strangling a woman and for raping another.

• A *bandido* by the name of Valdez, along with two accomplices, went on a crime spree, raping a woman in Teaneck,

New Jersey, while her husband lay handcuffed on the bed. Another woman who was slow in handing over her purse was shot. Two days later, this same trio entered a store in the Bronx and shot and killed the owner, William Belin, and wounded his fifteen-year-old nephew.

• A man known as Lazaro committed several armed robberies in New York in order to raise money to go on a gambling trip to Las Vegas. After he lost most of his money, he began robbing stores in Las Vegas to pay for the trip back to New York.

Dick Hafer. Reprinted by permission of AICF, Box 525, Monterey, VA 24465.

• One man in Newark, New Jersey, sponsored 35 Marielitos and used them to form his own gang of criminal drug dealers.

• In a random act of violence, Ramon Carrelero murdered three bar patrons in the Bronx, calmly shooting each in the head. . . .

Criminal activity by 1980 Caribbean "boat people" is increasing in scale and sophistication. *The New York Times* of March 31, 1985, published a long report, "Cuban Refugee Crime

Grows in U.S.," which pointed out that the "diplomatic agreement providing for the U.S. to deport back to Cuba 2,746 refugees classified as criminal or mentally ill offers little comfort to law-enforcement officials, who say that refugees who fled the port of Mariel in 1980 have been linked to an unusually large number of crimes. "

Cuban crime is no longer limited to a few cities, but has taken on a national character. A Las Vegas police report concluded that "Our observations confirm a national conspiracy exists" among Cuban "refugee" criminals. A report prepared by the Harrisburg police on crimes perpetrated by Marielitos reveals the existence of Cuban networks conducting such crimes as airline ticket fraud, credit card fraud, and cocaine and marijuana trafficking. . . .

Instead of expelling the Cubans and Haitians who arrived illegally in 1980, the politicians and the courts freed most of them from emergency compounds set up by the U.S. government. Those relatively few who have been kept in refugee camps, detention centers or federal prisons have shown their contempt for this country by repeatedly rioting. . . .

War Wagons

Gangs of Mexicans have repeatedly attacked Border Patrol officers with rocks and guns near the border. The Border Patrol has been forced to obtain some special armored vans—nicknamed "War Wagons"—in which to conduct border watches.

The millions of illegal aliens flooding our country by land, sea and air clearly have little respect for our laws—their very presence shows that. Many bring illegal drugs with them as they come. Immigration and Naturalization Service Commissioner Alan C. Nelson said in 1986 that 28% of the persons arrested for drug possession by the Border Patrol are illegal aliens.

In an affidavit filed in U.S. District Court in Portland, Oregon, in a 1986 heroin case, Neil Van Horn, a federal Drug Enforcement Administration agent, said, "I know that in and around the Portland metropolitan area, upper-level distributors often use illegal immigrants to transport heroin or other controlled substances into the United States from Mexico. . . . The illegal immigrants are then used to protect or distribute the heroin or other contraband substances and in that manner obtain their livelihood. Oftentimes, if arrested, the only action taken is deportation back to Mexico."

Many illegals engage in crime as soon as they are across the border. Charles Perez, INS director from the El Paso, Texas, area, says half of that city's downtown crime is related to illegal immigration. In Houston, more than 30 percent of the city's murders involve illegal aliens. And Denver Police Chief Art Dill notes that illegals who cannot quickly find work "steal to survive."

Of the more than 100,000 illegal aliens the INS suspects committed felonies in the U.S. between 1980 and 1987, only 12,000 have been prosecuted. Congress has failed to give the INS the resources needed to track down criminal aliens. Mexican gangs have already made large sections of East Los Angeles unsafe for law-abiding Americans, and the problem is bound to get worse as more illegals enter southern California from Mexico. As the Urban Institute explains in its study, *The Fourth Wave: California's Newest Immigrants*, "Youth gangs unquestionably pose a problem. Since the mid-1970s violent gang warfare resulting from drug usage and dealing have become common in the barrios and public housing projects."

The Drug Trade

For over a decade, Cubans, Colombians and other Hispanics have played a leading role in America's drug trade. Billions of dollars in illicit drug profits have created an economic miniboom in Miami. Drug dealers pay cash for condominiums, Mercedes-Benz automobiles, expensive jewelry and bribes to policemen. One drug dealer, Eduardo Orozco, came to the U.S. from Colombia in 1976, and over a four-year period used eleven U.S. banks and financial institutions to turn over more than $150 million in cash from his drug operations. According to the *Washington Post* of March 14, 1984: "Colombia's narcotics trade is thought to generate as much as $30 billion in revenue a year for that country, whose foreign exchange surplus with the U.S. has risen from $405 million in 1975 to more than $3 billion."

Aliens Commit More Crimes

Rep. Lamar Smith affirms that the nation has a "massive problem with potentially hundreds of thousands of illegal aliens . . . who have committed crimes." These include a growing number of serious offenses, such as murder, rape, and drug trafficking. The number of illegal aliens arrested by local authorities and turned over to the Immigration and Naturalization Service increased from 22,000 in 1985 to 51,154 in 1989.

Border Watch, May 1990.

Other "new immigrants" are taking advantage of our loosely enforced immigration laws: Japanese gangsters, members of a closely-knit, Mafia-like clan known as Yakuza, already heavily involved in prostitution and pornography rackets in Japan and Hawaii, have spread to California. Chinese gangs, manned by illegal aliens specializing in extortion, are today active in New York City, Boston, Miami and elsewhere. The *Jewish Press* of Brooklyn, New York, has reported on the "Israeli Mafia," composed of new immigrants from Israel whose criminal backgrounds are hidden from the American Embassy, which would not issue them visas if the truth were known. They have "continued their old ways," according to the *Jewish Press*, "preying on the Israeli immigrants first, and later, the Jewish community as a whole." Gangs of illegal aliens from Jamaica, known as "posses," were responsible for 600 homicides in 1986-1987, according to Jerry Rudden, a spokesman for the Bureau of Alcohol, Tobacco and Firearms. Jamaican gangs specialize in cocaine trafficking and are notorious for their use of violence and utter disregard for human life.

The problem posed by alien criminals is not new. From the early days of our Republic, foreign nations have often tried to dump their criminals here. Benjamin Franklin complained of this practice in an article entitled "On Sending Felons to America," published in the *Pennsylvania Gazette* in 1787.

In years past, our elected representatives passed laws to keep criminals out and then enforced those laws. Today the laws are still on the books but our leaders have lost the will to enforce them. There is scarcely a community in America that has gone untouched by alien-related crime—a crime-wave which will continue to worsen unless strong action is taken.

"The growing number of human rights violations . . . point to the xenophobic atmosphere rising out of baseless claims that migrant workers . . . are causing a national crime wave."

Illegal Immigrants Are Victims of Crime

Roberto Martínez

Roberto Martínez directs the U.S.-Mexico Border Program of the American Friends Service Committee in San Diego, California. The Program works to protect the human rights of illegal immigrants and migrant workers in the region. In the following viewpoint, he argues that most immigrants are not criminals, and that many of them are instead victims of crime brought on by racial prejudice. Martínez calls for the U.S. to be more open to and understanding of immigrants.

As you read, consider the following questions:

1. To what kinds of crimes are immigrants vulnerable, according to Martínez?
2. Why have hate crimes against immigrants been increasing, according to the author?
3. What does Martínez find ironic about the suggestion that the U.S. should build a wall on the Mexican border?

Roberto Martínez, "Migrants Are Falling Victim to Crimes of Hate and Violence," *San Diego Union,* July 8, 1990. Copyright 1990 Hispanic Link News Service. Reprinted with permission.

Jesús Reyes and his nephew, Andrés Valdes, left the poor *colonias* of Mexico City to try their luck in *El Norte*.

Originally from Oaxaca, one of the poorest states in Mexico, they moved with their families to Mexico City to escape its harsh poverty. They found 18 million people in the Federal District competing for jobs and housing. So Jesús, 18, and Andrés, 16, decided to do what thousands of their compatriots have done before them—head north.

Nothing, however, could have prepared them for what they would encounter once they reached the U.S.-Mexico border.

Danger at the Border

When they reached Tijuana, a city of almost 2 million bordering San Diego county, they had to decide where to cross. The area known as *El Bordo* (levee), popular because of its accessibility to freeways, was now lit by floodlights set up by the U.S. Border Patrol. Jesús and Andrés moved farther west.

The area they chose would take them through one of the most dangerous sections of the border, the scene of at least 10 shootings—six resulting in death—since January 1990. As Jesús and Andrés slipped through the torn fence and made their way down a path through a ranch, they heard a voice call out, *"Venga,venga, no migra"* (Come, come, we're not the Border Patrol).

When they moved closer to see where the voice was coming from, a white man in his early 20s stepped from behind a tree and pointed a high-powered bow and arrow at them. Then three men came out of the ranch house, pointed rifles and guns at them and demanded money. They took $50 and ordered the pair to run. As the boys ran, they saw another group of migrants approaching. They attempted to warn them, but the robbers waved them away with their weapons. From a safe distance, they saw the four men rob that group, too.

A week later, I was showing a CBS television crew a migrant camp in Carlsbad, a mixed farming and residential community in northern San Diego County. The correspondent requested that I ask two workers to relate their experiences as undocumented migrants. That's how I met Jesús and Andrés. They poured out their terrifying ordeal at the hands of the robbers.

More Tragedy

Two weeks later, tragedy struck in the area where they had been robbed. A 12-year-old boy crossing with relatives was shot to death. The shots reportedly came from the house the robbers had come out of to rob Jesús and Andrés. A 21-year-old man was arrested, and later released for lack of evidence, in the boy's death. The police, whom I had contacted about the ear-

97

lier incident, called me to bring Jesús and Andrés to look at suspects in a photo lineup. They identified the suspect as the man who had robbed them. He is still charged with robbing migrants.

Jesús and Andrés reside in the same camp where Cándido Galloso Salas lives. Galloso Salas recently was handcuffed, taped and beaten—with a bag fastened over his head—while seeking day work outside a rural store. An all-white jury found his assailant—twice his size at 6 feet, 6 inches and 220 pounds—guilty of a misdemeanor.

Joel Pett/*Lexington Herald-Leader*. Reprinted with permission.

Two other migrant workers in the camp described to me how they were attacked, robbed and beaten by six youths with guns and boards. A Mixtec organizer in nearby Vista also contacted me to say he had been shot in the face with a paint cartridge of the type used in war games. A similar projectile was used to injure 14 migrant workers in Poway, northeast of San Diego.

Hate Crimes

This sudden rise in hate crimes comes, not surprisingly, at a time when tensions and animosity are building in northern San Diego County against the growing presence and visibility of migrant Mexican and Guatemalan workers. Yet, it is nothing new.

In 1980 I began documenting shootings, killings and beatings of migrant workers by roving gangs of youth in the area. In November of 1988, two migrant workers were shot and killed on a lonely back road of Del Mar by two self-proclaimed white supremacists. That murder was classified as a "hate crime." The killer was sentenced to 50 years to life. His accomplice received 14 years.

Almost all the members of these gangs are between the ages of 14 and 22. It leads one to speculate whether they are carrying out their communities' fantasies, if the racism is so ingrained that they feel justified to the point that they think they are performing a community service.

The growing number of human rights violations, the use of a popular San Diego radio show to promote anti-immigrant sentiment, the hate calls and threats I receive at my office, the "light up the border" movement (private citizens park their cars, with headlights beamed at the border, to protest the so-called "invasion of Mexicans, drug traffickers and terrorists") all point to the xenophobic atmosphere rising out of baseless claims that migrant workers steal jobs and are causing a national crime wave, clogging our jails and courts.

As the surge of violence illustrates, those fears are being translated into physical attacks on defenseless people whose only crime is being poor, hungry and persecuted.

Need for Understanding

This fear and xenophobia should be replaced with an understanding of what drives people north. We are a nation of immigrants, and documented and undocumented workers contribute significantly to our economy, culture and history.

It is ironic that, while walls are crumbling in Eastern Europe, some conservative groups and government agencies here are calling for walls and ditches to be built at our border—sealing and militarizing it. Regular Army, Marines and National Guard troops are already patrolling the U.S.-Mexico border from San Diego to Brownsville, Texas.

The border is not a war zone. The people crossing are not the enemy. They are just people deserving of respect, dignity and all the rights afforded anyone who comes here to live and work.

a critical thinking activity

Recognizing Stereotypes

A stereotype is an oversimplified or exaggerated description of people or things. Stereotyping can be favorable. Most stereotyping, however, tends to be highly uncomplimentary and, at times, degrading.

Stereotyping grows out of our prejudices. When we stereotype someone, we are prejudging him or her. Consider the following example: Mr. Jones believes that all immigrants live on welfare. The possibility that many immigrants work hard at their jobs and shun welfare never occurs to him. He has prejudged all immigrants and will not recognize any possibility that is not consistent with his belief.

The following statements relate to the subject matter in this chapter. Consider each statement carefully. *Mark S for any statement that is an example of stereotyping. Mark N for any statement that is not an example of stereotyping. Mark U if you are undecided about any statement.*

If you are doing this activity as a member of a class or group, compare your answers with those of other class or group members.

S = stereotype
N = not a stereotype
U = undecided

1. Migrant workers are simply people looking for a place to live and work.
2. Illegal immigrants are often victims of violent crime as they cross the border.
3. People who oppose immigration are xenophobic racists.
4. Most undocumented aliens avoid criminal activities.
5. The Cubans who arrived in Florida in 1980 were hardened criminals—the dregs of Cuban society.
6. Asian immigrants provide us a shining example of how to succeed in America with hard work.
7. Many illegal immigrants engage in crime as soon as they cross the border.
8. Houston police statistics showing that 30 percent of murders involved illegal immigrants are not clear whether the immigrants were the victims or the perpetrators.
9. For over a decade, Cubans, Colombians, and other Hispanics have played a leading role in America's drug trade.
10. Most people, when they think of immigrants, think of their quaint grandparents and great-grandparents.
11. Because of their experiences, immigrants in general are good at adapting to new situations.
12. Children of immigrants always adapt better than their parents.
13. All of the world's great cultures were products of racially and culturally similar peoples.
14. The Tamils, Karens, Kurds, Sikhs, and other Third World tribal peoples think with their blood and with little else. That is why they are so ready to spill it.
15. Many immigrants now considered "mainstream" Americans were considered totally alien when they first arrived. Such a process will happen with today's immigrants.
16. The new throngs of foreigners are not absorbing the deeper aspects of American culture.
17. Immigrants are generally more patriotic than other Americans.
18. America's culture is threatened by massive levels of immigration.
19. Businesspeople who complain about the labor shortage simply want to pay less money for their workers.
20. Each additional immigrant, regardless of his or her personal qualities, swells the already too large U.S. population.

Periodical Bibliography

The following articles have been selected to supplement the diverse views presented in this chapter.

Jagdish Bhagwati	"Behind the Green Card," *The New Republic,* May 14, 1990.
Border Watch	"Criminal Aliens Fill U.S. Prisons," September 1989. Available from the American Immigration Control Foundation, PO Box 525, Monterey, VA 24465.
Business Week	"The Latest Huddled Masses," September 25, 1989.
Henry Cisneros	"The Demography of a Dream," *New Perspectives Quarterly,* Summer 1988.
Thomas Fleming	"A Not So Wonderful Life," *Chronicles,* July 1990.
Peter Francese	"Aging America Needs Foreign Blood," *The Wall Street Journal,* March 27, 1990.
Samuel Francis	"Principalities & Powers," *Chronicles,* July 1990.
Martin Hill	"The INS and Illegal Aliens: An Old Distorted Story," *Los Angeles Times,* October 19, 1986.
Kenneth S. Kantzer	"Has the Melting Pot Stopped Melting?" *Christianity Today,* March 3, 1989.
J. Michael Kennedy	"Border Has Worst of Both Worlds," *Los Angeles Times,* October 2, 1989.
Joel Kotkin	"Fear and Reality in the Los Angeles Melting Pot," *Los Angeles Times Magazine,* November 5, 1989.
Peter Marin	"Toward Something American," *Harper's Magazine,* July 1988.
Peter Passell	"So Much for Assumptions About Immigrants and Jobs," *The New York Times*, April 15, 1990.
Julian L. Simon, interviewed by James Cook	"The More the Merrier," *Forbes,* April 2, 1990.
Rita J. Simon	"Immigration and American Attitudes," *Public Opinion,* July/August 1987.
James J. Treires	"Dark Side of the Dream," *Newsweek,* March 20, 1989.
U.S. News & World Report	"The Great Melting Pot," July 7, 1986.
Thomas J. Ward	"Immigrants—America's Challenge or America's Opportunity?" *The World & I,* May 1989.

How Should U.S. Immigration Policy Be Reformed?

Chapter Preface

For the first one hundred years of its existence the United States essentially had no immigration policy. Anyone who wanted to immigrate to the U.S. could. Today the situation is much different. The U.S. sets annual limits on the number of immigrants it accepts, and every year more people apply than are accepted. In fact, many people throughout the world can wait for up to twenty years for permission to immigrate to the U.S.

It is clear, then, that the U.S. can pick and choose from a large number of would-be immigrants. The questions immigration policymakers face are twofold: how many immigrants should the U.S. accept, and what criteria should the U.S. use to select them? The viewpoints in the following chapter examine both questions while debating whether U.S. immigration policy needs reform.

"The United States does not need large numbers of new immigrants."

The U.S. Should Limit Immigration

Richard D. Lamm

Richard D. Lamm is director of the Center for Public Policy and Contemporary Issues at the University of Denver. He is a former governor of Colorado, and has written several books including *Megatraumas*. The following viewpoint is taken from testimony before Congress during hearings on revising U.S. immigration policy. Lamm argues that increasing immigration would worsen America's problems in education, health care and the environment. He concludes that the U.S. should limit the overall number of immigrants allowed in this country.

As you read, consider the following questions:

1. How does immigration contribute to America's social problems, according to Lamm?
2. Why does the author believe there is no labor shortage in the U.S.?
3. Why does Lamm call increased immigration a subsidy for business?

Richard D. Lamm, testimony before the U.S. House of Representatives Judiciary Committee's Subcommittee on Immigration, Refugees, and International Law, March 13, 1990.

I am here as a concerned citizen with an interest in immigration policy and its effects on the social, economic and environmental development of our country. My interest in immigration has grown, first out of my involvement in population and environmental issues, and later as a public servant who had to set priorities and make sometimes painful decisions about how to allocate society's limited resources.

During my 12 years as governor of Colorado, I came to recognize that people—regardless of race, religion, ethnicity or national origin—were our state's greatest resource. But I also came to realize that people were an asset that needed careful cultivation if their potential was to be realized. More people do not necessarily make for a better society. Better people do. And you get better people through better education, better health care, better environment, better housing, better public infrastructure and a better sense of community. To support a larger population, (if a larger population is our objective) a society must first improve the institutions that make for better, more productive citizens. To do otherwise, is to put the cart before the horse.

Over the years, I have earned the nickname "Governor Gloom" for my public admonitions about the perils facing the United States. In fact, what I have been talking about is our inability to set national priorities and make the hard choices necessary to achieve those objectives. All too often, I believe, those charged with making important national decisions say yes to the demands of a myriad of special interests and say no to the public interest by default. I believe the evidence is empirical: A nation that has amassed $2 trillion in debt in just the past decade, is a nation that cannot or will not establish priorities. We are a nation that has been saying yes to every worthy and not so worthy demand of vocal special interests and by default, saying no to the needs and aspirations of future generations who will have to pay the bills.

Saying Yes

Thus my assessment of the various bills before this committee is that they are, unfortunately, very much legislation for our times. They set no priorities and make no hard choices. They simply say yes to everyone who has a demand to make on our immigration system. They say yes to:
• more family-based immigration;
• more immigration from those countries that have unfairly dominated the immigration flow;
• more immigration from countries that have been unfairly shut out of the immigration process;

106

- more temporary workers to satisfy the demands of business interests;
- more long-term workers, who can eventually adjust to permanent status, to satisfy the demands of business interests; and
- more amnesties for illegal aliens.

In saying yes to virtually every interest group with a demand to make on the immigration process, Congress is, by default, cheating the public interest by saying no to:
- better education for America's children;
- better wages and working conditions for American workers;
- better training and retraining programs for displaced or underqualified American workers;
- better health care for America's disadvantaged;
- better and more affordable housing for young and poorer Americans; and
- better environment and more productive use of America's natural resources.

WOULD YOU WANT TO LIVE IN A HOUSE WITHOUT DOORS?

Dick Hafer. Reprinted by permission of AICF, Box 525, Monterey, VA 24465.

Let me emphasize that I do not believe immigrants are responsible for the social problems that afflict the United States. However, I do believe that population growth is a contributing factor to many of these problems and make their solution more difficult. Immigration now accounts for between one-third and one-half the population growth of the United States, and if this legislation should ever become law, it will account for an even greater share of more rapid population growth. As such, I believe immigration policy is inexorably linked to virtually every aspect of public policy in the United States. . . .

107

One of the most perplexing, and quite frankly, ludicrous, assertions I have heard is that the United States is now experiencing or is about to experience a shortage of labor. It is inconceivable to me that a nation of a quarter of a billion people can have a shortage of workers. Undeniably we have a skills and training shortage. Quite clearly we have problems of worker motivation and an erosion of the work ethic. There is also evidence that there is a maldistribution of jobs and workers to fill those jobs. We may lack for a lot of things in this country, but a sufficient supply of workers is not one of them.

At this very moment the United States has more than 6.5 million people who are officially categorized as unemployed. This figure does not even begin to take into account discouraged job-seekers who have given up looking for work, those who have never even entered the legitimate labor market, and those who are involuntarily working part-time. According to economist Robert Kuttner, taken together, Americans unemployed, underemployed and those who are presently unemployable, add up to more than 1.5 million people.

We do not have a labor shortage in the United States! What we have is a frightening social mess—a time bomb that will eventually explode in our midst if we do not take steps to diffuse it. America's growing, disenfranchised underclass is not simply going to disappear because we import foreign workers instead of training and retraining our own. They are going to move further to the fringes of our society and create problems that will ultimately be more costly in both monetary and social terms than bringing them into the economic and social mainstream.

Complaints of a Labor Shortage

In life, all things are relative, which is why we have been hearing complaints from many in the business community of a labor shortage. A quick look at the changing American demography explains why, to some, we appear to have a dearth of workers. Beginning in the mid-1960s through the mid-1980s, the enormous postwar baby boom generation entered the labor force skewing the laws of supply and demand in favor of employers. Ten or 15 years ago businesses did not have to go looking for workers; workers came to them begging for the chance to get a foot in the door. Wages and working conditions were dictated by the laws of supply and demand that existed at that time.

Now times have changed and the tables have turned somewhat, and the business community is understandably not as happy. The baby boom generation was followed by a baby bust generation who are now entering their working years. Instead of applicants beating down their doors, businesses have to go out and recruit workers and even train them themselves.

Moreover, today's laws of supply and demand mean that new job force entrants are in a more advantageous position when it comes to setting salaries and working conditions.

A Business Subsidy

Gentlemen, the businessmen and women testifying before your committees and cornering you at cocktail parties, asking for foreign workers, are simply one more special interest requesting a subsidy. Life has suddenly gotten a little tougher for them and rather than finding creative and innovative ways of dealing with a tighter labor market, they and their lobbyists are coming to you asking that you do in committee rooms what the American people failed to do in the bedroom in the late 1960s and 1970s.

An Immigration Ceiling

Polls . . . indicate that Americans favor reducing the number of legal immigrants admitted each year. While we may wish to continue to admit some immigrants, they should be from among the most talented segments of their respective societies, not the unskilled, marginally employable, as is the case with so many of the immigrants allowed into the United States today. Experts who have studied the impact of immigration on our population recommend that the number of new immigrants be equal to the number of American who emigrate each year. This would amount to around 100,000 per annum. . . . An iron-clad, loophole-free ceiling on all legal immigration, including immediate relatives of U.S. citizens, is a must.

Palmer Stacy and Wayne Lutton, *The Immigration Time Bomb*, 1988.

There is nothing wrong, per se, with a government stepping in to create an advantageous business climate. That is a legitimate function of government. However, for the past 20 years we have had exactly the kind of young, abundant labor force that the business community is asking you to recreate through immigration policy. What have been the results? By every yardstick, American competitiveness, wealth, and innovation has declined vis a vis our economic competitors. As Charles R. Morris pointed out in an article in the *Atlantic Monthly*:

New workers swelled the American labor force by about 50 percent in the past 20 years, shifting the average age and experience of workers sharply downward. Not surprisingly, with lots of cheap new workers mobbing the doorway, businessmen increased hiring instead of investing in labor-saving machinery— a fancy robot costs about as much as a year's wages for a hundred entry-level workers. Real wages and productivity were stag-

109

nant, and the business success stories were companies, like McDonald's, that learned how to pan for gold in that low-wage pool.

Ironically, Germany and Japan, which were experiencing an economic boom during this period, were experiencing exactly the demographic trend that the United States will face in the 1990s. "Personal savings are the ultimate source of all productive investment," writes Morris. "It is the high Japanese saving rate—as much as 18 percent of all personal income—that has financed Japan's global industrial conquest . . . plausibly enough, an older, more productive work force, with higher real incomes, will save more," he concludes.

Thus, after 20 years of trying to assimilate large numbers of new workers into productive jobs in the economy, a tighter labor market may be exactly what this country needs. During the past two decades we have had the type of rapid work force growth and demographic distribution that this bill would restore through immigration policy—and the results have been less than spectacular. Left alone, the demographic picture for the 1990s would resemble that of Japan and Germany in the 1970s and 1980s and the United States of the 1950s and 1960s. This country was at its most productive during a period when the Depression-era baby bust generation was young and entering the labor force.

What is wrong with returning to a period of population stability, full employment, stable housing costs and rising savings rates? These sound like laudable objectives to me.

Helping the Underclass

There is one more benefit to a tighter labor market that I would like to mention. The growth of this country's underclass, and the breakdown of social values in many communities is partially a result of demographics. We allowed large segments of our society to be relegated to the margins because they simply weren't needed. An economy that had more people entering the work force than jobs available could pick and choose from among the cream of those new workers. There was no need to reach out to those who, for a variety of reasons, did not possess the skills employers sought.

The changing demography of this country has now made these people important. This is the opportunity those who have been left behind have been waiting for. Every able body and mind is once again important. If the excess of new labor force entrants dries up, the American economy will have no choice but to find creative ways of bringing the 15 million Americans who are now outside the economic mainstream into it. By artificially reflooding the labor market, this Congress will be denying those people the opportunities they deserve.

I do not believe immigrants are responsible for the social problems that exist in this country. However, as I also stated, immigration is a population issue and population affects virtually every social and economic issue this nation faces.

There are those who have been making the rounds here on Capitol Hill espousing the "free lunch" theory of immigration—that immigrants are an unmitigated asset who contribute more to society than they use in public benefits. They even come with carefully selected statistics to back up their theories. Well, I am here to tell you that this free lunch theory has about as much merit as all free lunch theories.

As someone who has run a state government I can assure you that whatever small benefits that may be accrued at the federal level, are more than offset at the state and local levels. Immigrants are human beings and like all human beings they have needs that must be provided for. Their children need to be educated; they get sick and require health care; they become old and disabled; and they need places to live. The bulk of the burden for providing for these needs is absorbed at the state and local level. Los Angeles, a city with a huge immigrant population, found that it provides an average of $2,245 a year more in services to immigrant families than it collects in taxes. . . .

Education

American education is in drastic need of improvement. There isn't anybody who would disagree with that statement—it's kind of like saying the earth is round. We are, by all accounts and all objective standards of measurement, doing an abysmally poor job of educating our children. Yet while another committee is probably meeting across the hall or across the street to devise ways of improving our education system, we are here discussing not how to alleviate some of those problems, but how much greater burden we are going to impose on school systems around the country. Should a nation in which one-quarter of its youngsters fails to graduate high school, in which nearly half of minority students in some cities drop out of school, and in which 20 percent of the population is functionally illiterate, be thinking about new burdens it can place on its education system? . . .

Senator Connie Mack of Florida has stated that during the 1988-89 school year, Dade County public schools were registering new immigrant children (many of them illegal) "at a rate of 755 per month; that's virtually two new teachers per day and one new school per month." The cost says Senator Mack, "exceeds $27.5 million, or $3,900 per student." Even if the city of

Miami had that kind of money to spare, it couldn't build the schools and train the teachers fast enough. The real price is being borne by the schoolchildren of Dade County whose already inadequate education is being further devalued. . . .

We know, based on experience, that increasing immigration is going to increase the burdens of those school districts that can least afford to absorb them. It is also going to deny educational opportunities to those in our society who need them most. It's not the kids of Beverly Hills or Pacific Palisades who are going to suffer—they attend protected schools or their parents send them to private schools. It's the kids of Watts and East L.A. —those without options—who will suffer the consequences of large-scale immigration.

Health Care

During my years as governor of Colorado, some of my most difficult and painful decisions involved the closing of health care facilities for the poor. But invariably, the resources we had to work with were insufficient to provide the amount and quality of care we would have liked.

What turned pain into anger and frustration was the knowledge that while I was closing well-baby clinics in one part of the state, Denver General Hospital, the largest public health care facility in the state, was amassing millions of dollars in uncollectible bills for health services rendered to illegal aliens. Later you will hear from representatives of the Los Angeles County Department of Health Services who will tell you that they have had to absorb nearly three-quarters of a billion dollars in unreimbursable services for illegal aliens over the past six years. . . .

I could sit here all morning and cite examples of how the bills this committee is considering—which would raise immigration levels by anywhere from a few hundred thousand to more than a million people annually—would work to impede progress towards universally agreed upon goals.

The United States does not need large numbers of new immigrants. We are already adding more than 600,000 people—the population of Washington, D.C.—to our population through immigration each year. Some business interests may *want* more immigrants. Ethnic lobby groups may *want* expanded immigration. But I urge you to differentiate between what a few vocal and well-financed interest groups want, and what is in the best interests of the country.

I believe, as most proponents of immigration reform do, that immigration, at sensible levels, can be a positive force for the United States. Like anything else that is good and desirable, it is best when taken in moderation.

112

"We need not fear additional immigration to the United States. . . . We should positively welcome it."

The U.S. Should Encourage Immigration

Ben J. Wattenberg and Karl Zinsmeister

Every year, the United States admits around six to seven hundred thousand legal immigrants. One central question in forming immigration policy is whether that number should be increased or reduced. In the following viewpoint, Ben J. Wattenberg and Karl Zinsmeister argue that the U.S. should let in more immigrants. They state that in the past, immigrants made important contributions to society, and that increased immigration would ensure that the U.S. remains a prosperous and productive nation. Wattenberg and Zinsmeister are scholars at the American Enterprise Institute, a conservative public policy think tank in Washington, D.C.

As you read, consider the following questions:

1. How does present immigration compare with immigration in the past, according to Wattenberg and Zinsmeister?
2. What flaws do the authors find in the five main arguments against increased immigration?
3. In the opinion of Wattenberg and Zinsmeister, how do immigrants contribute to the U.S. economy?

Ben J. Wattenberg and Karl Zinsmeister, "The Case for More Immigration." Reprinted from *Commentary*, April 1990, by permission; all rights reserved.

The first thing to be said about current immigrant flows to this country is that in historical terms they are fairly moderate. While the actual number of foreign citizens now entering the U.S. may seem high—about 650,000 per year, counting legals, illegals, and refugees, and subtracting out-migration—it amounts all in all to an annual increase in the population of only about one-fifth of 1 percent. At the turn of the century, by contrast, when immigration was at its height, it increased the U.S. population by about 1 percent per year. Furthermore, the fraction of our current population that is foreign-born is not only well below earlier U.S. peaks, it is lower than the present levels in several West European nations, and considerably below the proportions in other immigrant nations like Australia and Canada. . . .

The numbers of people now entering the country are not distressingly high. In fact, they are lower than what, in our judgment, a wise policy would dictate.

Examining Arguments Against Immigration

Before considering what such a policy might look like, however, we need to attend to the arguments *against* substantial further immigration to this country.

The most widespread such argument is that America already has enough people, or too many people, or will soon have too many people unless the flow of new residents is stopped.

Yet according to medium-variant ("most likely") projections by the Census Bureau, at current levels of birth, mortality, and immigration, the U.S. over the next fifty years will experience relatively slow population growth, then slower growth, then no growth, and then decline. This is due primarily to the fact that, for fifteen years now, fertility rates have been below the replacement level. Even an immigration moderately higher than the current level would still leave us on a slow-growth path toward population stability in the next century.

The future can, of course, change. Suffice it to say that under current conditions there is no long-term population explosion under way in this country. Claims that immigration is going to bring about a standing-room-only America, or anything close to it, are bunk.

Beyond that, the risks and benefits of our current demographic trends are open to debate. Though much attention has been paid to the dangers of overpopulation and overimmigration, little notice has been directed to the dangers of stasis or decline. Over the last two centuries, America's prosperity and growing influence have coincided with the most significant long-term population boom in history. In the century to come the population of the planet as a whole will double; is it wise for America to be a no-growth player in a high-growth world?

A second, related argument against immigration focuses on potential damage to the environment. Former Colorado Governor Richard Lamm put the view clearly:

> With current levels of immigration, we will always be forced to use our resources at a faster and faster rate, to try to expand our economy to make room for more and more workers, to try to spread our suburbs, cutting down the forests and clearing out the farms that used to surround our cities.

The biologist Garrett Hardin recently blamed immigration for the fact that "Traffic problems are being replaced by rush-hour gridlock. Safe drinking water is scarcer every year. Forests are being killed by acid rain."

© Taylor/Rothco. Reprinted with permission.

Statements like these are flawed in many respects. To begin with the issue of resource depletion, the truth is that regardless of the level of population, we have always been and will always be "running out" of resources, but we will never hit empty. Under any intelligent market-based system, resource use is not a matter of draining down inherited reserves but a complex process of inherent rationing, constantly evolving new applications, and substitutions based on what makes economic sense plus what is feasible with contemporary technology. Among the once-dwindling resources that are now in "oversupply" are flint for arrowheads, farmland, acetylene for lamps, high-quality vacuum tubes, latex for rubber-making, trees usable for schooner masts, good mules, and copper ore. Moreover, as the economist Julian Simon has noted, the real costs of nearly all natural resources—measured in hours of human labor needed to acquire one unit—have fallen steadily and sharply in recent decades.

Similarly, ecological degradation is caused in large measure by what people do or fail to do, not by how many people there are. Within the last two decades, since America began spending significant sums on abatement, pollution has declined even as population has gone up. Recent concern about environmental trends like carbon dioxide build-up and alleged ozone depletion are particularly irrelevant to the immigration question. If, as some worry, an individual person adds to global warming, it does not matter whether that person is in South Korea or New York (unless it is beneficial for Third Worlders to stay poor, thereby using less energy). . . .

Social Spending

A third argument in opposition to immigration is that immigrants constitute a big drain on social spending

A series of recent economic studies challenge this notion. Immigrants tend to be disproportionately young, and as a result they draw very lightly on Social Security and Medicare—by far our largest social programs. Nor do they draw much more than natives on other kinds of welfare spending, like Aid to Families with Dependent Children, food stamps, and unemployment compensation. In all, immigrants actually consume smaller amounts of public funds than do natives for about their first dozen years in the U.S. After that, levels tend to equalize.

What is more, within eleven to sixteen years of coming to America the average immigrant is earning as much as, or more than, the average native-born worker. Immigrant *families*, who typically have more working members, outstrip native families in income in as little as three to five years. In this way, immigrants become above-average tax*payers*. Viewed strictly in terms of fiscal flows and social-welfare budgets, then, immigrants tend to represent a good deal for the nation.

A fourth argument directly contradicts the third: immigrants are such zealous workers that they deprive natives of scarce jobs. Here, too, major studies by the Urban Institute and by the Rand Corporation paint a different picture. Immigration to a given area can be quite compatible with job growth, and even with wage increases. Indeed, one finds little evidence of higher unemployment or of a serious depressive effect on wages even among the most vulnerable native groups—low-skill black workers or American-born Hispanics—when there is a rise in the proportion of immigrants in the local labor market.

Immigrants and Jobs

Immigrants seem generally to complement rather than compete with native workers. They often fill manual or specialized jobs for which domestic workers are in short supply. They sometimes attract minimum-wage industries which would otherwise have located elsewhere. They stimulate activity in the service economy. They start new businesses. As anyone who has lived in a neighborhood with such businesses can attest, these enterprises are largely original: far from driving someone else from a job, many immigrant entrepreneurs carve a narrow foothold for themselves out of the rubble of empty buildings and unserved needs.

Immigration Too Restricted

Immigration to the U.S. is now heavily restricted by Congress. The U.S. accepts only about 600,000 immigrants and refugees per year, or roughly 2.5 entrants for every 1,000 U.S. residents. This is only one-half the nation's historical rate of immigration and one-tenth the rate in peak years at the turn of the century. The U.S. now has a smaller percentage of foreign born relative to its population than most industrialized countries—including Australia, Britain, Canada, France, and West Germany.

What America needs is a pro-family, pro-growth immigration policy for the 1990s. The centerpiece of immigration reform legislation, therefore, should be gradual immigration expansion.

Stephen Moore, The Heritage Foundation *Backgrounder*, November 6, 1989.

A fifth and final argument against immigration, perhaps the most venerable of all, is cultural: immigration on a large scale will eventually disrupt societal coherence, "swamp" the national culture, and imperil our sense of shared history and unity. Benjamin Franklin was an early articulator of this view; the targets of his ire were Germans, whom he criticized as clannish, ignorant, and intent on maintaining their own language. Since Franklin's time, the targets have varied—Irish, Italians, Jews, Hispanics, and others have each taken their turn—but the charges have remained remarkably consistent.

Yet, Benjamin Franklin and a host of other critics notwithstanding, the integration of immigrants into the national ethos has not proved notably difficult in the past. We did not develop a German-language province, or any other separate enclaves;

new arrivals, certainly after a generation or two, have tended to disperse fairly broadly across the land. Immigrants have not succeeded in introducing monarchism into this country, or for that matter Bolshevism (to mention only two once-widespread fears). Our founding fathers, were they able to pay a visit, would find many of our basic social and political institutions rather familiar. American ethnic history has for the most part followed the wise old dictum, "In all things essential, unity, in other things diversity.". . .

Continued emphasis on English-language proficiency and other essentials of the collective American identity is obviously wholly desirable, not only from the perspective of the larger American interest but from the point of view of immigrants anxious to make progress in society. Militant advocates of linguistic and cultural separatism are, as it happens, out of step with the actual practices of most immigrants. It is in fact newcomers who often have the most powerful interest in the creation of common cultural ground—one reason Spanish is not going to become California's co-official language is that new Californians from Korea, Taiwan, the Philippines, Vietnam, the USSR, India, and Cambodia would not stand for it.

A Labor Shortage

These, then, are some of the reasons why we need not fear additional immigration to the United States. Beyond these, there are other reasons why, especially in the period just ahead, we should positively welcome it. . . .

Many, though not all, economists believe we may be entering an era of long-term labor deficit. Business cycles may rise and fall, they maintain, but the long-term trend will probably be one of too few qualified workers for the positions available. From mid-1985 to 1990, eleven million new jobs opened up while the total working-age population grew by only five million. If that squeezing trend continues, it will become harder and harder for employers to fill positions. . . .

Possible Penalties

A future of more jobs than workers may sound like a happy circumstance, but it reflects imbalances for which there can also be penalties. One such penalty is deteriorating service, and an increase in underqualified, rude, and weakly committed employees. Another is the cancellation of expansion plans for many businesses. Still another may be the advent of wage inflation, which could damage not only the U.S. but also other nations in both the Western and developing worlds.

Many of these dislocations could be avoided by immigration,

118

a superb smoother of economic and demographic swings. Immigrants flow not to areas of labor surplus but to the regions and the occupations where demand is greatest. In this way they serve as a natural shock absorber in the U.S. labor market.

The most immediate beneficiaries of immigrant enterprise, moreover, are often the very individuals who are assumed to be their competitors—the poor. Ghetto stores are perhaps the clearest example. In vast stretches of low-income inner cities all across America, the most striking fact of life, aside from the staggering crime incidence, is the underprovision of basic services. In Washington, D.C., for instance, in the large poor neighborhood east of the Anacostia River, home to a significant portion of the city's population, there are only a handful of decent sit-down restaurants and grocery stores. Block after block passes unpunctuated by commercial operations. To obtain even the simplest of goods and services often requires a long bus ride.

More Immigrants Are Better

The most general policy issue concerns the total number of immigrants. Taking in immigrants at a rate equal to, or even far above, our present admission rate improves our average standard of living, on balance. American citizens even do well while doing good when admitting refugees. Rather than being a matter of charity, we can expect our incomes to be higher rather than lower in future years if we take in more immigrants. Therefore, increasing the total immigration quota is recommended.

Julian L. Simon, *The Economic Consequences of Immigration*, 1989.

The absence of provisioners is not conspiratorial, but "rational." With the harassments of crime and the low spending habits of the residents, only long hours of unpleasant work can make inner-city businesses succeed. And in Anacostia, as in many other places, it is largely immigrants who are opening establishments in the commercial desert. It is easy to downplay the significance of their contribution, and their motive is not altruism. But for residents who can buy milk and newspapers and hay-fever pills at 2 A.M. where before there was nothing, they make a significant addition to the quality of life. . . .

Of course, immigrants provide our society and economy with other, more ineffable, benefits than these. It is often said, for example, that America's future depends on our ability to cultivate strengths and bolster weaknesses in an increasingly competitive global arena. Even though current immigration policies give inadequate consideration to occupational qualifications—a subject to which we will return—the U.S. still gets more than 11,000 engineers, scientists, and computer specialists per year. We also get future practitioners of these professions; of the 40 finalists in the 1988 Westinghouse high-school science competition, 22 were foreign-born or children of foreign-born parents: from Taiwan, China, Korea, India, Guyana, Poland, Trinidad, Canada, Peru, Iran, Vietnam, and Honduras. In Boston, 13 of the 17 public high-school valedictorians in the class of 1989 were foreign-born. Researchers at San Diego State University report that "immigrants and refugees to the U.S.—whether from Asia, Europe, or Latin America—are systematically outperforming all native-born American students in grade-point averages despite . . . English-language handicaps." Beyond the specific contributions made by such people, we may also consider the salutary shock effect their presence in our schools could have on young native-born Americans.

Fulfilling Our Mission

Immigration, then, can bring us significant numbers of bold creators and skilled workers. It can diminish whatever labor shortages may be coming our way. Immigration can keep America from aging precipitously and fill in the demographic holes that may harm our pension and health-care systems. Immigration can energize whole communities with a new entrepreneurial spirit, keeping us robust and growing as a nation. At a time when the idea of competitiveness has become a national fixation, it can bolster our competitiveness and help us retain our position as the common denominator of the international trade web. And as most Americans continue to believe that we have a mission to foster liberty and the love of liberty throughout the world, immigration can help us fulfill that mission through successful example. . . .

Our immigration policies ought not be conceived as some kind of messianic international public service. From our inclusionism we reap rich fruits, bolstering our numbers, enhancing our competetiveness, increasing our influence. A nation like ours functions best when confident, welcoming progress and growth, and demonstrating a willingness to absorb the lessons of outsiders. It wounds itself when it turns inward—excluding foreigners, protecting its markets, resisting fresh ideas and infusions. We would dilute both our own prosperity and our reason for being were we to fail to extend, and widen, our gangplank to the world.

"The immigration of more highly skilled workers has . . . beneficial effects."

The U.S. Should Admit Immigrants on the Basis of Job Skills

Barry R. Chiswick

The United States admits non-refugee immigrants on the basis of two primary criteria: the presence of relatives already in this country, and the possession of skills and education deemed economically beneficial to the U.S. In the 1970s and 1980s the vast majority of immigrants were admitted on the basis of family reunification. In the following viewpoint, taken from testimony before Congress on immigration reform, Barry R. Chiswick argues that the U.S. should place more emphasis on economic skills. He recommends establishing a point system in which people applying for immigration are rated for their education, skills, job experience, and knowledge of English. Chiswick is a professor of economics at the University of Illinois in Chicago, and has written numerous books and articles on immigration.

As you read, consider the following questions:

1. How has the U.S. economy changed since the 1965 immigration reforms, according to Chiswick?
2. Why should family reunification issues be considered less important now than in the past, in the author's opinion?
3. Which skilled immigrants does Chiswick wish to attract?

Barry R. Chiswick, testimony before the U.S. House of Representatives Judiciary Committee's Subcommittee on Immigration, Refugees, and International Law, March 1, 1990.

It has been a quarter century since the passage of the landmark 1965 Amendments to the Immigration and Nationality Act of 1952. The 1965 Amendments abolished the pernicious "national origins" quota system enacted in the 1920's to severely limit Southern and Eastern European immigration and the remaining racist features of the "Asiate Barred Zone" that allowed only negligible immigration from Asia. The mid-1960's was a period of economic euphoria. Americans felt that we had reached a "golden growth path" that would guarantee high growth rates of productivity, low inflation, continuously rising real incomes, and the elimination of economic deprivation and poverty.

It is appropriate for Congress to reassess the mechanism for admitting non-refugee immigrants as developed in the 1965 Amendments and subsequent amendments. Both the passage of time and the obvious invalid assumption regarding the future performance of the economy call for this reassessment.

The United States admits legal immigrants for two primary reasons. The first is humanitarian. We accept refugees—that is, those with "a well-founded fear of persecution" for political, racial, religious and other reasons—to aid those in distress and to promote freedom. We also accept the immediate relatives of U.S. citizens for humanitarian reasons. It pains us to know that political boundaries can separate parents from young children and husbands from wives.

Immigrants are also accepted for economic reasons. A primary function of our government is to help create an environment in which our largely free-market economy can grow and provide the population with higher levels of economic and social well-being. Immigration has historically been one of the policy instruments used to promote economic growth in America.

Current U.S. Policy

The current system for regulating non-refugee legal immigration is based on the 1965 Amendments to the Immigration and Nationality Act (1952), and related subsequent amendments. These visas are issued nearly entirely on the basis of kinship with a citizen or resident alien of the United States. There is very little scope for allocating visas on the basis of the contribution the applicant is likely to make to the economy of the United States.

Of the more than 643,000 persons who received an immigrant (permanent resident alien) visa in fiscal year 1988, only 22,454 were admitted on the basis of their own skills. Of these, 11,758 were occupational preference principals under the third preference ("professional or highly skilled immigrants") and

10,696 were occupational preference principals under the sixth preference ("needed skilled or unskilled workers"). These 22,454 "skill-tested" immigrants were a mere 3.5 percent of total legal immigration. (These data exclude illegal aliens granted amnesty under the 1986 Immigration Reform and Control Act.)

Although those admitted under occupational preferences are numerically few, the occupational preferences are a key source of skilled workers. Of the 8,081 engineers who immigrated to the United States in 1988, 36 percent were occupational-preference recipients, as were 38 percent of the 1,198 natural scientists, 49 percent of the 1,164 mathematical and computer scientists, 30 percent of the 4,063 nurses, and 32 percent of the 3,223 college and university teachers.

Outdated Laws

America's outdated immigration law simply is not geared to admit the very ones the country needs most. Following a principle that has remained unchanged since 1952, the law offers the right of immigration based on family preference. As a result, the vast majority of new arrivals are spouses, children, and siblings of earlier immigrants—and the system self-perpetuates: Once they become citizens, they in turn bring in *their* families. Since these immigrants' skills are never a factor in whether or not they are admitted, any benefits that they bring to the U.S. economy are coincidental. Of 1989's 650,000 new immigrants, just 54,000 qualified solely on the basis of their education or ability.

A more sensible policy would be to expand opportunities for those immigrants who possess skills in short supply, as Canada and Australia have recently done.

Louis S. Richman, *Fortune*, January 29, 1990.

The immigrant engineers, natural scientists, computer scientists and mathematicians, are essential if we as a nation are to remain at the cutting edge in the development and implementation of new technology. It is this new technology that creates employment opportunities for lesser-skilled workers. The immigrant nurses are essential in the staffing of our hospitals and nursing homes, particularly in the less-advantaged inner-city neighborhoods. The immigrant college and university teachers are crucial both in developing a more highly skilled workforce and through their own research in the natural, health, behavioral and social sciences, as well as in the humanities.

The immigration of more highly skilled workers has two beneficial effects. One is expanding the productive potential of the American economy. In particular the potential for job creation

123

by immigrant scientists, engineers and entrepreneurs can be substantial. The second effect is the narrowing of economic inequality. The immigration of more highly skilled workers tends to reduce relative differentials in wages and employment across skill groups, thereby promoting the policy objective of narrowing the inequality of income, reducing poverty and welfare dependency. The immigration of low-skilled workers has the opposite effect on income inequality, poverty and welfare dependency. The research studies that have addressed the issue show consistently that those admitted to the United States on the basis of their own skills have a greater productivity in the U.S. economy (as measured by their earnings or occupational attainment) than those admitted on the basis of other criteria.

Too Much Family Emphasis

Current immigration policy places an inordinate emphasis on rationing non-refugee visas on the basis of kinship. There are however, two important ways in which the decade of the 1990's and beyond differs from the past that compels a rethinking of this policy. The middle 1960's was a period of: low and declining real costs for energy, unprecedented growth in productivity, shrinking unemployment, and rapidly expanding real GNP [gross national product] per capita. Most important, it was a period during which Americans believed all of these trends would continue indefinitely. In such an environment it might have been quite appropriate to downplay economic considerations in reformulating immigration law, and to expand the scope for immigration based on kinship.

The result, however, is an immigration policy that is not relevant to the coming decades. It is more reasonable to expect slow economic growth, low increases in productivity, and increasing international competition from the newly industrialized countries of the Third World and from the politically and economically freer countries of Eastern Europe. America's declining position as a world leader in technology and international competitiveness requires a rethinking of all policies, including immigration.

There is another way in which the past differs from the future. Immigration to the United States used to be a gut-wrenching experience. It meant the virtual severance of all ties with family members who remained behind. This has not been the case for several decades and will be even less relevant in the future. The real costs of transportation and communication have plummeted. It is now relatively inexpensive in both time and money to fly to Europe, Asia or any place in Latin America. Thanks to modern technology, international telephone communication is quick, clear and cheap for voice communication and for facsimile transmission of printed matter, letters, photos, etc. And although postal services in every country are charged with being slow and inefficient, this is largely because our rising expectations outdistance their performance. Furthermore, the United States and most of the countries from which the U.S. receives immigrants have very few restrictions on nationals from one country visiting another. The recent relaxation of political tensions, particularly in Eastern Europe, has expanded opportunities for international visits.

We have become a small world in which family ties can be maintained with relative ease even when family members live on opposite sides of national boundaries. In a real sense, Chicago is now no further from Mexico City, Berlin, Taipei or Casablanca than it is from San Francisco.

Nuclear Family Only

The concept of family reunification can apply only to the nuclear family. Expanding it is a disguise to get around the rules. Applying it to nieces, nephews and assorted in-laws ridicules its real purpose, which is to bring together spouses and their dependent children. We should not confuse family reunifications with family reunions.

There are prospective immigrants longing to come to the United States. They have the drive to make it on their own. We should stop discriminating against such skilled, qualified and enthusiastic people whose only lack is relatives already here.

Luis Acle Jr., *Los Angeles Times*, July 5, 1989.

This calls into question the need, and the wisdom, of some of the kinship categories in the preference system. In 1988, nearly 21,500 brothers and sisters of U.S. citizens immigrated, about the same as the number of occupational preference principals. In addition, these brothers and sisters were accompanied by nearly 14,500 spouses and nearly 28,000 children. The nearly 64,000 immigrants who entered under the fifth preference for siblings of U.S. citizens can be compared with only 53,607 immigrants who were occupational principals or their spouses and children.

Rationing by Skills

The relevant policy question is the following: How can we develop a mechanism for rationing immigration visas so as to accommodate both the humanitarian and the economic objectives? For this discussion I will assume that two features of current immigration law will remain in place. One is that adult citizens of the United States will be able to bring to this country their bona fide spouses, minor children and aged parents without numerical limit. The other is that we will continue to have a generous refugee policy, although its particular features may differ from what exists under current law.

For other immigration visas, the policy objective should be to place the emphasis on skill, with perhaps some weight for other kinship relationships. Skills are, however, multidimensional. They include formal schooling, technical training, occupational attainment, on-the-job training, being in a prime age group, and knowledge of written as well as spoken English. Each of these skill characteristics has been shown to be an important determinant of economic adjustment and earnings in the United States. Even bona fide pre-arranged employment may be viewed as a characteristic enhancing one's likely productivity in the United States, although this is subject to more abuse.

To combine the multidimensional aspects of skills into a criterion for rationing immigration visas necessitates the adoption of a point system. This requires a list of readily measured characteristics that are expected to enhance the productivity of immigrants, along the lines suggested in the previous paragraph. For each characteristic, points would be assigned to reflect the applicant's traits, within the pre-determined ceiling for that characteristic. For example, each level of schooling completed may be worth a few points. Apprenticeship training, vocational training, and relevant on-the-job training would also earn points for the applicants. Points could be earned for fluency in written and spoken English, among other characteristics. Points might also be awarded if the visa applicant would be accompanied by a spouse with a high level of skill.

Attracting Entrepreneurs

The 1965 Amendments provided for the immigration of investors ("entrepreneurs"). These are individuals who would be investing funds in and managing a business in the United States that would create jobs for American workers. The 1965 Amendments put investors in the residual non-preference category, and in recent years there have been no residual visas available—and hence no investor immigrants. Entrepreneurs need to be explicitly brought back into the immigration stream. These individuals can be returned to the immigration system if points are provided for entrepreneurs who will be investing in and managing a U.S. business. Alternatively a separate explicit investor category can be created. Either way, these policy changes would provide a clear recognition of the importance of entrepreneurial immigration and would allow a substitution of entrepreneurial skill (and financial resources) for the skills acquired in school and through job training.

The point system can recognize that relatives already in the United States may provide assistance to a new immigrant. A small number of points could be awarded, for example, to applicants with close relatives in the United States who will guarantee their financial support for a period of, say, five years, by the posting of a bond. In this manner, applicants who fall short of the general productivity criterion by a few points but whose presence is of considerable value to their relatives in this country would be better able to immigrate legally. Such a provision, however, should be retained only so long as the guarantee of support by sponsoring relatives is legally enforceable by a bond or other mechanism.

It is essential to preserve the non-racist character of the plan. Points should *not* be awarded on the basis of the applicant's race, religion, ethnicity or country of origin. Indeed, under this plan the country limit on numerically restricted visas in current immigration law, of 20,000 visas per year, should be removed. The current country ceiling discriminates against individual applicants from countries with large populations and from countries in which a larger proportion of the population migrates to the United States. It violates the principle that it is who you are that matters, not where you are from.

A threshold number of points would be determined for each year. Immigrants receiving more than this number would receive visas for themselves and for their spouses and minor children. The annual flow of non-refugee legal immigrants could be regulated by altering the threshold. This would permit, as the current system does not, an explicit tailoring of immigration to the business cycle and other economic criteria. Whereas Congress should set the upper and lower limits to immigration from the point system, annual immigration within these limits should be determined administratively.

Not Anti-Family

Some may argue that an immigration policy based on the applicant's contribution to the American economy is "anti-family." This is not the situation. Foreigners with more kinsmen in the United States would still be more likely to apply for an immigrant visa; coming to the United States is more attractive to them than to others in their home country. The immediate relatives of adult U.S. citizens (the spouse, minor children, and aged parents) would still be eligible for admission without numerical restrictions. For other applicants, kinsmen in the United States could still assist their immigration by accepting the financial responsibility of serving as sponsors, financing the applicants' skill acquisition (e.g., schooling, technical training, English fluency), and arranging employment. The willingness of U.S. citizens and resident aliens to engage in these activities is a better test of their interest in the immigration of their relatives than exists in current policy.

A unique feature of current immigration law is that it differentiates among applicants for non-refugee visas primarily on the basis of to whom they are related. Nowhere else in U.S. economic or social policy does official nepotism take center stage over evaluating an individual on the basis of his or her own characteristics and behavior. It is a policy that is fundamentally contrary to the American spirit, as well as to its self-interest.

Basing immigration policy on the productivity characteristics of the applicant does not, as some might believe, tend to favor European immigrants. The U.S. experience with the occupational preferences, as well as the experiences of Australia and Canada with their highly successful skill-based point systems, are instructive. In each of these instances, the shift to issuing visas on the basis of skill has tended to favor Third World applicants rather than Europeans. Furthermore, the skill-based system opened immigration channels for applicants from ethnic groups and countries of origin which, for one reason or another, had not been present in previous immigration streams. . . .

Immigrant Productivity

There may be many who could immigrate under the current kinship criteria but not under productivity criteria. The immigration of these persons is at the expense of the U.S. population, which accepts less productive workers. The largest adverse impact is borne by low-skilled workers and disadvantaged minorities who face greater competition in the labor market and in the allocation of income-contingent transfers. A system based on productivity would reverse this pattern. Furthermore, by increasing the overall skill level and hence the productivity of immigrants, there would be greater public support for increasing annual immigration.

A productivity-based point system is not a "pie in the sky" idea. The United States experience with the occupational preferences and the Australian and Canadian experiences with their own productivity-based point systems are relevant guides to the future. Increasing the emphasis on the applicant's likely contribution raises the skill level of immigrants and expands the range of countries from which immigrants are drawn.

128

4

"Protection of family unity is and must remain a prominent theme in U.S. immigration policy."

The U.S. Should Admit Immigrants on the Basis of Family Ties

Arthur C. Helton

Arthur C. Helton directs the Political Asylum Project of the Lawyers Committee for Human Rights, and teaches immigration and refugee law at the New York University School of Law. In the following viewpoint, he argues that family reunification should remain a fundamental part of U.S. immigration policy. He writes that immigrants do better economically and socially when they have family support.

As you read, consider the following questions:

1. How does the author define a family?
2. In what specific ways do family members help immigrants, according to Helton?
3. Why does Helton object to attempts to cut back on family-motivated immigration?

Arthur C. Helton, a paper presented to the Conference on the Purpose of Legal Immigration in the 1990s and Beyond, sponsored by the Federation for American Immigration Reform, June 10, 1988. Reprinted with permission.

Family reunification has long been part of U.S. immigration policy. While it might be difficult to describe as a "purpose" of immigration policy, protection of the family is a firmly established tenet which has been respected in the formulation of such policy. For example, preference admission for brothers and sisters was included after World War II, because it was thought that such siblings were in many cases the only surviving members of families.

Indeed, the admission of siblings has recently been the focus of some controversy. In 1954, the first full year of operation under the Immigration and Nationality Act of 1952 (INA), less than 2 percent of the total number of quota immigrants admitted were brothers and sisters of U.S. citizens. Subsequent amendments to the INA altered that situation and, by 1977, 41 percent of the immigrants admitted under the total annual immigration ceiling were charged to the fifth preference category —brothers and sisters of U.S. citizens. This rise in the percentage and the increasing backlog of applicants wishing to enter under the fifth preference have inspired concern.

How important is family unity? What is the family? How should governmental authorities determine family closeness for immigration purposes? Guidance in answering these questions can be found in international and domestic law, social science studies, policy debate, and the practices in other countries similar to the United States.

Family Unity in International Law

Protection of the family has been recognized for some years as a proper goal of international law, including immigration and refugee law. A number of the major documents of international law contain references to the family.

In the preamble of the Universal Declaration of Human Rights, the unity of the family is stated as the "foundation of freedom, justice and peace in the world." Article 16(3) of the Universal Declaration further defines the family as "the natural and fundamental group unit of society and is entitled to protection by society and the State." The International Covenant on Economic, Social and Cultural Rights expands on the concept, stating that "[t]he widest possible protection and assistance should be accorded to the family," and expresses particular concern for the establishment of the family and the care of dependent children. The American Declaration of the Rights and Duties of Man states in article VI that "[e]very person has the right to establish a family, the basic element of society, and to receive protection therefore.". . .

Moreover, the United Nations High Commissioner for Refugees (UNHCR) has given particular attention in recent years to the problem of family reunification. In 1981, in response to the problem of the boat people, the Executive Committee of UN-HCR adopted a number of conclusions on the reunification of separated refugee families. Included in the recommendations of the committee are provisions encouraging asylum countries to apply "liberal criteria" in identifying family members and to grant family members the same legal status as the head of the family who was designated a refugee.

Table 1

U.S. Immigration Law and Number of Immigrants Admitted in 1987

Preference	Number Admitted (in 1,000s)
Immigrants Subject to Numerical Restrictions (270,000 Visas)	
First: Unmarried adult children of U.S. Citizens and their children (20 percent of visas are allocated to this category)	11.4
Second: Spouses and unmarried children of permanent resident aliens and their children (26 percent and any visas not used above)	110.8
Third: Professional or highly skilled persons and their spouses and children (10 percent)	26.9
Fourth: Married children of U.S. citizens and their spouses and children (10 percent and any visas not used above)	20.7
Fifth: Siblings of adult U.S. citizens and their spouses and children (24 percent and any visas not used above)	69.0
Sixth: Needed skilled and unskilled workers and their spouses and children (10 percent)	27.0
Nonpreference and other (visas not used above, and other special admissions)	5.4
Immigrants Not Subject to Numerical Restrictions	
Spouses, parents, and minor children of adult U.S. citizens	218.6
Refugees and asylees	96.5
Other	15.3
Subtotal	330.4
TOTAL	601.5

U.S. Immigration and Naturalization Service.

While there are no specific treaty provisions involving the principles favoring family unity which bind the United States, the general principle can be considered so basic as to have achieved the status of a norm under customary international law.

U.S. Law

U.S. constitutional law is fundamentally in accord with international human rights principles. While there is no express constitutional right to family unification, family relations in our constitutional scheme have been regarded as sacrosanct. In Moore vs. City of East Cleveland (1977), the Supreme Court went so far as to extend judicial protection in a zoning dispute to a non-traditional family unit consisting of a grandmother and her two grandsons, basing its decision on substantive rights emanating from the Fourteenth Amendment's Due Process Clause specifically, and from our history, traditions, and values more generally.

Our decisions establish that the Constitution protects the sanctity of the family precisely because the institution of the family is deeply rooted in this Nation's history and tradition. It is through the family that we inculcate and pass down our most cherished values, morals and cultural.

Ours is by no means a tradition limited to respect for the bonds uniting members of the nuclear family. The tradition of uncles, aunts, cousins, and especially grandparents sharing a household along with parents and children has roots equally venerable and equally deserving of constitutional protection.

In the immigration context, however, the jurisprudential solicitude given to protecting the family has not been wholly consistent. Just how far family ties may be extended is an open question. Part of the problem stems from the inevitable difficulties the judiciary faces when it attempts to apply concepts ostensibly grounded in a "tradition"—it is no easy task determining what constitutes a traditional family in the United States, and the task is even more difficult when attempting to define the family for new arrivals who come from different traditions or who, in the absence of their families, have established important but less traditional association. . . .

Is emotional closeness the criterion for determining family relationships? Is it a matter of establishing blood relations, or conforming to a statutory definition? What do we mean by "family"?

What Constitutes a Family?

Of course, the "family" is an ancient institution found in all human societies However, there is controversy over just what constitutes the family unit.

The word "family" can refer to a number of different groupings of people. It has its origin in a Latin word which could be roughly equated with "domestic group" or "household." Households may be made up of individuals between whom no kinship ties exist, and, conversely, members of one "biological family" (related by blood or marriage) may be distributed over several households. "Nuclear family" is most frequently used to refer to a group consisting of a husband, wife, and their socially recognized children. The group need not be coresidential provided regular relationships are maintained among its members. It need not exist as a separate and isolated entity but may be contained within more extensive groups provided it is given some recognition. A "compound family" is a group formed through the amalgamation of nuclear-family units or parts of them. For example, a family group of remarried widowers or divorcees with children from a previous marriage would constitute a compound family whether or not they all lived together. "Joint families" grow as younger members bring in spouses rather than setting up independent households. A joint family may be such a cohesive unit that it is difficult to see nuclear families within it as separate groups. Finally, an "extended family" is a dispersed version of the joint family. That is, the members do not all live together in one dwelling, but may engage in common activities.

Keep Family Preferences

Our system of giving preference to close relatives of U.S. citizens and lawful permanent residents has worked well, both for these immigrant families and for the country as a whole. It would not be in our national interest or be consistent with our family values to severely alter our system of family preference immigration. . . .

As Rep. Howard L. Berman has stated, "To cut back on the ability of new Americans to be with their family members betrays the core American value and tradition of emphasizing the integrity of the family."

Stewart Kwoh, *Los Angeles Times*, September 14, 1989.

Today's modern society, with its emphasis on individualism, cosmopolitanism, and change, is in tension with traditional familism. The family has historically functioned as a support system for its members. For example, much attention has been focused on the sibling relationship in the childhood and adolescence years but, unfortunately, the relationship's importance and persistence is overlooked in the later years of the life cycle. "Siblingship [is] recognized as unique and influential." Allowing siblings to immigrate can promote the successful adaptation and integration of these immigrants into our society.

Immigrants Need Family Support

Upon arrival in the United States, immigrants experience a cultural shock which proves to be quite difficult for them to overcome. Unifying extended families allows immigrants to support each other socially, emotionally, and even financially. The unification provides stability and familiarity, lessening the feeling of alienation. This unification not only prevents a loss of identity, but actually functions to maintain and promote ethnic identity.

A case study comparing the successful adjustment of Italian immigrants in Louisiana to those of Italian immigrants in New York during the same time period exemplifies the important results familism can have on a society. The immigrants settled in Louisiana with their families during the nineteenth century.

The Louisiana Italians, who came from Sicily, employed themselves as shopkeepers, merchants, and peddlers, and they were more successful generally than their New York contemporaries. This "success was, at least in part, due to their familistic orientation." The Louisiana Italians were better able to support and cooperate with each other. Their familial bonds allowed them to better integrate their culture and values into their new lives, and familism lead to their successful adaptation into American society which, in turn, promoted their rapid upward mobility.

The case study suggests that familism may above all promote the economic progress of the immigrant, his family, and society rather than retard it. "Familism may be a fruitful variable to investigate the mobility of present day immigrants."

The Family in U.S. Immigration Policy

Immigration policy in the United States has evolved slowly with a general consensus as to who is and who is not part of an immigrant's "family." Included as essential members, and exempt from numerical quotas or ceilings, are spouses, children, and since 1965, parents of adult U.S. citizens. Excluded from family reunification provisions so far are grandparents, nieces, nephews, cousins, or other more distant relatives. Numerically restricted preferences are assigned to other close family members, including unmarried children of citizens and permanent residents, followed by married children of citizens.

Siblings have always been a relatively low priority—in fourth or fifth place—but were allocated a relatively large proportion of immigrant visas in the 1965 quota revision that they felt would be quickly revamped.

The Select Commission on Immigration and Refugee Policy (SCIRP) and Congressional hearings in 1981-1983 were an occasion to rethink the priorities and proportions assigned in 1965. They attempted to tilt the selection system back towards a greater emphasis on meeting U.S. labor needs, with proposals to reduce allocations to siblings.

SCIRP was established in 1978 by P.L. 95412 to conduct a study and evaluation of immigration laws, policies and procedures. The Commission assumed that:

The reunification of families should remain one of the foremost goals of immigration not only because it is a humane policy, but because bringing families back together contributes to the economic and social welfare of the United States. Society benefits from the reunification of immediate families, especially because family unity promotes the stability, health and productivity of family members.

The Commission did, however, add the important caveat that it was more important "to reunify close family members than those that are less closely related to a U.S. sponsor." However, one commentator in testimony before the Select Commission said:

> We, as a nation, cannot only accept, but are enriched in countless ways, by traditions which honor the family and stress close ties not only within the nuclear family of spouses and children but also among generations and among brothers and sisters. Attacks on family reunification beyond the immediate family as a form of nepotism are empty posturing.

The Commission submitted its final report to the President and Congress in March 1981. It recommended that the current policy admitting brothers and sisters of adult U.S. citizens within the numerical limitations be continued. It noted that this was "one of the most difficult issues" they faced and indicated that a large minority of the Commissioners favored extending this preference only to unmarried brothers and sisters. The report noted that the recommendation to include all brothers and sisters continues to promote national interest "as it recognizes the closeness of the sibling relationship and the broader concept of family held by many nationalities."

The Preference System

Following the report of the Select Commission, legislation was introduced which did not propose any changes in the existing preference system. In November 1981 and January 1982, the Subcommittee on Immigration and Refugee Policy of the Senate Judiciary Committee held hearings on the preference system, during which the question of the future status of fifth preference for brothers and sisters of adult U.S. citizens was addressed. Reverend Joseph Cogo of the American Committee on Italian Migration testified that for many ethnic groups, brothers and sisters, whether or not they are married, are an integral part of the family reunion concept. Elimination of this preference category would violate a sacrosanct human right of an American citizen to live with his [or her] own traditional lifestyle. Esther Kee of the U.S.-Asian Institute said that those admitted as fifth preference immigrants are the easiest entries to resettle, have little need of public assistance, and are thus assets to the United States.

135

Others countered, saying that fifth preference entries result in exponential immigration growth and contribute to large backlogs. Also, it was asserted that the large number of people admitted as relatives are displacing what could be admissions based on skills likely to benefit the United States. . . .

No legislative formulation, however, is assured of speedy enactment. No doubt this is due, at least in part, to the uncertainty of the factual predicate which serves as the impetus to reform. In 1987, a senate staff report found:

> Recent concerns over massive fifth preference backlogs may be exaggerated, and suggest that a balanced assessment of recent evidence indicates that the fifth preference is functioning largely as it was intended. It serves as a low level admission priority attracting additional family members but requires that they wait in relatively long lines in order to obtain the benefits of an immigrant visa. Potential beneficiaries often do wait the necessary years but some reject visa applications for reasons plausibly tied to their increasing age and the decreasing priority of uprooting their families.

In the absence of a strong case for reform, proposals to revise the basis for immigration take on the character of utopian "social engineering" which politicians perhaps understandably shy away from. . . .

Family Unity

Protection of family unity is and must remain a prominent theme in U.S. immigration policy. The principle is fundamental and universal. Family unity promotes the stability, health and productivity of family members, which in turn promotes stability and productivity in the community and nation. The term "family" can have varied meanings. A married brother or sister need be no less "close" or important to a sibling because he or she is married. Absent compelling evidence that a real threat is posed to the general welfare of the United States, and that reform is thereby warranted, the fifth preference specifically should remain intact.

"America's refugee admission policy has lost much of its compassion and reason."

The U.S. Should Accept More Refugees

Stephen Moore

Refugees differ from immigrants in that they are forced out of their native country by political persecution, famine, or civil war. There are over fifteen million refugees in the world today, many of whom live in makeshift camps in Third World countries. The United States let in 106,000 refugees in 1989, but turned down applications from many more. In the following viewpoint, Stephen Moore argues that the U.S. should greatly increase the number of refugees it admits. He contends that the costs of letting in refugees could be minimized by replacing welfare assistance with loans. Moore is director of the American Immigration Institute, a Washington, D.C. research organization that supports increased U.S. immigration.

As you read, consider the following questions:

1. What three revisions to U.S. refugee policy does Moore recommend?
2. Why is the distinction between economic and political refugees obsolete, according to Moore?
3. How does welfare assistance harm refugees, in the author's opinion?

"Flea Market: More Refugees at Lower Cost," by Stephen Moore is excerpted, with permission, from the Spring 1990 issue (No. 52) of *Policy Review*, a publication of The Heritage Foundation, 214 Massachusetts Avenue NE, Washington, DC 20002.

America's refugee admission policy has lost much of its compassion and reason. In 1990 tens of thousands of freedom seekers—including Poles, Hungarians, and other newly freed Eastern Europeans, Vietnamese boat people, Soviet Jews, and Central Americans—who in previous eras would have been warmly accepted in the United States, will be turned away. The United States admits roughly half the number of international refugees that it admitted in 1981, and fewer than a fifth as many as at the turn of the century. This restrictive policy is imposed even when all evidence demonstrates that accepting refugees is not merely an act of humanitarianism, but also a direct long-term benefit to the U.S. economy and culture.

Three Needed Revisions

America could reopen its gates to many more international victims of political, religious, and economic persecution—at no cost to U.S. taxpayers—by making three long-overdue revisions in refugee admission policy. First, for victims of Communism, such as the Vietnamese boat people, the United States should stop pretending that there is a moral distinction between those fleeing for political reasons and those fleeing for economic reasons. America now accepts the former and turns away the latter, even though in both cases, these casualties of Communism are fleeing for their lives. The boat people awaiting to be deported in Hong Kong should be sent to the United States, not to Vietnamese reeducation camps.

Second, the United States should adopt a policy allowing entry of emigrants from newly freed Communist countries. The U.S. State Department declared that as a result of the "democratic evolution" in Poland, Hungary, and Czechoslovakia, citizens of these nations will no longer be granted refugee status. They are the latest victims of the Catch-22 of a U.S. refugee policy that states, in effect: if you are free to leave, you are no longer free to come. America should respond to the emergence of freedom and liberty around the world by opening the immigration gates wider, not slamming them shut. Congress should provide each newly democratized nation, depending on its size, 20,000 to 50,000 "freedom visas" annually for the next five years to restore normal immigration flows.

Most important, the United States should terminate federal grant programs that pay for refugees' resettlement costs. Refugees come to the U.S. seeking opportunity, not a handout. Careful research demonstrates that these well-intentioned public aid programs hurt refugees in the long run by encouraging welfare dependency and delaying entry into the labor force. Moreover, the $500 million price tag for these assistance programs ensures that U.S. refugee policy is driven by federal bud-

138

get worries, not humanitarian concerns.

Most resettlement costs could be eliminated by replacing federal grants for refugees with temporary low-interest guaranteed loans—to be paid back when these new Americans are integrated culturally and economically into U.S. society. Loan repayments would then be used to finance the resettlement expenses of future refugees, thus minimizing the taxpayer cost of absorbing these émigrés while making room for many more.

Obsolete Distinction

In 1989 some 50,000 Vietnamese refugees crammed onto small, overcrowded fishing boats and journeyed to Hong Kong, where they thought they would find freedom. The inhospitable reception the boat people have received in Hong Kong is by now well known. Immediately seized and placed in refugee camps, they are treated as illegal aliens and now await forced repatriation—despite their protests that "we would rather die than return." Several already have committed suicide rather than be sent back to spend months or years in Vietnam's nightmarish reeducation camps.

The U.S. response to the tragedy has been anything but commendable. While angling moral aspersions at Britain and Hong Kong for the harsh insensitivity of involuntary repatriation, the

Chuck Asay, by permission of the *Colorado Springs Gazette Telegraph*.

U.S. government essentially has joined a multinational chorus of agreement that there is simply no room in the free world for the Vietnamese.

The sad plight of the Vietnamese boat people has dramatized an increasingly obvious defect of U.S. (and worldwide) refugee standards: the distinction between an economic migrant and a political refugee is no longer very useful—if it ever has been —in evaluating whom America should welcome and whom it should reject. Under U.S. and international law, political refugees are people with "a well-founded fear of persecution in their country of residence because of their race, religion, nationality, or political opinion." Refugees are eligible for immediate entry into the United States, while the normal immigration process can take up to 20 years (except for those who have immediate family members in the United States or possess highly specialized labor market skills).

America must begin to acknowledge that the distinction between a person fleeing Communism for political motives and one fleeing for economic motives is merely semantic, not moral. Should a teacher fleeing Vietnam because of his or her political beliefs be generously accepted by the United States, while a peasant farmer who leaves because his nation's centralized economic system does not allow him to adequately feed his family is spurned as an "economic migrant"? In effect, our refugee policy says to the exile: we will not let you die at the hands of the executioner, but are ambivalent to your death from economic deprivation. If today's admission criteria were applied in earlier times, one can imagine the U.S. government turning back the ships from Ireland carrying hundreds of thousands of Irish fleeing the great potato famine 100 years ago. . . .

America's Iron Curtain

What should U.S. immigration and refugee policy be with respect to nations where Communism already has collapsed, as in Eastern Europe? For some four decades, immigration and refugee flows from nations such as Poland, Hungary, and Romania have slowed to a trickle because of tight emigration restrictions and strict penalties against illegal departure. As a consequence, over the past decade only a tiny proportion of immigration to the United States—3 percent of the total—has come from the Eastern bloc. The number of immigrants from all of Eastern Europe in the 1980s was roughly the same number that arrived from the single island of Jamaica.

The sudden triumph of liberty in Eastern Europe would seem to naturally loosen government barriers to the free movement of people across borders. Yet tens of thousands of frustrated East Europeans who have waited 40 years for the opportunity to emigrate to the United States now find that the Iron Curtain of Communism has been replaced by an impenetrable iron curtain around the U.S. visa office. In November 1989, less than a month after the shattering of the Berlin Wall, the U.S. State Department permanently revoked refugee status for some 20,000 East Europeans waiting to resettle in the United States. Since they are no longer fleeing persecution, they can now only come to the United States as immigrants. Yet under America's current immigration system, most East Europeans do not qualify because, after four decades of severed immigration channels with America, very few East Europeans have immediate family members living in the United States.

Living Up to Our Heritage

After spending so many years demanding free immigration for oppressed peoples, America's reluctance to accept those who are now being released is both tragic and cheap. It is time that we lived up to our immigrant heritage, offering a haven to those so desperately in need around the world.

Douglas Bandow, *American Legion Magazine,* August 1989.

The United States should immediately establish a policy of reserving 20,000 to 50,000 additional "freedom visas" each year for people from newly democratized nations where freedom of emigration had been restricted. Congressman William Lipinski, a Democrat from Chicago, who by unofficial count represents more Poles than any elected official outside Warsaw, has introduced legislation that would launch such a program to reopen immigration from Eastern Europe for the first time since the end of World War II. This special immigration policy could then be extended to Cubans, Albanians, Russians, Chinese, and other nationalities when Communism is repudiated in their countries.

The predictable complaint of the "freedom visas" program is that the United States is already overwhelmed with immigrants. Yet the percentage of foreign-born people living in the United States, the best measure of our ability to absorb immigrants, is only half of what it has been in most earlier periods in this century. Each year the United States admits fewer than three refugees and immigrants for every 1,000 U.S. residents—a very small immigration rate historically and in relation to many other industrialized nations that do not pride themselves on being nations of immigrants. The major effect of the "freedom visas" would be to expand the ethnic diversity of

141

America's newest immigrants, thereby enhancing one of America's greatest strengths. . . .

Most of the 2.5 million refugees who have resettled in the United States since the late 1940s have been net economic contributors. Miami is clearly richer with the presence of the Cubans who fled Castro than without them; the Poles and Hungarians who escaped the Iron Curtain have brought new economic vitality to those American cities with proud ethnic heritages, most notably Chicago. The Vietnamese have contributed mightily to the economic prosperity of Southern California in the 1980s. In general, Southeast Asian refugees—and now their children—have proved to be model citizens: highly resourceful and motivated, family-oriented, pro-American, and strongly anti-Communist. A RAND Corporation study of immigrants in California describes Asians as "one of the most skilled immigrant groups ever to come to the United States."

Although not as upwardly mobile as economic immigrants —who tend to bring to the United States considerable wealth, skill levels, and immediate job prospects—most recent refugee groups are climbing the traditional immigrant ladder to success in America, too. It would be easy to be misled into concluding otherwise. Inspecting a snapshot at a single point in time would reveal a seemingly bleak picture of how the whole refugee population is faring: more than one-quarter of all refugees are dependent on some form of public assistance, their labor force participation rate is about 30 percent below that of the U.S.-born population, and of those refugees that are counted in the labor force, their unemployment rate (8 percent) is significantly higher than that of natives (5 percent). Yet this analysis shields from view the steady economic progress refugees make over time.

Making It

A 1984 study entitled "Making It on Their Own," by one of the nation's largest private refugee assistance groups, Church World Services, documents the rapid economic and social transition of refugees in their new homeland. This survey of more than 2,100 political exiles and their sponsors found that over their first four years in the United States, refugees' "use of cash assistance" dropped from 24 percent in their first year to 7 percent in their fourth year; their "knowledge of English" rose from 56 percent to 70 percent; and their rate of "self-sufficiency" climbed from 44 percent to 70 percent. An exhaustive study by Rita and Julian Simon of Soviet Jews, the very group whose entry the State Department is now restricting, found an especially steep economic climb over a short period for this mostly highly skilled and educated population. Those who arrived in the 1970s had high rates of welfare dependency, but after only two years in the United States they received less public assistance than the average American-born family. . . .

A 1988 survey by the federal government's Office of Refugee Resettlement (ORR) discovered that unemployment among Southeast Asian refugees who arrived in 1985 plummeted from 50 percent in their first year in the United States, to 20 percent in 1986, to 9 percent in 1987, to 5 percent in 1988—right at the national average. Even more impressive, after 12 years in the United States, the Indochinese refugees who arrived in 1975 had incomes and tax payments that exceeded those of the median U.S.-born family.

Leo Cherne of the International Rescue Committee explains that refugees, by necessity, bring with them unique survival skills that account for this encouraging economic progress. "Starting from scratch, refugees have to be more inventive and more determined," states Cherne. They have to be more frugal and work harder. This is the secret of their success—success that over the years has been the trademark of all identifiable refugee groups, starting with the displaced persons of the post-World War II years.

Still, beneath this good news is a stubbornly persistent high rate of dependency for some recent refugee groups. About one of every four refugees continues to receive public aid, even after three years in the United States. Some analysts have hypothesized that this excessive dependency rate is due to a decline in employment skills, knowledge of English, and educational level of the more recent arrivals from Southeast Asia and the Soviet Union. There is some evidence of this. But the far more convincing explanation is that most refugees today, unlike earlier uprooted groups, are almost immediately acquainted upon their arrival to these shores with the welfare state and the work disincentives it creates.

Welfare Trap for Refugees

Under the provisions of the 1980 Refugee Assistance Act, each newly arriving refugee receives about $5,000 in federal assistance during his resettlement period in the United States. This money covers the refugee's transportation costs to the United States, 12 to 24 months of refugee cash assistance, medical coverage, vocational and language training, and most important, federal reimbursement of state welfare payments. The philosophy underlying this broad safety net is that most refugees arrive in the United States in a "traumatized condition," and thus need immediate access to public aid and job training to prepare themselves for the future. The explicit ob-

143

jective of the resettlement assistance is to "help refugees achieve economic self-sufficiency within the shortest time possible following their arrival in the United States." In practice, these programs have had precisely the opposite effect.

The most dramatic evidence that welfare has stifled the economic vigor of refugees is seen in the extremely high dependency rate of newcomers who settle in California—the state that offers a public aid benefit package that is 65 percent more generous than the average for the rest of the nation. Some 80 percent of California refugees are on public assistance during their first two years in the United States, while in other states an average of 33 percent of refugees collect benefits. Refugees locating in California have four times as high a dependency rate and only half the labor force participation rate as do those in Texas, where benefits are less than half as generous. . . .

Clearly, America must begin to restructure these refugee resettlement programs to reduce the costs and work disincentives and to restore public support for higher refugee admissions. . . . The most important reform is for the U.S. government to stop treating able-bodied refugees like welfare recipients.

Loans for Refugees

Under a reformed public assistance program, all public aid programs for able-bodied new refugees, except Medicaid, would be eliminated and replaced by a low-interest federal guaranteed loan of up to $5,000. The loans would be financed by private refugee resettlement agencies or banks, in much the same way the Guaranteed Student Loan program operates. The refugees could use these funds for any variety of purposes: job placement, language training, housing, or even as start-up capital for a small business. After five years in the United States, the refugees would begin to repay these loans, unless they still had very low incomes. The resettlement groups could then use repayment funds to make new loans. In this way, past refugees would help finance the costs of succeeding waves of newcomers. . . .

A loan program would shift much of the primary caretaker responsibility from the shoulders of the government back to where it has traditionally rested: with the network of private voluntary groups, churches, ethnic communities, and families. To be sure, hundreds of groups already generously provide hundreds of millions of dollars in financial aid and in-kind assistance to America's refugees. But more needs to be done by private citizens and ethnic groups.

"There are real limits on how many refugees we can resettle in the United States, and we must learn to respect these limits."

The U.S. Should Not Accept More Refugees

Gerda Bikales

What to do about the world's fifteen million refugees from the Soviet Union, Eastern Europe, Africa, Asia, and Latin America remains an important issue for American immigration policy. In the following viewpoint, Gerda Bikales argues that the U.S. lacks the space and resources to take in more refugees. She believes that instead of letting in more refugees, the U.S. should aid international organizations that help them, and work to change the international conditions that create refugees. Bikales is a consultant on public policy issues and former executive director of U.S. English, an organization which seeks to establish English as the official language of the U.S.

As you read, consider the following questions:

1. What personal background does Bikales cite as relevant to her present opinions on U.S. refugee policy?
2. How many refugees should the U.S. admit, according to the author?
3. What criteria does Bikales believe should be used in determining which refugees to admit into America?

Gerda Bikales, a paper presented to the Conference on the Purpose of Legal Immigration in the 1990s and Beyond, sponsored by the Federation for American Immigration Reform, June 10, 1988. Reprinted with permission.

I was a refugee in four countries, ultimately, in the United States. It was here that I ceased being a refugee, finding a people willing to include me on equal terms in its evolving destiny. . . .

My own life experiences have naturally conditioned me to empathize deeply with those who are uprooted and living in fear. Had America (or England, or Canada, or Australia) been willing to give refuge to my family in 1938, I would have had a far more normal childhood, without death and destruction as my constant companions.

America's unwillingness to play a role in the protection of Europe's endangered Jewry remains a dark page in our history. But what might have been a righteous and possible solution in 1938 can no longer form the basis of American refugee policy in 1988. The world has changed in these past fifty years. We were wrong in 1938, but if we don't learn the full lessons of that failure, we risk being wrong in 1988 as well.

It seems to me that there are, or should be, two components to American refugee policy:

1. How many refugees do we admit, under what conditions, and by what selection criteria? and—this is most important:

2. How do we discharge our moral obligations toward the many more million refugees awash in the world, those who would like to resettle in the United States but will never gain admission?

Immigration Policy

It is fitting that we discuss refugee policy as part of overall U.S. immigration policy. Policy-makers and refugee lobbies have always insisted on separating the issue of refugee admissions from immigration policy, as if the compelling needs of people in distress elsewhere in the world somehow canceled out their domestic impact. Unfortunately, that is not so, and we may as well admit at the outset that refugees impact heavily upon public welfare programs.

What are the goals of immigration today? What benefits do we, as a people, expect to flow from the admission of immigrants at this time? How can immigration policy best serve the national interest? The answers to these questions must inform our formulation of refugee admissions policy.

To start with the obvious, we no longer need people to settle the land. The land is settled, crowded, expensive, unavailable— the thousands of homeless people in America today bespeak of that truism. The era of inviting newcomers for the purpose of settling the land formally ended in 1935, when the Homestead Act was repealed. In reality, the availability of free land as an inducement to settlement had ended long before its official repeal.

146

We have no need to import massive manpower, though there are shortages in some sectors of the labor market. It makes good sense to reserve a substantial portion of our immigrant admissions for those with skills that are in demand.

U.S. Goals

The reunion of families remains a prime objective of immigration policy. But unless we limit ourselves to the nuclear family unit, our well-meaning attempts at reunification are self-defeating: every act of reunion in our country becomes an act of separation in the sending country. We can never hope to have every one happily reunited in this country.

A Refugee Ceiling

The United States should continue to provide a haven for some refugees. But the number we accept should be included in an annual ceiling set by Congress which includes all entrants—immigrants, refugees, and persons granted asylum. We must decide what flow of newcomers we can afford, and can assimilate into our culture. Then the US administration would be required to operate within this ceiling. . . .

Like all countries, we have limits. We can't be the world's welfare agency. We cannot eliminate third-world poverty and oppression by opening our door to all who would like to escape. Switzerland and Norway have reputations of being among the most humanitarian nations in the world, but they know that they cannot accept hundreds of thousand of refugees without destroying their way of life and their ability to provide an acceptable safety net for their own employed and poor.

Richard D. Lamm, *The Christian Science Monitor*, June 11, 1986.

For some time now, diversity has been a goal of our immigration policy. We have been very successful in this endeavor, and have indeed enriched our core culture with the contributions of people from many different cultural traditions. In the future, non-discrimination on the basis of race, religion and national origin must remain a hallmark of immigration policy, thus assuring a continued inflow of people from many different backgrounds.

There is another goal still that we wish to fulfill through immigration. It has nothing at all to do with practical concerns, and everything to do with sentiment and a healthy desire to feel good about ourselves. We are a nation of immigrants, and we wish to honor this immigrant tradition by keeping the door open. Not as wide as we once did, but open to at least some people desperate to remake their lives with us. This objective we can accomplish through refugee admissions.

The American people's humanitarian concerns and generous impulses toward the oppressed and dispossessed are, in fact, the sole justification for maintaining a policy of refugee admissions, and a relatively generous one at that.

How Many?

How many refugees should we admit?

Before answering this question, we must decide how many immigrants we are prepared to accept annually, deduct from that the number we shall need for the reunification of conjugal families, decide how many slots we want to allocate to immigrants with job skills in short supply, and keep the rest for refugees.

As is the case with other would-be immigrants, refugees are unfortunately in plentiful supply. There are far more of them than we can ever hope to accommodate. In many ways we find ourselves in a shopper's market, and this reality should shape our immigration selection process and our refugee selections as well.

In general, refugees who have close relatives here are prime candidates for admission. So are refugees with training that meets a need in the labor market.

Foreign Policy Concerns

More controversial, perhaps, is the notion that refugees should also be selected with some sensitivity to political foreign policy implications. No one has an intrinsic "right" to be resettled as a refugee in America, and there is no compulsion to follow a policy of absolute political blindness in deciding admissions. If it reinforces our foreign policy objectives to accept fugitives from one regime but not from another, it makes good sense to go that route. To bring that point home bluntly, it means that if the United States supports the government of El Salvador as a struggling democracy but perceives Nicaragua as a cruel oppressor, it is logical to accept Nicaraguans but not Salvadorans. You or I may or may not like the Administration's Central American policies, and we are not afraid to say so. But there is a lot to be said for consistency in public policy, and a refugee policy that complements foreign policy is better than one that doesn't.

As with immigration policy, we should aim toward diversity in refugee admissions. Not only Russian Jews, but also Iranian Bahais. Not only released political prisoners from Cuba, but also from Ethiopia and Cambodia. We should avoid building up

148

large concentrations of any one refugee group. Ethnic groups tend to cluster in one area, burdening local schools and social services. Also, such build-ups are a prescription for the emergence of spontaneous lobbies for more refugee admissions along ethnic lines, substituting special interests for the national interest in this issue.

Economic Refugees

The news media portray all the "Joses" in our country as hard-working, scared refugees from oppression. In reality, most of these people are simply economic refugees who only serve to take jobs from American citizens and drain our Social Security, welfare and other benefit programs.

Palmer Stacy and Wayne Lutton, *The Immigration Time Bomb*, 1988.

Having offered a policy that would unashamedly favor the refugee with American relatives, with useful skills, and whose admission would not run counter to our foreign policy objectives nor magnify adverse impacts upon local communities, I would like to propose a subcategory of refugees, limited to perhaps three percent of our overall refugee admissions. People in this subcategory would be admitted strictly on the basis of humanitarian concerns—people who are ill and in need of long-term extensive rehabilitation. Norway took in a few desperate concentration camp survivors after World War II, and succeeded in giving a new lease on life to people rejected by everyone else. Today, several Scandinavian countries are again accepting a small contingent of the most hopeless refugees for rehabilitation. Following this course would pay homage to our humanitarian tradition, and most unambiguously meet our collective impulse to reach out to the most wretched of the earth.

Political Asylum

Life does not always arrange itself quite so neatly, of course. It doesn't always provide us with the opportunity to make deliberate choices. Not all would-be refugees are patiently awaiting our decision in a country of first asylum. More and more, people make their way into the United States, and eventually ask for political asylum.

In determining who is eligible for political asylum, we may at times have to relax on requirements relating to professional training and American relatives. However, to truly distinguish between illegal aliens and genuine asylees, politics and foreign policy considerations must necessarily be the primary determi-

149

nant in such cases.

Here again, those we accept should be deducted from our overall refugee admission totals. An asylee is in fact a refugee, who got here by a different route.

But what about those others, those who will not make it in the intense competition for resettlement in the United States? The United States, the world's most powerful democracy and defender of freedom, cannot discharge its obligations simply by taking in x number of refugees, no matter how generous that number may be. It must assume a much larger role than mere resettlement.

U.S. Role

As I reflect upon the events relating to the Nazi persecutions of the late thirties, in which my own family was caught up, I have come to see that the failure of the United States was not only that it refused to give refuge to even a small number of the persecuted. The real failure was that it turned its back completely. In 1938, a conference was called in Vichy, France, at which the world's democracies came together to discuss the fate of Europe's Jews, who were openly threatened with extinction. It was decided not to decide—to do nothing. No nation offered to take in any of the endangered people. Hitler correctly interpreted the indifference of the democracies as carte blanche to do as he pleased with Europe's Jews. And he did.

There was no United Nations at the time, no High Commissioner for Refugees. The Vatican was silent. The democracies didn't choose to be bothered. The Jewish organizations in America were barely whispering their concern. As the darkening clouds engulfed Europe, the Jews felt abandoned. And, indeed, we were.

I don't believe that we would have had Auschwitz and Treblink, Maidanek and Bergen Belsen, if the symbolic protection of a High Commissioner for Refugees had been bestowed upon the Jews under Nazi rule, if the Vatican had used its moral authority on their behalf, if the democracies had shown interest at Vichy.

A model of what we can do to help oppressed people is what we have done in the Soviet Union. In response to pressure brought by successive presidents and by the weight of world opinion, conditions are at last improving in the Soviet Union. Every week brings word of greater freedom, and hope of economic improvement. Vietnam is eager to resume diplomatic contacts with the U.S. and for economic assistance, so that here again we can pressure for better conditions that will allow the repatriation of the thousands of Vietnamese refugees now languishing in camps in Thailand and elsewhere.

This, then, is the essential role that the United States can and must play—to contribute financially to the maintenance of refugee camps, to build the prestige of the UN High Commissioner of Refugees, to rally world opinion against the oppressors, whether of the right or left, and press on for changed conditions in the home countries so as to avoid the making of more refugees and permit the eventual repatriation of those in exile.

The Costs of Refugees

The cost of these hundreds of thousands of "refugees" to U.S. taxpayers is staggering. The federal government has been spending billions of dollars on refugee-related programs in recent years. The State Department has specific multi-million-dollar annual programs for "refugee" transportation to the U.S., reception and placement grants and "English as a Second Language" courses. The Department of Agriculture's Food Stamp program provides additional millions of dollars of assistance to "refugees" every year. And the Department of Health and Human Services conducts a wide range of programs for the exclusive benefit of "refugees.". . .

Hundreds of millions of dollars more are spent by state and local governments for aid to "refugees" and illegals. Although Congress must accept responsibility for unwillingness to enforce our immigration laws, the federal government provides relatively little assistance to states which bear the brunt of the alien invasion.

Palmer Stacy and Wayne Lutton, *The Immigration Time Bomb*, 1988.

There are real limits on how many refugees we can resettle in the United States, and we must learn to respect these limits, despite the temptation to ignore them "just this once." But there are no limits to the moral pressure we can bring to bear on behalf of the exiles, and those suffering oppressed people still in the homeland.

There are few satisfying answers, and no satisfactory ones. But as long as we do not turn a deaf ear and indifferent heart to the world's refugees, we can be a force for good on this earth.

a critical thinking activity

Distinguishing Between Fact and Opinion

This activity is designed to help develop the basic reading and thinking skill of distinguishing between fact and opinion. Consider the following statement: "The United States admits far more immigrants than Japan." This is a fact which can be checked by comparing the immigration records of both countries. But the statement, "The United States should learn from Japan not to take in so many immigrants," is an opinion. Whether the U.S. should restrict immigration or not is a debatable issue on which many people disagree.

When investigating controversial issues it is important that one be able to distinguish between statements of fact and statements of opinion. It is also important to recognize that not all statements of fact are true. They may appear to be true, but some are based on inaccurate or false information. For this activity, however, we are concerned with understanding the difference between those statements which appear to be factual and those which appear to be based primarily on opinion.

Most of the following statements are taken from the viewpoints in this chapter. Consider each statement carefully. *Mark O for any statement you believe is an opinion or interpretation of facts. Mark F for any statement you believe is a fact. Mark I for any you believe is impossible to judge.*

If you are doing this activity as a member of a class or group, compare your answers with those of other class or group members. Be able to defend your answers. You may discover that others come to different conclusions than you. Listening to the reasons others present for their answers may give you valuable insights into distinguishing between fact and opinion.

O = opinion
F = fact
I = impossible to judge

152

1. Through immigration, the U.S. acquires 11,000 engineers and scientists each year.

2. A nation like America functions best when it confidently welcomes the contributions immigrants can bring.

3. The United States should accept more refugees than it does now.

4. Welfare programs can be demoralizing for immigrants. Immigrants come with dreams of great success and end up relying on handouts.

5. The fraction of the U.S. population that is foreign-born is lower than that of Canada and Australia.

6. Many immigrants have started shops in the inner cities, providing services where none had existed before.

7. The U.S. admits roughly half the number of refugees that it admitted in 1981.

8. The distinction between "economic migrants" and "political refugees" is no longer useful.

9. Immigration now accounts for one-third to one-half of the population growth in the United States.

10. A nation of 250 million people simply cannot have a shortage of workers.

11. America is taking in more than enough immigrants already.

12. Extended family ties help immigrants adjust to life in the United States. The U.S. should accept anyone who has family ties here and wishes to immigrate.

13. Family reunification should remain one of the important principles of American immigration policy.

14. About three-quarters of all immigrants in 1988 had relatives living in the U.S.

15. Under U.S. immigration rules, unmarried children of U.S. citizens have a higher immigration priority than married children of U.S. citizens.

16. Current immigration policy places too much emphasis on kinship as a basis for admitting immigrants.

17. The number of visas issued each year by the U.S. is far less than the number of visas demanded.

18. No refugee has an automatic right to resettle in the U.S.

19. The United States admitted over 100,000 refugees in 1986.

20. U.S. immigration law is unfair and impractical. Thousands of people come to the U.S. illegally because the law unfairly bars their entry.

Periodical Bibliography

The following articles have been selected to supplement the diverse views presented in this chapter.

Luis Acle Jr. — "Reunification, Not Reunions," *Los Angeles Times*, July 5, 1989.

Gary S. Becker — "Why Not Let Immigrants Pay for Speedy Entry?" *Business Week*, March 2, 1987.

George J. Borjas — "The U.S. Takes the Wrong Immigrants," *The Wall Street Journal*, April 5, 1990.

Kevin Clarke — "Who's Welcome in America?" *Salt*, June 1990. Available from *Salt*, 205 W. Monroe, Chicago, IL 60606.

Congressional Digest — "Immigration Reform," October 1989.

Roger L. Conner — "Answering the Demo-Doomsayers," *The Brookings Review*, Fall 1989.

Mario M. Cuomo — "The American Dream and the Politics of Inclusion," *Psychology Today*, July 1986.

Bill Frelick — "Refugees in the '90s," *The Christian Science Monitor*, June 14, 1990.

Morton M. Kondracke — "Borderline Cases," *The New Republic*, April 10, 1989.

Stewart Kwoh — "Family Unity Ranks First in Immigration," *Los Angeles Times*, September 14, 1989.

Kenneth Labich — "Let's Let Asians In," *Fortune*, September 17, 1989.

William O. Lipinski and Lamar Smith — "Should Immigration Quotas for Soviet-Bloc Refugees Be Increased?" *American Legion Magazine*, January 1990.

Scott McConnell — "The New Battle over Immigration," *Fortune*, May 9, 1988.

Jonathan Moore — "Update on Immigration and Refugee Issues," *Department of State Bulletin*, July 1989.

Stephen Moore — "Put Green Cards Up for Sale," *The Wall Street Journal*, September 13, 1989.

Stanford S. Penner — "Tapping the Wave of Talented Immigrants," *Issues in Science and Technology*, Spring 1988.

Robert B. Reich — "Huddled Masses or Elite Classes?" *The Washington Monthly*, February 1990.

Steven V. Roberts — "The Hunt for New Americans," *U.S. News & World Report*, May 14, 1990.

Saskia Sassen — "America's Immigration 'Problem,'" *World Policy Journal*, Fall 1989.

How Should the U.S. Respond to Illegal Immigration?

Chapter Preface

The U.S. has a large population of immigrants who are in the country illegally. Some enter on temporary student or tourist visas and remain in the U.S. Others arrive with forged visas or no documentation at all. Many enter the U.S. at some point on the 1,936 mile border between Mexico and the U.S. How the U.S. should treat these illegal immigrants is a controversial and divisive issue.

Many people argue that the U.S. should not accommodate illegal immigrants at all. They fear that such a response would simply attract more illegal immigrants to the U.S. They view these immigrants as lawbreakers who should be expelled from this country. But others argue that illegal immigrants are simply looking for work and a better life, and should not be treated as outlaws. They advocate passing laws to ensure that these people are not discriminated against or exploited. Between these two positions there seems little room for compromise.

Yet, Congress made an attempt at compromise in 1986 when it passed the Immigration Reform and Control Act (IRCA). To satisfy those who said illegal immigration must be halted, the law made it a crime to hire illegal immigrants. Congress believed that if employers were discouraged from hiring illegal immigrants, the flow of immigrants would be reduced as these illegal immigrants found there were few jobs in the U.S. To satisfy the demands of those who said illegal immigrants should not be treated as outlaws, the law granted amnesty to large numbers of illegal immigrants, specifically those who could prove they had lived in the U.S. since 1982. While the law had some initial success in slowing illegal immigration, it has failed to stop it or to settle the issue. The viewpoints in this chapter examine the continuing controversy over how illegal immigrants should be treated.

"Crisis. That's the word to describe the situation on our borders and our immigration dilemma."

Illegal Immigration Is a Crisis

William F. Jasper

In the following viewpoint, William F. Jasper calls illegal immigration an invasion which threatens the U.S. He argues that the U.S. Border Patrol has too few people and resources to effectively enforce immigration laws, and that illegal immigration creates economic and social problems for the U.S. Jasper is a contributing editor to *The New American,* a conservative news and opinion magazine.

As you read, consider the following questions:

1. How many illegal immigrants enter the U.S. each year, according to Jasper?
2. What kinds of problems do illegal immigrants cause, according to the author?
3. What does Jasper mean by the "Third World colonization" of the U.S.?

William F. Jasper, "Out of Control: The Immigration Invasion," *The New American,* September 12, 1988. Reprinted with permission.

Invasion. That's what we are witnessing: an ongoing invasion that has been escalating for over a decade. Each day, at hundreds of points along our southern border, thousands of people from countries all over the world are entering the United States illegally. Most will enter along the U.S.-Mexican border. Some will be smuggled across in secret compartments in some of the thousands of vehicles that cross the border each day. Others will enter using forged documents. Still others will fly into this country on student or tourist visas and never leave. The vast majority, however, will simply walk in, wade in, or float in. Their chances of escaping apprehension are quite good. The U.S. Border Patrol is, in some cases, too short on men and resources even to give chase.

Even so, the Border Patrol has apprehended well over one million illegal aliens per year. In 1986 the Border Patrol's arrests totaled almost 1.8 million—nearly two million people caught entering this country in violation of our law in a single year!

By the most conservative and optimistic estimates, one or two illegal aliens successfully penetrate our border and escape inland for each illegal alien that is arrested and deported. Many Border Patrol officers have told us that the successful entry-to-arrest ratio is much higher, more on the order of four or five to one.

That means that—at the least—well over one million illegal aliens make it into this country annually. Who are these people that make up this surging tide of humanity breaking on our shores? Are they refugees fleeing political or religious persecution? Desperate peasants seeking work so they can feed their starving families? Economic pilgrims seeking a more affluent lifestyle, perhaps intending to live off the welfare state? Hardened criminals who will victimize other aliens or American citizens? Drug pushers? Agents of hostile foreign powers? Terrorists? They are all of these, and more. And they continue to come by the hundreds of thousands.

No One Knows How Many

As long ago as 1975, then-Commissioner of the Immigration and Naturalization Service (INS) General Leonard Chapman warned that "illegal immigration is out of control." The following year Commissioner Chapman said: "There are today in the United States six to eight million illegal aliens, and that number is increasing by half a million to a million each year."

Despite the growing crisis, Congress refused to act. President Reagan was merely stating what had been painfully obvious for many years when he said in October 1983: "This country has lost control of its own borders, and no country can sustain that kind of position."

Proponents of the controversial Immigration Reform and Control Act of 1986 assured us that their measure would remedy the problem. That bill is now law, but the invasion continues on a massive scale. . . .

Downplaying the Number of Illegals

No one knows for sure just how many foreign nationals have illegally entered the United States and taken up residence here on a permanent or semi-permanent basis. Commissioner Chapman, in 1976, put the total at six to eight million. President Jimmy Carter replaced General Chapman with Leonel J. Castillo, who put the "rights" of illegal aliens above enforcement of the law and attempted to downplay the seriousness of the situation by claiming that there were only three to six million illegals in the U.S.

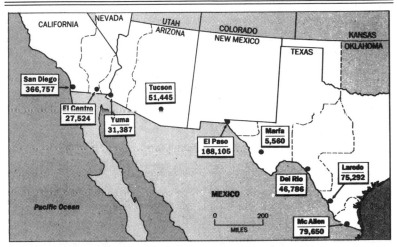

Number of arrests for illegal border crossing for fiscal year ended September 30, 1989.

Victor Kotowitz/*Los Angeles Times*, © 1990. Reprinted with permission.

Regardless of which figures one accepts, the numbers involved are enormous. Even if we go with the most conservative estimates of "only" three to six million, we're still talking about an invasion in numbers potentially greater than the total manpower of the Soviet armed forces (5.9 million) and greater than the population count of most of our individual states.

An influx of this magnitude over such a short time frame has enormous economic, social, political and national security ramifications. . . .

We are indeed a nation of immigrants. We are rightfully proud of our distinctive heritage—rich in the cultures, tongues, and contributions of peoples from many nations. For more than three centuries America has been a refuge, and a beacon, indeed a magnet to peoples the world over.

The first permanent English settlement in America was founded at Jamestown, Virginia in 1607. Thirteen years later the Pilgrims established their settlement at Plymouth, Massachusetts. By 1640 the North American colonies had a population of around 25,000. A century later the colonists numbered almost one million.

Our first national census, conducted in 1790, placed our population at 3.9 million, including nearly three-quarters of a million slaves. During the 18th and 19th centuries there was little reason to be concerned about immigration. America had vast, open frontiers and was in need of new hands that were willing to work.

Even though there were few restrictions placed on immigration during the first century of our Republic, there was never any question that immigration to this country was a *privilege* not a *right*. There are many now, however, who claim that immigration is indeed a right. This notion, of course, is absurd: As a sovereign nation, the people of the United States, through their elected representatives, have a right (1) to determine who may immigrate to this country and (2) to establish the criteria for admission. This is the right of all sovereign nations. . . .

The Border Patrol

The INS (including the Border Patrol) operates out of the Department of Justice on a budget of less than $1 billion. . . . With these relatively puny resources the INS/Border Patrol is charged with securing our thousands of miles of border, inspecting several million places of employment, and maintaining records on millions of foreign visitors, not to mention numerous other responsibilities.

Along our 2,000 mile border with Mexico, where over 95 percent of our illegal alien arrests are made, the Border Patrol operates with fewer than 2,500 officers. That means that probably no more than 500 to 600 agents are actually manning our entire southern border during a normal work shift. By the end of the 1988 fiscal year, the Border Patrol on the U.S.-Mexican border is scheduled to be augmented to a total of 3,600 officers—a significant increase, but still far from adequate. (By contrast, New York City has a police force of nearly 27,000 officers. The Los Angeles Police Department has nearly 7,400 men in uniform.)

The border fence, erected by the United States in 1975, at the cost of $5 million dollars, is virtually non-existent, or severely damaged at most points along the border. In some areas, the smugglers are so brazen that they bring in bulldozers to demolish the fence and to make roads for their vehicles. . . .

Our men and women in green are in constant danger and nearly all carry visible battle scars. For their personal safety, they should be assigned to the field in two-man teams, but the standard is still one officer per vehicle. These lone agents, often with inoperable radios and unreliable vehicles, regularly patrol remote and dangerous areas where they may be outnumbered by as much as 100 to one. Along some stretches of our border, our officers dare not venture except in "war wagons" outfitted with special screens for protection against barrages of rocks, bottles, and chunks of metal and concrete.

Borders Out of Control

"This country has lost control of its own borders, and no country can sustain that kind of position," declared President Reagan in 1983. Since that time, the border situation has steadily worsened as the immigration flow continues unchecked. While the U.S. has always been a generous nation eager to harbor the "downtrodden" and "huddled masses," the nation is witnessing an uncontrollable tide of illegal immigration, generating far-reaching social, economic and political problems yet difficult to gauge.

J. Michael Rodriguez, *The Mindszenty Report*, June 1989.

Our thin green line is simply being overwhelmed; they cannot keep up with the surging tide of aliens. Every hour of every day, busloads of Mexican nationals are returned to the border and released into Mexico. Within hours, many of them will be back in the United States. Our nation's busiest port of entry, San Ysidro, California, handles some 12 million vehicle crossings and 10 million pedestrian crossings a year. Across the border is Tijuana. Much smuggling of both drugs and aliens goes undetected here because we have the enforcement manpower for only cursory, sporadic checks of vehicles and foot traffic. Customs officers are limited to approximately 30 seconds per vehicle and only a second or two per person. The INS in 1986 inspected in excess of 320 million aliens and returning U.S. citizens at our borders. More than ten and one-half million visitor visas are issued to foreign tourists, business travelers, and students each year. In the border areas fraudulent documents are easy to obtain and often are very difficult for officers to detect.

Many are the ramifications of this massive influx of both legal and illegal immigrants. One of the most important factors in the immigration equation today—not present when earlier immigrant waves hit these shores—is our gargantuan welfare state. Previous generations of immigrants arrived here as destitute as any of those arriving today. They had to work to survive. There was no alternative. There was no free lunch. What assistance was available came from friends, relatives, church and private charities.

That is a far cry from today. Booklets such as *El Otro Lado (The Other Side—A Guide for the Undocumented)* are distributed by the thousand to illegal aliens, refugees, and other recent immigrants. Published by the radical Resource Center in Albuquerque, New Mexico, *El Otro Lado* provides the illegal aliens with an extensive list of organizations, addresses, and telephone numbers—many of them toll free—in almost every state in the Union that they can contact for legal assistance in fighting deportation. They are told how to apply for all of the welfare and medical benefits available to them in this land of plenty. . . .

A study conducted in 1986 by the Chief Administrative Office of Los Angeles County determined that services to illegal aliens were costing county taxpayers $172.8 million per year. That total did not include the tax dollars paid to the sixty thousand citizen children in Los Angeles County who receive federal Aid to Families with Dependent Children. These are children (allegedly) born in the United States to illegal aliens. Under current law, being born here is sufficient for citizenship. . . .

County hospitals and health delivery systems have been particularly hard hit. Jackson Memorial Hospital in Florida's Dade County provides health services to thousands of refugees and illegal aliens. Besides receiving the bulk of the 150,000 Cuban refugees from Mariel in 1980, Dade County is host to 50,000 to 75,000 illegal aliens from Nicaragua, and many thousands more from Haiti, Jamaica, El Salvador, Mexico, and elsewhere. After receiving reimbursement from the Federal Government, Jackson Memorial is still looking at an $8-10 million shortfall for unpaid services rendered to illegal aliens. . . .

Los Angeles public schools are bursting at the seams and are going on year-round rotating class schedules to accommodate the tremendous numbers of children of illegal aliens, refugees, and immigrants who have settled there in recent years. The cost to the county and city school districts for services provided to undocumented aliens is estimated at close to $570 million.

Third World Colonization

A visible effect of our uncontrolled immigration is what is increasingly referred to as the "Third World colonization" of the United States. Large sections of major U.S. cities now resemble Mexico City, San Salvador, Bombay, and Calcutta—with tens of thousands of people living in cardboard and tin shanties, or sleeping in the streets. California, which has been especially hard hit by the recent immigration waves, has been christened by *Time* magazine as our first "Third World state." Many of our small towns and rural areas have also been severely impacted. Several thousand migrant farm workers live in settlements without sanitation or potable water, in conditions that breed sickness and disease.

Out of Control

On the border, with Mexico in various stages of collapse and its population hemorrhaging, things are totally out of control. Whole businesses have sprung up, producing every type of Social Security card, voting card, green card, driver's license, and passport. Despite liberal disclaimers, illegals are taking jobs across the spectrum—and, according to apprehension statistics of the Immigration and Naturalization Service, in nearly exactly the same proportion of industrial and agricultural jobs as other Americans—and they are getting welfare, Social Security, bilingual education, and hospital care, among other things.

Georgie Anne Geyer, *The Washington Times,* March 24, 1986.

Of course, many immigrants are already infected with serious diseases before they arrive here. Applicants for immigration who come through legal channels receive only a cursory health examination; illegal aliens receive no inspection whatsoever. The upsurge of tuberculosis and leprosy cases in recent years is almost completely attributable to our resident alien population.

Crime

The alien influx has also contributed greatly to our spiraling crime statistics. Most illegal aliens are not criminally inclined, and, other than violating our immigration laws, do not engage in illegal activities. But when we're dealing with millions of aliens, it does not take a large percentage to add up to a sizeable criminal element. Here are some figures compiled in 1987 by the INS from law enforcement agencies in southern California:

- Illegal aliens are involved in one-third of the rapes and murders and one-fourth of the burglaries in San Diego County.
- Aliens account for over half of the homicides in Orange County.
- Aliens are responsible for about 90 percent of the narcotics traffic in the city of Santa Ana, and 80 percent of the same in Fullerton.
- Four hundred illegal aliens a month are added to the Califor-

nia prison system for serious crimes.

• The cost to California taxpayers for incarceration of illegal aliens is at least $136 million per year.

During 1987, the INS's Western Regional Office (covering California, Nevada, Hawaii, and Arizona) deported ten thousand illegal aliens for criminal activities, and most of them were serious felony offenses. Half of these cases were drug-related.

Our uncontrolled borders are an open invitation to the international drug cartels to flood the American markets with their deadly wares. And they have done just that. Our backroads, our interstates, and our airways in the Southwest have become cocaine corridors and heroin highways, transporting billions of dollars worth of narcotics transshipped through Mexico. The Border Patrol accounts for 70 percent of the drug interdiction on our southern border, even though that is not their primary responsibility. . . .

A Crisis

Crisis. That's the word to describe the situation on our borders and our immigration dilemma. As political and economic instability in many areas around the world continues to worsen, the ranks of those seeking entry (legally and illegally) to this country will continue to swell.

What can be done? First of all, we must recognize that we have arrived at our present predicament because the "Silent Majority" has been just that—silent—while the vocal, radical minority has maintained a high-visibility campaign, including a steady barrage of letters and communications to Congress. Find out how your Congressman voted on amnesty and other immigration votes. If he has sided with those who are committed to "breaking down the border," set to work to change his voting habits, or vote him out of office.

Ultimately, it comes down to this: We should either abandon our borders altogether—even the very concept of borders—and allow everyone and anyone who wishes to enter to do so; or we should establish reasonable criteria and quotas and an orderly process for entry, and then commit sufficient manpower and resources to enforce the law.

"If every Mexican in this country went home next week, Americans would starve."

Illegal Immigration Is Not a Crisis

Pete Hamill

Pete Hamill writes a column for *Esquire*, a monthly men's magazine, and is the author of *Loving Women*. In the following viewpoint, he argues that illegal immigration contributes to the U.S. economy and does not constitute a crisis. He states that those who want increased barriers at the U.S.-Mexico border are racists who want to keep non-whites out of the U.S.

As you read, consider the following questions:

1. What is the typical illegal immigrant like, according to Hamill?
2. Why does Hamill believe illegal immigrants help the U.S.?
3. According to the author, what two possible events must happen before illegal immigration can be stopped?

You move through the hot, polluted Tijuana morning, past shops and gas stations and cantinas, past the tourist traps of the Avenida Revolución, past the egg-shaped Cultural Center and the new shopping malls and the government housing with bright patches of laundry hanging on balconies; then it's through streets of painted adobe peeling in the sun, ball fields where kids play without gloves, and you see ahead and above you ten-thousand-odd shacks perched uneasily upon the Tijuana hills, and you glimpse the green road signs for the beaches as the immense luminous light of the Pacific brightens the sky. You turn, and alongside the road there's a chain link fence. It's ten feet high.

On the other side of the fence is the United States.

The Tortilla Curtain

There are wide gashes in the fence, which was once called the Tortilla Curtain. You could drive three wide loads, side by side, through the tears in this pathetic curtain. On this morning, on both sides of the fence (more often called *la linea* by the locals), there are small groups of young Mexican men dressed in polyester shirts and worn shoes and faded jeans, and holding small bags. These are a few of the people who are changing the United States, members of a huge army of irregulars engaged in the largest, most successful invasion ever made of North America.

On this day, they smoke cigarettes. They make small jokes. They munch on tacos prepared by a flat-faced, pig-tailed Indian woman whose stand is parked by the roadside. They sip soda. And some of them gaze across the arid scrub and sandy chaparral at the blurred white buildings of the U.S. town of San Ysidro. They wait patiently and do not hide. And if you pull over, and buy a soda from the woman, and speak some Spanish, they will talk.

"I tried last night," says the young man named Jeronimo Vasquez, who wears a Chicago Bears T-shirt under a denim jacket. "But it was too dangerous, too many helicopters last night, too much light. . . ." He looks out at the open stretch of gnarled land, past the light towers, at the distant white buildings. "Maybe tonight we will go to Zapata Canyon. . . ." He is from Oaxaca, he says, deep in the hungry Mexican south. He has been to the United States three times, working in the fields; it is now Tuesday, and he starts a job near Stockton on the following Monday, picker's work arranged by his cousin. "I have much time. . . ."

Abruptly, he turns away to watch some action. Two young men are running across the dried scrub on the U.S. side, kicking up little clouds of white dust, while a Border Patrol car goes after them. The young men dodge, circle, running the broken field, and suddenly stand very still as the car draws close. They are immediately added to the cold statistics of border apprehensions. But they are really mere sacrifices; over on the left, three other men run low and hunched, like infantry-men in a fire fight. "*Corre, corre,*" Jeronimo Vasquez whispers. "Run, run. . . ." They do. And when they vanish into some distant scrub, he clenches a fist like a triumphant fan. He is not alone. All the others cheer, as does the woman selling tacos, and on the steep hill above the road, a man stands before a tar-paper shack, waves a Mexican flag, and shouts: "*Gol!*" And everyone laughs.

We've all read articles about the 1,950-mile-long border between the United States and Mexico, seen documentaries, heard the bellowing rhetoric of the C-Span politicians enraged at the border's weakness; but until you stand beside it, the border is an abstraction. Up close, you see immediately that the border is at once a concrete place with holes in the fence, and a game, a joke, an affront, a wish, a mere line etched by a draftsman on a map. No wonder George Bush gave up on interdiction as a tactic in the War on Drugs; there are literally hundreds of Ho Chi Minh trails leading into the United States from the South (and others from Canada, of course, and the sea). On some parts of the Mexican border there is one border patrolman for every twenty-six miles; it doesn't require a smuggling genius to figure out how to get twenty tons of cocaine to a Los Angeles warehouse. To fill in the gaps, to guard all the other U.S. borders, would require millions of armed guards, many billions of dollars. And somehow, Jeronimo Vasquez would still appear on a Monday morning in Stockton.

Those young men beside the ruined fence—not the *narcotraficantes*—are the most typical members of the peaceful invasion. Nobody knows how many come across each year, although in 1988 920,000 were stopped, arrested, and sent back to Mexico by the border wardens. Thousands more make it. Some are described by the outnumbered and overwhelmed immigration police as OTMs (Other Than Mexican, which is to say, Salvadorans, Guatemalans, Nicaraguans, Costa Ricans fleeing the war zones, and South Americans and Asians fleeing poverty). Some, like Jeronimo Vasquez, come for a few months, earn money, and return to families in Mexico; others come to stay.

"When you see a woman crossing," says Jeronimo Vasquez, "you know she's going to stay. It means she has a husband on the other side, maybe even children. She's not going back. Most of the women are from Salvador, not so many Mexicans. . . ."

Tijuana is one of their major staging grounds. In 1940 it was a town of seventeen thousand citizens, many of whom were employed in providing pleasure for visiting Americans. The clenched, blue-nosed forces of American puritanism gave the town its function. In 1915 California banned horse racing; dance halls and prostitution were made illegal in 1917; and in 1920 Prohibition became the law of the land. So thousands of Americans began crossing the border to do what they could not do at home: shoot crap, bet on horses, get drunk, and get laid.

Movie stars came down from Hollywood with people to whom they weren't married. Gangsters traveled from as far away as Chicago and New York. Women with money had abortions at the Paris Clinic. Sailors arrived from San Diego to lose their virgin status, get their first doses of the clap, and too often to spend nights in the Tijuana jail. The Casino of Agua Caliente was erected in 1928, a glorious architectural mixture of the Alhambra and a Florentine villa, complete with gambling, drinking, a nightclub, big bands, tennis, golf, a swimming pool, and fancy restaurants. Babe Ruth and Jack Dempsey were among the clients, and a young dancer named Margarita Cansino did a nightclub act with her father before changing her name to Rita Hayworth. The casino was closed in 1935 by the Mexican president, and only one of its old towers still remains. But sin did not depart with the gamblers or the end of Prohibition. The town boomed during the war, and thousands of Americans still remember the bizarre sex shows and rampant prostitution of the era and the availability of something called marijuana. Today the run-down cantinas and whorehouses of the Zona Norte are like a living museum of Tijuana's gaudy past.

"It's very dangerous here for women," Jeronimo Vasquez said. "The coyotes tell them they will take them across, for money. If they don't have enough money, they talk them into becoming *putas* for a week or a month. And they never get out. . . ."

Although commercial sex and good marijuana are still available in Tijuana, sin, alas, is no longer the city's major industry. Today the population is more than one million. City and suburbs are crowded with *maquiladora* plants, assembling foreign goods for export to the United States. These factories pay the highest wages in Mexico (although still quite low by U.S. standards) and attract workers from all over the republic. Among permanent residents, unemployment is very low.

Skilled Immigrants

But it's said that any given time, one third of the people in Tijuana are transients, waiting to cross to *el otro lado*. A whole subculture that feeds off this traffic can be seen around the Tijuana bus station: coyotes (guides) who for a fee will bring them across; *enganchadores* (labor contractors) who promise

168

jobs; rooming-house operators; hustlers; crooked cops prepared to extort money from the non-Mexicans. The prospective migrants are not simple field hands, making the hazardous passage to the valleys of California to do work that even the most poverty-ravaged Americans will not do. Mexico is also experiencing a "skill drain." As soon as a young Mexican acquires a skill or craft— carpentry, wood finishing, auto repair—he has the option of departing for the north. The bags held by some of the young men with Jeronimo Vasquez contained tools. And since the economic collapse of 1982 hammered every citizen of Mexico, millions have exercised the option. The destinations of these young skilled Mexicans aren't limited to the sweatshops of Los Angeles or the broiling fields of the Imperial Valley; increasingly the migrants settle in the cities of the North and East. In New York, I've met Mexicans from as far away as Chiapas, the impoverished state that borders Guatemala.

Such men are more likely to stay permanently in the United States than are the migrant agricultural laborers like Jeronimo Vasquez. The skilled workers and craftsmen buy documents that make them seem legal. They establish families. They learn English. They pay taxes and use services. Many of them applied for amnesty under the terms of the Simpson-Rodino Act; the new arrivals are not eligible but they are still coming.

I'm one of those who believe this is a good thing. The energy of the Mexican immigrant, his capacity for work, has become essential to this country. While Mexicans, legal and illegal, work in fields, wash dishes, grind away in sweatshops, clean bedpans, and mow lawns (and fix transmissions, polish wood, build bookcases), millions of American citizens would rather sit on stoops and wait for welfare checks. If every Mexican in this country went home next week, Americans would starve. The lettuce on your plate in that restaurant got there because a Mexican bent low in the sun and pulled it from the earth. Nothing, in fact, is more bizarre than the stereotype of the "lazy" Mexican, leaning against the wall with his sombrero pulled over his face. I've been traveling to Mexico for more than thirty years; the only such Mexicans I've ever seen turned out to be suffering from malnutrition.

But the great migration from Mexico is certainly altering the United States, just as the migration of Eastern European Jews and southern Italians changed the nation at the beginning of the century and the arrival of Irish Catholics changed it a half century earlier. Every immigrant brings with him an entire culture, a dense mixture of beliefs, assumptions, and nostalgias about family, manhood, sex, laughter, music, food, religion. His myths are not American myths. In this respect, the Mexican immigrant is no different from the Irish, Germans, Italians, and

Jews. The ideological descendants of the Know-Nothings and other "nativist" types are, of course, alarmed. They worry about the Browning of America. They talk about the high birthrate of the Latino arrivals, their supposed refusal to learn English, their divided loyalties.

Much of this is racist nonsense, based on the assumption that Mexicans are inherently "inferior" to people who look like Michael J. Fox. But it also ignores the wider context. The Mexican migration to the United States is another part of the vast demographic tide that has swept most of the world in this century: the journey from the countryside to the city, from field to factory, from south to north—and from illiteracy to the book. But there is one huge irony attached to the Mexican migration. These people are moving in the largest numbers into precisely those states that the United States took at gunpoint in the Mexican War of 1846-48: California, Arizona, New Mexico, Texas, Nevada, and Utah, along with parts of Wyoming, Colorado, and Oklahoma. In a way, those young men crossing into San Ysidro and Chula Vista each night are entering the lost provinces of Old Mexico, and some Mexican intellectuals even refer sardonically to this great movement as *La Reconquista* —the Reconquest. It certainly is a wonderful turn on the old doctrine of manifest destiny, which John L. O'Sullivan, the New York journalist who coined the phrase in 1845 said was our right "to overspread the continent allotted by Providence for the free development of our yearly multiplying millions."

Immigration Will Continue

The yearly multiplying millions of Mexico will continue moving north unless one of two things happens: the U.S. economy totally collapses, or the Mexican economy expands dramatically. Since neither is likely to happen, the United States of the twenty-first century is certain to be browner, and speak more Spanish, and continue to see its own culture transformed. The Know-Nothings are, of course, enraged at this great demographic shift and are demanding that Washington seal the borders. As always with fanatics and paranoids, they have no sense of irony. They were probably among those flag-waving patriots who were filled with a sense of triumph when free men danced on the moral ruins of the Berlin Wall; they see no inconsistency in the demand for a new Great Wall, between us and Mexico.

The addled talk goes on, and in the hills of Tijuana, young men like Jeronimo Vasquez continue to wait for the chance to sprint across the midnight scrub in pursuit of the golden promise of the other side. *Corre*, hombre, *corre*. . . .

170

"Let us close our national borders to any further mass immigration . . . as does every other nation on earth."

Illegal Immigration Should Be Stopped

Edward Abbey

Edward Abbey, who died in 1989, was a noted and sometimes controversial author and essayist who often wrote on environmental themes. In the following viewpoint, he argues that both U.S. society and its natural resources are threatened by illegal immigrants. He argues that the U.S. should use its military forces to close off its borders.

As you read, consider the following questions:

1. Why do both liberals and conservatives support immigration, according to Abbey?
2. How does Abbey characterize illegal immigrants?
3. How would ending immigration help Third World countries, according to the author?

Edward Abbey, "Immigration and Liberal Taboos," from *One Life at a Time, Please*. New York: Henry Holt & Company, 1988. Copyright © 1988 by Edward Abbey. Reprinted by permission of Don Congdon Associates, Inc.

In the American Southwest, where I happen to live, only sixty miles north of the Mexican border, the subject of illegal aliens is a touchy one—almost untouchable. Even the terminology is dangerous: the old word *wetback* is now considered a racist insult by all good liberals; and the perfectly correct terms *illegal alien* and *illegal immigrant* can set off charges of xenophobia, elitism, fascism, and the ever-popular genocide against anyone careless enough to use them. The only acceptable euphemism, it now appears, is something called *undocumented worker*. Thus the pregnant Mexican woman who appears, in the final stages of labor, at the doors of the emergency ward of an El Paso or San Diego hospital, demanding care for herself and the child she's about to deliver, becomes an "undocumented worker." The child becomes an automatic American citizen by virtue of its place of birth, eligible at once for all of the usual public welfare benefits. And with the child comes not only the mother but the child's family. And the mother's family. And the father's family. Can't break up families, can we? They come to stay and they stay to multiply.

Are More People Necessary?

"What of it?" say the documented liberals; ours is a rich and generous nation, we have room for all, let them come. And let them stay, say the conservatives; a large, cheap, frightened, docile, surplus labor force is exactly what the economy needs. Put some fear into the unions: tighten discipline, spur productivity, whip up the competition for jobs. The conservatives love their cheap labor; the liberals love their cheap cause. (Neither group, you will notice, ever invites the immigrants to move into their *homes*. Not into *their* homes!) Both factions are supported by the cornucopia economists of the ever-expanding economy, who actually continue to believe that our basic resource is not land, air, water, but human bodies, more and more of them, the more the better in hive upon hive, world without end—ignoring the clear fact that those nations which most avidly practice this belief, such as Haiti, Puerto Rico, Mexico, to name only three, don't seem to be doing well. They look more like explosive slow-motion disasters, in fact, volcanic anthills, than functioning human societies. But that which our academic economists will not see and will not acknowledge is, painfully obvious to *los latinos*: they stream north in ever-growing numbers.

Meanwhile, here at home in the land of endless plenty, we seem still unable to solve our traditional and nagging difficulties. After forty years of the most fantastic economic growth in the history of mankind, the United States remains burdened with mass unemployment, permanent poverty, an overloaded

SURF'S UP

ILLEGAL ALIENS

Bill Garner. Reprinted with permission.

welfare system, violent crime, clogged courts, jam-packed prisons, commercial ("white-collar") crime, rotting cities and a poisoned environment, eroding farmlands and the disappearing family farm, all of the usual forms of racial, ethnic, and sexual conflict (which immigration further intensifies), plus the ongoing destruction of what remains of our forests, fields, mountains, lakes, rivers, and seashores, accompanied by the extermination of whole species of plants and animals. To name but a few of our little nagging difficulties.

End Immigration

This being so, it occurs to some of us that perhaps ever-continuing industrial and population growth is not the true road to human happiness, that simple gross quantitative increase of this kind creates only more pain, dislocation, confusion, and misery. In which case it might be wise for us as American citizens to consider calling a halt to the mass influx of even more millions of hungry, ignorant, unskilled, and culturally-morally-genetically impoverished people. At least until we have brought our own affairs into order. Especially when these uninvited millions bring with them an alien mode of life which—let us be honest about this—is not appealing to the majority of Americans. Why not? Because we prefer democratic government, for one thing; because we still hope for an open, spacious, uncrowded, and beautiful—yes, beautiful!—society, for another. The alternative, in the squalor, cruelty, and corruption of Latin America, is plain for all to see.

Yes, I know, if the American Indians had enforced such a policy none of us pale-faced honkies would be here. But the Indians were foolish, and divided, and failed to keep our WASP ancestors out. They've regretted it ever since.

To everything there is a season, to every wave a limit, to every range an optimum capacity. The United States has been fully settled, and more than full, for at least a century. We have nothing to gain, and everything to lose, by allowing the old boat to be swamped. How many of us, truthfully, would *prefer* to be submerged in the Caribbean-Latin version of civilization? (Howls of "Racism! Elitism! Xenophobia!" from the Marx brothers and the documented liberals.) Harsh words: but somebody has to say them. We cannot play "let's pretend" much longer, not in the present world.

Therefore—let us close our national borders to any further mass immigration, legal or illegal, from any source, as does every other nation on earth. The means are available, it's a simple technical-military problem. Even our Pentagon should be able to handle it. We've got an army somewhere on this planet, let's bring our soldiers home and station them where they can be of some actual and immediate benefit to the taxpayers who support them. That done, we can begin to concentrate attention on badly neglected internal affairs. *Our* internal affairs. Everyone would benefit, including the neighbors. Especially the neighbors.

Poverty

Ah yes. But what *about* those hungry hundreds of millions, those anxious billions, yearning toward the United States from every dark and desperate corner of the world? Shall we simply ignore them? Reject them? Is such a course possible?

"Poverty," said Samuel Johnson, "is the great enemy of human happiness. It certainly destroys liberty, makes some virtues impracticable, and all virtues extremely difficult."

You can say that again, Sam.

Poverty, injustice, overbreeding, overpopulation, suffering, oppression, military rule, squalor, torture, terror, massacre: these ancient evils feed and breed on one another in synergistic

174

symbiosis. To break the cycles of pain at least two new forces are required: social equity—and birth control. Population control. Our Hispanic neighbors are groping toward this discovery. If we truly wish to help them we must stop meddling in their domestic troubles and permit them to carry out the social, political, and moral revolution which is both necessary and inevitable.

Do Not Open Borders

"Open borders" is one of the rallying slogans of America's powerful alien lobby. It translates to mean uncontrolled borders and unlimited immigration. The phrase has a nice sound, suggesting "open-hearted" and "open-minded.". . .

Open borders is the pleasant slogan; the loss of national sovereignty is the unpleasant reality. Most people agree that America is unique and attractive. These are the traits that draw so many people here. Opening our borders is erasing our borders. This would erase our national identity and its most attractive and distinctive features, namely freedom and prosperity.

John Vinson, *Border Watch,* May 1990.

Or if we must meddle, as we have always done, let us meddle for a change in a constructive way. Stop every *campesino* at our southern border, give him a handgun, a good rifle, and a case of ammunition, and send him home. He will know what to do with our gifts and good wishes. The people know who their enemies are.

"Most of the substantive problems associated with immigration are caused by attempts to restrict immigration."

Illegal Immigration Should Be Legalized

Alan W. Bock

In the following viewpoint, Alan W. Bock argues that many of the social problems caused by illegal immigrants arise from their illegal status. He proposes that the most direct way to solve the illegal immigration problem is to open U.S. borders and make all immigrants legal. He asserts that immigration cannot be stopped as long as the U.S. remains an attractive place to live. Bock is senior columnist for *The Orange County Register,* a daily newspaper published in southern California.

As you read, consider the following questions:

1. What kinds of people should the U.S. not allow to immigrate, according to Bock?
2. How does the author characterize immigrants?
3. What does Bock believe would be the most effective way to stem immigration?

Alan W. Bock, "Open Borders: The Real Immigration Solution," *The World & I,* January 1987, © 1987 Alan W. Bock. Reprinted with the author's permission.

The immigration problem in the United States—insofar as we accept conventional wisdom by calling immigration a problem—has a simple cause. Immigration is a problem because the American Dream, although tattered around the edges and undermined by an accretion of rules, regulations, and conventions, is still alive. Those of us who have lived in this country all our lives may have complaints about many things, but for those who view us from afar—whether from across the oceans or from across the border—this is still as close to a Promised Land as this troubled world affords.

The American Dream

So long as this country continues to honor the American Dream of opportunity and liberty, and as long as other countries provide less of a measure of these advantages, people will want to come here. Some call this a problem; others view it as an exhortation both to be true to the principles that have made this country so attractive and to continue to benefit from the inpouring of dynamism, variety, new ideas, and willingness to work that have contributed so much to the uniqueness of America.

All that may have been true when Emma Lazarus wrote that nice sonnet, some may say, but things have changed. This country can no longer afford to absorb all the wretched and tempest-tossed of the earth. Immigrants take jobs from native-born Americans, especially black Americans and those who are already living on the economic margin; they overload an already overburdened welfare system, harm the economy, depress wage levels, and deplete natural and sociological resources. Illegal immigrants then become an underclass subject to exploitation. They stretch the limits of tolerance in a society already struggling with racial, ethnic, and cultural divisions unique in the world's history.

Even if all these contentions were true, they would not justify the abandonment of our heritage. In fact, though, most objections to immigration are based on myths and unfounded fears. Most of the substantive problems associated with immigration are caused by attempts to restrict immigration or by a welfare system out of control.

Most of the subjectively valid objections to immigration would disappear if we set up stations at convenient intervals along our borders with a mandate to check for infectious diseases and affiliation with known subversive or terrorist groups. (The latter criterion should be fairly tightly defined: Being a member of an opposition party in Mexico or Guatemala should not qualify.) Those who fail to meet physical and political standards would be sent packing, and everybody else would be

177

granted legal entry, without eligibility for welfare or public support for a period of at least five years.

Such a system would permit the supply of immigrants to meet the demands of labor in the most flexible manner possible without the interposition of an arbitrary quota set up by wise men in Washington. It would defuse the two most common and valid objections I hear from outraged readers on the phone whenever I write such irresponsible claptrap for a newspaper: "I don't mind their being here so much as their being lawbreakers," and "I don't mind if they come to work, but too many of them suck up welfare."

Where's the Limit?

Critics contend that under such conditions everybody in the world would want to come. Although we could deal with that if it started to happen, it is a rather unlikely possibility.

© Margulies/Rothco. Reprinted with permission.

Immigrants must first be emigrants—people who decide to pull up roots, sever ties with the place where they were born, where all their friends and memories are, then learn a new language, deal with new customs, and go to a new and unfamiliar place, where they are likely to be despised and scorned.

Great waves of emigration/immigration usually come in response to cataclysmic political or natural upheavals—from the Irish potato famine to the communization of Vietnam to the reign of hopelessness in Mexico. Even in such hard times, however, only a minority choose to emigrate. They tend to be a special type—unusually restless, resourceful, adaptable, and ambitious. Such people, as U.S. history records, tend to add dynamism and entrepreneurial zeal to the land they choose as a destination.

For some, of course, the very recognition of these facts is their unspoken reason for opposing immigration. Many fear competing with these resourceful, highly motivated immigrants. While such fears may be well-founded in some individual cases, in the larger societal picture, they prove groundless. In contributing to the dynamism of an economy, immigrants create more opportunities for others than they take for themselves; a free, growing economy is not a zero-sum society.

Pushing Everyone Up

A surprising illustration of this principle was witnessed when economists of the Urban Institute studied Mexican immigration in Southern California. Wage levels for black people were higher in Los Angeles, which has experienced a great deal of illegal immigration from Mexico, than in San Francisco, which had experienced hardly any. Their conclusion: Illegals, rather than displacing native-born workers, were pushing them up into better jobs.

This is not an isolated phenomenon. Most areas with a large illegal population, including Houston and Dallas before the collapse of oil prices, have had generally higher wage levels and lower unemployment levels than the country as a whole during the "illegal invasion." That could be a tautological statement. Why would illegals go where there weren't any jobs available? But if immigration really wrecked an area's economy, some deterioration would be obvious.

It is likely, in fact, that illegal immigration has contributed to economic dynamism and even kept a number of domestic industries from moving overseas. The garment industry in New York, the garment and furniture industries in Southern California, and electronic assembly in Silicon Valley, to name a few, would have all but disappeared or have moved to Hong Kong or Korea if not for immigrants, legal and illegal, willing to work for relatively low wages. Those industries also employ native-born Americans, but often in higher-paying management or skilled support positions. If a magic wand could be waved to send all the illegals back where they came from in an instant, the economic effects on many industries could be devastating.

There is a virtual consensus among those who have studied the phenomenon in any depth—from the Urban Institute to the Rand Corporation to dozens of academic economists to the president's own Council of Economic Advisers—that immigrants, legal and illegal, are a boon to the economy, and that the boon would be greater if they were all legal.

There is dispute over the effect of illegal immigration on welfare, public assistance, public schools and hospitals, and various elements of local infrastructure. Some economists, like Julian Simon, contend that illegals pay into the Social Security and income tax systems for fear of making themselves conspicuous and take little from the government for the same reason, giving the government a nifty profit. On the other hand, local government officials often complain of the drain illegals place on their resources.

Stop Smuggling of Immigrants

Is there a solution to alien-smuggling that won't bleed taxpayers? Only one: Let more aliens in. Illegals now make up as much as 6% of the U.S. work force. . . .

If so many people are desperate to enter the U.S. by any means possible, then the best way to fight the black market in human cargo is to open up more legitimate means of entry.

Richard Behar, *Time*, May 14, 1990.

Both contentions may be true. It seems almost certain that illegals pay more into Social Security and other federal programs than they withdraw. At the same time, local governments—often as a result of federal or state government mandates—are often obliged to provide services to illegals while being unable to tax them effectively, except through sales taxes. This inequity could be alleviated by legalizing immigration, thus converting most illegals into honest, taxpaying residents. Some changes in the way mandates and resources are allocated among levels of government might also be called for, but this is a problem that pervades more issues of intergovernmental policy than just illegal immigration.

Many people express concern that illegal immigrants are subject to exploitation by unscrupulous employers due to their dicey legal status. There is little doubt that such exploitation occurs, though most people would probably be surprised at the efficiency of the information network among illegals, letting novices know which employers give them a fair shake. The simplest way to eliminate this problem almost entirely, however, is to liberalize or eliminate quotas. Finally, the argument that the first duty of a sovereign nation is to protect its borders clearly applies to a foreign military invasion for the purpose of conquering the resident government. The military metaphor is hardly appropriate in the case of people who want to come do an honest day's work for an honest day's pay. Most immigrants don't want to overthrow this government; they want to benefit from the opportunities created by its policies. As proof, most immigrants become almost exaggeratedly patriotic. The majority understand the importance of learning English, and even if they never master it fully, take pains to see that their children do.

All this is not to say that open immigration will not result in some culture clashes and tensions that will require tolerance, patience, and understanding on the part of the native-born and immigrants alike. But the current wave of immigration is less, as a percentage of total population, than the great wave that this country handled between 1890 and 1910. Today's immigrants also have resources earlier immigrants often lacked: established communities of their countrymen in many American cities to ease the transition, and the more widespread use of English as a lingua franca in many parts of the world.

The Final Solution

The most effective way to stem immigration into the United States is to make this country uglier and less prosperous, and therefore less attractive as a destination for emigrants. However, even at the time of the Great Depression, thousands of Jews who were being persecuted in Germany and other countries overrun by the Nazis sought refuge in the United States but were unable to enter because of rigid quotas that discriminated particularly against Central European countries.

The immigration bill passed in 1986—with its employer penalties, beefed-up enforcement, and built-in pressures militating toward a national identification system with all kinds of authorities able to demand to "see your papers, please"—will contribute to making this country a little uglier, less free, and less prosperous. It will not do enough to stem the tide, however, and its amnesty provisions—probably necessary to avoid widespread economic dislocation—provide an incentive for a whole new generation of illegals to take the risk of working underground until their very numbers demand another amnesty.

How much better it would have been if this country had rediscovered and reclaimed its heritage of nourishing liberty and opened its borders to those seeking that same heritage.

"Employer sanctions will be an important addition to America's efforts to stop illegal immigration and regain control of its borders."

Employers Who Hire Illegal Immigrants Should Be Punished

Daniel A. Stein

Daniel A. Stein is executive director of the Federation for American Immigration Reform, an organization which seeks to limit U.S. immigration. In the following viewpoint, he argues that laws prohibiting the employment of illegal immigrants have been successful in deterring illegal immigration. Stein contends that while specific laws and rules might have to be modified, the main idea of punishing employers who hire illegal immigrants is good public policy.

As you read, consider the following questions:

1. How have employer sanctions helped U.S. workers, according to Stein?
2. According to the author, what is the key to successfully implementing employer sanctions?
3. How in Stein's opinion might the enforcement of employer sanctions be improved?

Daniel A. Stein, testimony before the U.S. House of Representatives Judiciary Committee's Subcommittee on Immigration, Refugees, and International Law, May 17, 1989.

Employer sanctions represents the most significant change in American labor law in the last twenty years. Mindful of this fact, we are not surprised that there have been a few "glitches" in the implementation of sanctions. Considering the magnitude of the job, in these first years the Immigration Service has done an excellent job informing employers of the new law's requirements (compared to the compliance rate with new tax law changes). Now, that's not to say that there is not a lot more to be done. And that's not to say that there are not some employers who remain ignorant—either inadvertently or intentionally—of the new law's requirements. But thus far, the record shows that the vast majority of the nation's major employers are aware of the requirements and most employers have adjusted to employer sanctions without incident.

Amidst all the bickering and trifling minutiae one hears from those who oppose sanctions for a living, there are some positive observations that can already be made.

Improved Wages and Working Conditions

One is that the net effect of employer sanctions has been to improve the welfare of the American worker. Employers often point out how difficult it is to find legal workers in some sectors. The tried and true method for attracting legal workers is to increase wages and benefits and to improve working conditions. In many cases, that's precisely what's happening. American businesses continue to display remarkable adaptive powers in the face of the new prohibition. Anticipating the December 1, 1988, start of enforcement against agriculture, one farmer in California's Central Valley has tried to make farm work more palatable for legal workers by planting 6-foot high peach trees that can be harvested without ladders. Elsewhere in California, a strawberry grower has sought to retain workers by reorganizing the system of harvesting and by shortening the workday. Another firm is developing a power harvest clipper to help students and women to quickly harvest citrus fruits.

Legitimate food service employers are also coping with the new law. The owner of a personnel agency notes in *Western Food Service* that, "Hourly wages for some pantry and line positions have risen by as much as 30% since 1986." A hotel in San Francisco has little difficulty in hiring and keeping good people, because it responds to the "kitchen staff's desire to learn by assuring all applicants of rotation and training possibilities. . . ." Others manage by "using the resources of the training programs for the mentally handicapped for dishwashing staff," or contacting urban retraining programs. In short, "the labor market will find equilibrium again, and healthy businesses will have no trouble adapting to the situation as it exists today."

Other businesses are seeking to draw refugees and asylees into the labor market to replace illegal aliens, and many businesses are offering improved family benefits to try to retain more women workers. These companies are offering day care for the children of employees, paternal leave, flexible working hours and a program that enables employees to work part-time by sharing a job.

Employer Sanctions Are Effective

Employer sanctions have proven themselves to be generally effective and enforceable, and the vast majority of American employers seem to be in compliance. Nevertheless, as with any new law, some problems exist.

The problems, while disturbing, are all remediable. Simply by adhering to the recommendations of the law itself and utilizing existing technology, employer sanctions can effectively do what they were intended to do—protect American jobs for American workers and ensure that every individual who has the legal right to work in the United States can compete for a job without fear of discrimination.

Federation for American Immigration Reform, *Making Employer Sanctions Work: The Next Three Years,* 1990.

Amidst the cries of gloom and doom over a purported labor shortage, I note a comment by Allen Murray in *The Wall Street Journal* (October 24, 1988).

As labor becomes scarcer, companies will have to make more efficient use of their workers. Particularly in labor intensive service industries, managers will have to seek new ways to use technology and better ways to organize their businesses. The result: job growth may slow, but productivity would rise. And that means higher earnings and higher standards of living.

So, by and large, we see the overall effects of employer sanctions to be positive.

Eliminating Sweatshops

Not surprisingly, the concentration of fines is located in the service industry. These are the sectors that are likely to experience the greatest stress with the imposition of sanctions. The General Accounting Office (GAO) identified these sectors in March 1988 when it concluded:

[These findings] identify industries likely to experience stress, if the Immigration Reform and Control Act of 1986 is implemented successfully. These industries, which are in declining business environments and, at least in places, employ large proportions of international migrant workers, are shoes, garments and auto parts production. Other, unstudied sectors, which prior to 1987 had high concentrations of illegal workers, may also feel pressured to raise wages to the reservation level (i.e., the level at which unemployed are attracted to jobs) and experience consequent difficulty in meeting foreign competition unless corresponding increases in productivity can be obtained.

Many of these industries are likely to experience substantial stress and, in some cases, may even be forced out of business. As the equilibrium in the labor market shifts as a result of sanctions, marginal or unproductive sectors are bound to be affected. First and foremost, we must be vigilant to fight any efforts by marginal employers to continue running slave houses. In 1988 the GAO studied the development of sweatshops and found them alive and well in key cities. (A sweatshop is defined as a business that regularly violates both health or safety and wage or child labor laws.) The GAO looked at restaurants and apparel manufacturers in New York City and Los Angeles, and surveyed federal and state officials. It identified three major factors which contribute to the existence of sweatshops:

1) the presence of large numbers of immigrants, exploitable either because they are illegally in the US or, if they are legal, because they do not speak enough English to find better jobs;

2) the reliance of labor intensive industries on low wage and low skilled workers, usually immigrants; and

3) a growing number of small subcontractors in labor intensive industries—especially now that businesses can now use subcontractors as a way to dodge employer sanctions.

The existence of sweatshops in the US is unconscionable. Sanctions are an integral part of the effort to put these owners of the slave shops out of existence. Despite a few problems in the implementation of sanctions, we must keep in mind that at bottom the new law has had, and will continue to have an ameliorative effect on the welfare of American workers. Make no mistake, the arrival of employer sanctions has brought with it new employment opportunities for America's poor and its disadvantaged minorities and handicapped.

Sanctions Enforcement

But for sanctions to succeed, we must have adequate resources for sanctions enforcement. In that regard, FAIR [Federation for American Immigration Reform] has testified on many occasions for more investigators to enforce employer sanctions, and we do not support *any* budget decrease for the INS [Immigration and Naturalization Service] under any circumstances.

In the years since employer sanctions were enacted, public

support for the concept has grown. A poll in California, conducted by V. Lance Tarrance and Associates, finds that 79% of Californians approve of the law to strictly enforce sanctions against employers hiring illegal aliens. Among Hispanic Americans, the polls show that support among those living in California has also grown, since the last time their views were measured in 1983. These data suggest that Americans are as supportive as ever of employer sanctions, as well as overall efforts to end illegal immigration and place a cap on the annual level of legal immigration.

Problems with Sanctions

The problems encountered in enforcing employer sanctions are minor and manageable. In all cases, education about the new law's requirements is the key to success. For large employers with manpower and personnel specialists on staff, all indications are that the relatively simple requirements have been mastered. Most of the problems identified by GAO in its last survey can be remedied by education: the objectionable practices were related to ignorance of the law, not any desire to discriminate unlawfully. Further, most of the problems constituted "non-material" errors, i.e., no one was ultimately denied a job solely because of the sanctions requirements.

Sanctions Have Worked

Employers must now verify that their employees are U.S. citizens, or that they are documented aliens with permission to work in this country. Failure to do so can result in stiff penalties. Most employers appear to be obeying the law. Thus there are fewer jobs available for undocumented aliens. The message has gotten back to Mexico, where . . . many who otherwise would take the trek north have decided not to risk the expense if it is dubious that they will find employment once they get here.

William F. Jasper, *The New American*, February 15, 1988.

To the extent there are significant problems, they lie among the small business owners. There is, in our view, a need for a permanent component of the educational how-to-reach program that is dedicated to informing the employers of 15 or fewer employees about the new law. These employers tend to be novices or somewhat more cavalier about detailed compliance. They should be targeted. It is also very important for the success of sanctions that the message from all government agencies be consistent. . . .

At the root of the success of employer sanctions, is the perception among the nation's employers that not only they, but their competitors, will be held to high standards of compliance. Consistency in the message is vital if sanctions are to succeed. . . .

The track record on discrimination cases filed with the Office of Special Counsel attests to the fact that most forms of alienage discrimination that have occurred can be rectified by the following:

1) the use of a consolidated uniform work authorization document that will enable the employer to determine who is work authorized quickly, efficiently; and

2) by making it clear to all employers that a pattern of wilful paperwork violations will be fined, notwithstanding the absence of an underlying hiring violation.

It is very important that employers be left with the impression that all employers are held to the same high standards for paperwork compliance. Only in this way can invidious discrimination be minimized and sanctions truly effective. We are surprised that many of those organizations which are purportedly concerned about discrimination are not more concerned about the universal nature of the paperwork requirement. Rather than spend millions of dollars in a search for any evidence of inconsistencies, they would be better served to try to come up with constructive remedies to make the law work.

Unclear Standards

To the extent that there has been any alienage discrimination under the new law, it is directly traceable to the existence of the unclear standards for the issuance and evidence of work authorization. . . .

The problems we have experienced with sanctions thus far can all be remedied by clarity, consistency, and comprehensiveness.

• Clarity in the employer requirements to create an affirmative defense when screening applicants and to avoid unlawful hiring practices;

• Consistency and firmness in the manner of enforcement, the exercise of prosecutorial discretion, as well as in the definitions of statutory terms; and

• Comprehensiveness in the ultimate development of a single work authorization document for all US employees.

Experience in Europe and in Canada suggest it takes several years of experience and refinement before sanctions are truly effective. That experience is sure to be duplicated here. But . . . we are sure that employer sanctions will be an important addition to America's efforts to stop illegal immigration and regain control of its borders.

"Rather than causing undocumented immigrants to return home, the net effect of employer sanctions is to trap them in substandard jobs and inhuman living conditions."

Punishing Employers of Illegal Immigrants Is Counterproductive

Aurora Camacho de Schmidt

Many illegal immigrants come to the U.S. to find jobs. One of the sections of the 1986 Immigration Reform and Control Act tried to curtail illegal immigration by making it a crime for employers to hire illegal immigrants. In the following viewpoint, Aurora Camacho de Schmidt argues that such employer sanctions have caused discrimination against foreign-looking workers. Camacho de Schmidt is a staff writer for the American Friends Service Committee. A Mexican citizen and permanent U.S. resident, she has written extensively on immigration.

As you read, consider the following questions:

1. According to the author, why do illegal immigrants migrate to the U.S.?
2. What effects have employer sanctions had on the U.S., according to Camacho de Schmidt?
3. What solutions to illegal immigration does Camacho de Schmidt propose?

Aurora Camacho de Schmidt, "Battling Unjust Immigration Laws," *The Witness*, March 1989. Reprinted with permission.

When the new Immigration Reform and Control Act (IRCA) was signed into law in November 1986, some three and a half million Latin American undocumented immigrants were in the United States. They were here and have kept coming here because of what author Gabriel Garcia Marquez calls "the persistent advantage of life over death." They came mostly because they had to, not because they wanted to.

The immigrants came to a nation increasingly intent on fortifying itself against their presence, and yet eager to use their cheap and reliable human power. They saw themselves as saving their lives, feeding their families, surviving. But some of their hosts saw them as a danger to national unity and sovereignty, usurping jobs, spoiling neighborhoods, taxing social services, useful only as a disposable labor supply.

They crossed the border aided by smugglers and often risked their lives in the process. Over one million of them fled war and had to traverse more than one foreign country to find refuge. Young men turned the hunt by the U.S. Border Patrol into a game of high stakes requiring wit and resolve. But helicopters, electronic sensors and weapons made for unequal encounters.

When women arrived in large numbers, the United States knew this migration was permanent. Women came to build a community, to plant the seed of their children in the new, hostile home. Not even a law designed to starve them out could uproot them again. They came to stay.

What the Law Said

President Reagan signed the Immigration Reform and Control Act in 1986. The law offered the possibility of legalization to undocumented people who had arrived before January 1982, and to farmworkers who could prove they had worked for at least 90 days during the year before May 1986. At the end of the application period, close to three million immigrants—perhaps less than half the total undocumented population, which also includes Asians, Europeans, Caribbean peoples, etc.—had applied for temporary residence. This program could not have been implemented without the help and constant vigilance of organizations representing the immigrants' interests. The lure of legalization attracted support for a legislative package that contained a dangerous provision: employer sanctions.

The logic of employer sanctions is simple and one-dimensional—if we want to stop illegal immigration, let's stop employers from giving jobs to illegal immigrants. Too bad things just don't work that way. During eight years of debate, churches, civil liberties groups, minority organizations, and lawyers' organizations—not to mention employers—have opposed employer

189

"OK, YOU HUDDLED MASSES. I KNOW YOU'RE IN HERE."

BY WILKINSON

Signe Wilkinson/*Philadelphia Daily News.* Reprinted with permission.

sanctions. They warned Congress about the discriminatory power of the policy: All minorities and foreign-looking persons could be suspect at the job site. Some opponents explained that the nature of a restructuring global economy is extreme flexibility. In the name of higher profits, transnationals can send jobs abroad—to Taiwan, northern Mexico, South Korea—or create substandard jobs in its nooks and crannies, where workers have no protection. The idea that employer sanctions would "save jobs for Americans" and stem the flow of illegal migration was unfounded.

Yet the precarious political balance of legalization and employer sanctions allowed a bad law to pass. Growers, the most notorious employers of undocumented labor, lobbied hard and got to have their cake and eat it too. Employer sanctions were not implemented in the fields until December 1988, and several programs make it possible for agricultural employers to recruit new legal temporary foreign workers.

The sponsors of IRCA wanted "to regain control of our borders." The ostensible motive for immigration reform was "to protect jobs for Americans," but the old racism and chauvinism of the Nativist movement was at work again. Even the legalization program was reluctantly given, and thus fraught with problems. There is no way of estimating how many applications will be successful and how many will be denied in the end. IRCA became the expression of the fears of people who could not imagine a future pluralistic society.

Effects of the Law

Employer sanctions make IRCA an instrument for *control.* Every employer must check documents that prove authorization to work in the United States for anyone hired after November 1986. The employee and employer must both sign a piece of paper, the I-9 form, attesting to the fact that documents have been presented and the employee has a legal right to work. Failure to ask for documentation or to sign and keep the I-9 form results in fines and even prison terms. False attestation or use of fraudulent documentation by the employee can bring even heavier penalties.

According to a November 1988 survey conducted by the General Accounting Office (GAO), which must study the implementation of employer sanctions and report to Congress once a year for three years, a large proportion of all employers—22%—do not know anything about the law. Half of those who do know are not in compliance before inspection. And, more disturbing, of all employers surveyed by the GAO, 16% are engaged in illegal discriminatory practices as they attempt to comply with the law—for example, refusing to hire legal residents who are not citizens.

The law has effects the GAO research team did not see: loss of jobs, and, more frequently, the acceptance of substandard jobs by many undocumented people. The GAO has the authority to recommend termination of the employer sanctions provisions if they cause "widespread discrimination," but not if they simply oppress undocumented immigrants. The organizations that helped implement the first phase of the legalization program refer to the people not included as "residual population," estimated to number over three million. These people have always lived clandestine lives, but the law has given them a new degree of illegality, and this makes them vulnerable to exploitation. At the same time, the existence of this large group as a labor reserve jeopardizes the interest of poor U.S. workers, who cannot compete with them for substandard wages.

Refugees

Central American refugees are not recognized as such by the U.S. government, and thus fall under the category, "undocumented worker." IRCA hurts these refugees by destroying their

191

livelihood in the United States when they cannot go home.

Legislators are surprised that people would not choose to go home in spite of such hardship. But the new level of difficulty must be endured, because there are no options. The war in Central America has intensified, and the prospect of economic recovery is farther away than ever. For example, U.S. dollars sent home by Salvadoran refugees are now the third largest source of revenue for the country. The capacity of Salvadoran refugees to contribute to the life of those at home is an element in the political equation.

Unintended Consequences

Employer sanctions are causing employers to discriminate against workers through the selective screening of work documents. Such discrimination appears to disproportionately affect racial minorities and those who are perceived as foreign. At the same time, sanctions also contribute to the erosion of federal and state labor laws by further entrenching undocumented immigrants in substandard or marginalized employment. The evidence compels the conclusion that sanctions are having a host of impacts unintended by Congress while there is scanty evidence of its effectiveness at making it impossible for undocumented immigrants to find jobs in the U.S.

Center for Immigrants Rights, *Employer Sanctions: An Update on Its Impact upon Authorized and Unauthorized Workers in the New York Metropolitan Area,* 1989.

Mexico is another case. Its crushing foreign debt means no margin of subsistence for poor people and no prospects of growth in the near future. But while U.S. foreign policy wastes opportunities to cooperate in Mexico's economic stability and to help end the war in Central America, the government treats refugees and immigrants—the symptoms of these problems—as a plague to be eradicated.

Rather than causing undocumented immigrants to return home, the net effect of employer sanctions is to trap them in substandard jobs and inhuman living conditions. For my employer, the American Friends Service Committee (AFSC), an organization working for peace and justice, this is hard to accept. . . .

The AFSC has been involved with Mexican farmworkers for three decades, and its Mexico-U.S. Border Program has observed the development of immigration policy reform and the changes in Latin American immigration since 1979. Later on the AFSC started programs in public education and networking on Central American refugee issues, bringing a direct understanding of the region based on AFSC's international programs.

Working with the Border Program, I was part of that history for five years. And I have come to agree with Catholic theologian Henri Nouwen's statement that the spiritual destinies of the United States and Latin America are intimately bound. I see this in the phenomenon of undocumented immigration, in the mystery of people twice rejected who dwell among us.

No Solution in Sight

Because of employer sanctions, the IRCA is an explosion with aftershocks. Federal policy is designed to eradicate a class of human beings from U.S. society, giving the signal that it is appropriate and good to do so. . . .

No easy solution is in sight. Ironically, as long as the war in Central America continues, a harvest of refugees will come to the center of power. As long as communities in Mexico are unable to sustain young life, undocumented workers will follow the steps of other generations going north. As long as the economy of the United States functions in a way that inexhaustible labor reserves can be marginally incorporated, the illegal workers will serve an economic purpose and continue to boost profits.

The fact of the matter is that over three million men, women and children who live in the United States have been declared legally expendable. Over one million of these are refugees from Central America. If the people of the United States cannot see their way through all the dilemmas posed by undocumented migration, they can now see the effects of a law built on injustice. . . .

Taking exceptions to employer sanctions, the AFSC stands with undocumented men, women and children. It affirms their act of migrating as an option for life.

Recognizing Statements That Are Provable

From various sources of information we are constantly confronted with statements and generalizations about social and moral problems. In order to think clearly about these problems, it is useful if one can make a basic distinction between statements for which evidence can be found and other statements which cannot be verified or proved because evidence is not available, or the issue is so controversial that it cannot be definitely proved.

Readers should constantly be aware that magazines, newspapers, and other sources often contain statements of a controversial nature. The following activity is designed to allow experimentation with statements that are provable and those that are not.

The following statements are taken from the viewpoints in this chapter. Consider each statement carefully. *Mark P for any statement you believe is provable. Mark U for any statement you feel is unprovable because of the lack of evidence. Mark C for any statement you think is too controversial to be proved to everyone's satisfaction.*

If you are doing this activity as a member of a class or group, compare your answers to those of other class or group members. Be able to defend your answers. You may discover that others come to different conclusions than you. Listening to the reasons others present for their answers may give you valuable insights into recognizing statements that are provable.

P = provable
U = unprovable
C = too controversial

1. The Immigration Reform and Control Act [IRCA] was signed into law in 1986.
2. IRCA is unfair to illegal immigrants.
3. IRCA has had no effect on the rate of illegal immigration to the U.S.
4. The Border Patrol made almost 1.8 million arrests in 1986.
5. For every illegal immigrant the Border Patrol catches, one or two others make it into the U.S.
6. If illegal immigrants who work on U.S. farms all went home, America would starve.
7. There are over ten million illegal immigrants in the U.S.
8. Polls show that the majority of Americans favor sanctions against employers who hire illegal immigrants.
9. The net effect of employer sanctions has been to improve the welfare of the American worker.
10. A 1986 study by Los Angeles County found that illegal immigrants were costing county taxpayers $172 million a year.
11. Immigrants take jobs from native-born Americans.
12. Illegal immigrants now make up as much as 6 percent of the U.S. labor force.
13. An urban study found that wages for black people were higher in Los Angeles, which has a large illegal immigrant population, than in San Francisco, a city with fewer illegal immigrants.
14. Opening our borders to all immigrants would ultimately destroy our freedom and prosperity.
15. Children of illegal immigrants become U.S. citizens if they are born in the U.S.
16. The United States has been more than full for at least a century.
17. The border between the U.S. and Mexico is almost two thou-sand miles long.
18. Only half of the nation's illegal immigrants are Mexican.
19. Illegal immigrants take jobs that other people do not want.
20. The majority of America's people favor strict enforcement of immigration laws.
21. Many Mexican immigrants are simply returning to territory that the U.S. took from Mexico in 1848.
22. The border fence erected in 1975 between Mexico and the U.S. is severely damaged at many points.

Periodical Bibliography

The following articles have been selected to supplement the diverse views presented in this chapter.

America	"California Indicts the New Immigration Law," February 24, 1990.
Richard Behar	"The Price of Freedom," *Time*, May 14, 1990.
Tom Bethell	"A New Statute of Liberty," *National Review*, December 18, 1987.
Gregory J. Boyle	"Still They Come; There Is No Choice," *Los Angeles Times*, May 3, 1990.
Patrick Buchanan	"Question of a Secure Southern Border," *Conservative Chronicle*, February 15, 1989. Available from *Conservative Chronicle*, Box 11297, Des Moines, IA 50340-1297.
William L. Chaze	"What It Was Like to Fear 'A Knock on the Door,'" *U.S. News & World Report*, January 19, 1987.
Nathan Glazer	"New Rules of the Game," *The National Interest*, Summer 1987.
William F. Jasper	"Making Ourselves Vulnerable," *The New American*, February 15, 1988.
Jane Juffer	"Abuse at the Border," *The Progressive*, April 1988.
George C. Larson	"Holding the Line," *Air & Space*, December 1988/January 1989.
Jay Matthews	"It's Border Patrol 712, Illegal Immigrants 35,000," *The Washington Post National Weekly Edition*, November 20-26, 1989.
W.P. Norton	"Border Crossing," *The Progressive*, October 1989.
Mark Olson	"Open the Border!" *The Other Side*, March 1986.
Phyllis Schlafly	"Alien Threat," *The New American*, February 3, 1986.
David Shaw	"Take a Number and Wait," *The Washington Monthly*, September 1989.
Earl Shorris	"Raids, Racism, and the INS," *The Nation*, May 8, 1989.
Abel Valenzuela	"A Borderline Case," *Dollars & Sense*, May 1989.
David Whitman	"The Unstoppable Surge of Illegal Aliens," *U.S. News & World Report*, June 6, 1988.

What Policies Would Help Immigrants Adapt to the U.S.?

Chapter Preface

Although immigrants to the U.S. come from diverse backgrounds and cultures, many of them face similar challenges upon arrival here. Some must learn a new language; others must learn new jobs. All face the simple but profound challenge of forsaking the old home for the new. Henry Grunwald, former editor of *Time* and an immigrant from Austria, has written, "Every immigrant leads a double life. . .being suspended between an old and a new home, an old and a new self."

Some immigration critics, such as scholar Glenn Dumke, believe that today's immigrants are not adapting to American life as well as previous immigrants did. Past immigrants, according to Dumke, "came here to 'be Americans.' Today some of the arriving groups are not agreed on this goal; they want top priority to be given to preservation of their own culture." Dumke and others believe that such attitudes threaten to divide the U.S. These attitudes are particularly prevalent in the Hispanic community, they contend. Some Hispanic immigrants do not learn English but instead continue to speak Spanish and interact mainly in the Hispanic community. Dumke maintains that the U.S. should enact policies to ensure that immigrants become Americans and adapt to American society. One such policy would be to declare English the official language of the United States.

But others believe fears of cultural separatism are unfounded. Author James Fallows argues that many similar fears were expressed during the turn of the century when new ethnic groups from Europe arrived in the U.S. Such misgivings turned out to be a false alarm, as eventually members of these ethnic groups became accepted and established in American society. "There is no evidence," Fallows writes, "that Spanish-speaking immigrants are behaving differently from the way Italian, Polish, or German immigrants behaved several generations earlier." Fallows and others argue that even if some immigrants never fully adapt to American life, their children complete the process.

The viewpoints in this chapter examine several questions on how to help immigrants adapt to their new lives in the U.S.

"School success is tragically undercut when children do not receive basic instruction in their own language."

Bilingual Education Helps Immigrants

National Coalition of Advocates for Students

The National Coalition of Advocates for Students (NCAS) is a national nonprofit network of child advocacy organizations. The following viewpoint is excerpted from *New Voices,* the result of a two-year study on immigrant children and the public schools. The study, conducted by the Immigrant Student Project, included surveys of educational research and public hearings with immigrant students, parents, and teachers. The report argues that language barriers are one of the main problems facing immigrants, and recommends bilingual education programs to ensure that immigrant children are properly educated. It recommends that immigrant children be encouraged to study their native languages and cultures, and that immigrants be used to help other students learn foreign languages.

As you read, consider the following questions:

1. What are some of the obstacles immigrant children face, according to NCAS?
2. According to the authors, what flaws exist in current bilingual programs?
3. What are the costs of "monolingualism" according to NCAS?

National Coalition of Advocates for Students, *New Voices: Immigrant Children in the Public Schools.* Boston: NCAS, 1988. Excerpted with permission.

The great immigration wave of the 1970s and 1980s has dramatically changed U.S. public schools. At the same time, the United States is increasingly becoming a multicultural and multilingual nation, transformed by its changing demographics, and in turn transforming those who come here.

As the nation has learned from previous periods of great migration, young immigrants contribute great energy, cultural richness, strength, and maturity to the schools. They also bring new challenges which U.S. schools, for the most part, are not meeting well; rather, the U.S. public education system appears unprepared and overwhelmed.

Despite the fact that every immigrant child has the legal right of access to a free public education, serious problems with access exist. Many schools discourage immigrant children from enrolling. Once inside the schoolhouse, these children continue to experience barriers to a comprehensible and effective education. . . .

Immigrant students need years to learn a new language and make difficult adjustments; but most U.S. schools are not structured to provide this time. Immigrant students are more likely to be retained in-grade, inappropriately placed in special education, and are at a double risk for being placed in low academic tracks on the basis of language limitations or slow academic progress. The cumulative effects of these experiences often cause immigrant students to leave school early, and create great emotional stress.

Immigrant students lack the quality language assistance programs they need to develop effective skills in reading comprehension, writing, and speaking to ensure their school success and provide access to the full curriculum while they are learning English. Large numbers of limited English proficient students do not have access to language assistance services at all; and additional large numbers are in poorly implemented and underfunded programs. . . .

Impact on Local Schools

Documented and undocumented immigrant children represent about 6% of precollegiate students. While not an unmanageable number as a total, geographic concentration has greatly increased the impact of recently arriving immigrants on some schools. Testimony at public hearings sponsored by the Immigrant Student Project illustrates the severity of the impact:

> More than a third of San Francisco Unified School District's student population's primary language is other than English . . . the immigrant students coming to the district represent 20 or more different language groups. Roughly one-third of [the district's] population of 65,000 has immigrated here within the

200

last five years, the two largest groups being Asian and Hispanic . . . the school district's ethnic distribution has changed dramatically over the past twenty years . . . the Spanish-surname population has increased from 11.5% to 18.3% . . . the White population has decreased from 45.3% to 15.6% . . . the Black population has decreased from 25.6% to 20.6% . . . the Chinese population has increased from 13.3% to 25.5% . . . [and the Filipino population from 2.5% to 8.9%].

The [school district's] intake center processed over 6,000 new students, 31% of them being Chinese and 33% of them being Hispanic. Filipinos made the third largest group at 12.4%. . . . *Ramon Cortines, Superintendent, San Francisco Unified School District.*

A Sixth-Grade View

Two years ago in Seattle, I got off a plane. In front of me was a whole new world. I wondered if I would survive in this world, a world where the people, the language and the whole environment were different than mine. I had a question in my mind about what my future was going to be.

I found myself as a deaf person in a strange world. I started to go to school and participated in the bilingual program where I would learn both English and my own language. Bilingual education brought back my hearing. It helped me to survive in the new world. It helped my family adapt to the new environment. The bilingual program introduced me to American people and taught me their way of life and their language. It brightened up my future. It helped me to climb up the "vocabulary ladder" to show the Americans that I was not a useless person, no matter what country I came from. It supplied me with a good education and a better chance to achieve my goals. It assisted me in looking forward to my future in America. I knew that I could do and be whatever I wanted.

Mai Nguyen-Huynh, National Association for Bilingual Education *Newsletter,* vol. 7, no. 4, 1984.

In 1980, there were almost 2.8 million households total in New York City, of which 781,000 or 28% were headed by an immigrant . . . when we look at the schools themselves, we find that a little more than a quarter of the city's public school children— 27.2%—came from households that were headed by an immigrant . . . in addition to the 273,000 children of immigrant families in the public schools, the schools are also educating 174,000 children whose parents were born in Puerto Rico, bringing to a total of nearly 450,000 the number of children whose parents' native language and culture was not English . . . that was, in 1980, almost half the schools' total enrollment. . . . *Elizabeth*

Bogen, Director, New York City Office of Immigrant Affairs.

. . . in 1970, the school population was 73% White and 27% minority . . . [by] the year 2000, we will have a school population which is mainly made up of Black, Hispanic, Asian, Filipino, Pacific Island students, with a minority being Anglo . . . now of course, among those minority students are substantial numbers of limited English proficiency students, specifically immigrant students . . . something like 70,000 to 80,000 students entering kindergarten every year. . . are limited English proficient . . . Los Angeles in 1980 had 106,000 LEP students—it was 260,000. In the Bay Area here, Santa Clara County had 14,000 [in 1980], and now almost 26,000. San Francisco . . . had 10,000 in 1980 [and that] almost doubled to 20,000. And so on. . . .
Norman Gold, California Department of Education.

As children enter the United States from distant lands, their first experience is the clash between their primary cultures and the norms of their new home. In a land where relatively few citizens can speak or write anything but English, language is a primary source of conflict. The behaviors and traditions carried here from native lands also act to magnify the friction between newcomers and native-born Americans.

Language as a Barrier

"I know that despite the English language, I am a very intelligent girl," states a Laotian student from Greenfield, Mass.

The cultures of immigrant children are embedded in their mother tongue. Each language holds a world view, and the identity of the speaker. To learn a new language in a new environment, a child must develop a new identity.

Nevertheless, in all of the interviews with immigrant families and at all of its public hearings, the Project found unanimous agreement that learning English is important. The Project commonly heard comments like one offered by a 12-year-old Hmong girl who said she came to America "to learn English." A young Vietnamese girl noted that to be successful in the United States, "you have to know English."

Limited use of English, or none at all, is a common problem for immigrant students. As previously noted, many first-wave immigrants arrived with some command of English—certainly superior skills with a foreign language than is exhibited by the average American student. Subsequent arrivals, however, have less and less ability with English, and, in many cases, are not fully literate in their own language.

An 18-year-old Cambodian girl from a small rural town in Battambang Province explained that she never went to school before she came to Philadelphia (PA) because, "there were no schools at all under the Pol Pot regime" (1975-1979) and reading was forbidden. Even after six years in a Thailand camp where

202

some schooling took place, she did not learn English because "my father (could) only afford to pay the school fee for my older brother."

A 14-year-old Hmong boy now living in St. Paul (MN) explained, "In Laos, there was a school that some farm children walked to, but it was too far [for me]." At the school, students studied math, art and other subjects in Lao, but English lessons were offered only privately and cost $3 a week—too expensive for most refugees.

Immersion Approach No Alternative

Immersion is often only a new term for what previously had been called a "sink or swim" approach. Unfortunately, most students subjected to this approach had no alternative but to sink. The high dropout rate of Mexican Americans, Puerto Ricans, Native Americans and others is certainly one indication of the educational failure spawned by this approach.

Sonia Nieto, *Interracial Books for Children Bulletin,* vol. 17, nos. 3 & 4, 1986.

For some immigrants, the problem of learning a new language is particularly difficult. Asian children, even those from stable backgrounds with well-educated parents must develop two strategies because of fundamental orthographic differences between their first language and English. Children from the Pacific Islands, Laotian hill tribes, and Montagnards from Vietnam have "dual handicaps" by coming from oral traditions with little exposure to written materials. Rarely, if ever, has anyone read to them. As education consultant Sister Lumina O'Sullivan noted, this can be particularly hard on already struggling students:

The Khmuu people live in the highlands of Laos, and most of these parents . . . cannot read and write in their own language . . . some of the children have never been to school.

Until the parents complained, the Boston school district was teaching these kids in Lao, neither the language of their home nor the language of the United States. The kids had to learn two languages simultaneously—English and Lao.

Complicating matters further, English—like any language —has differing forms. The style of English which must be mastered for the classroom is very different from the style of English which is spoken by children to each other on the playground. . . .

One of the great ironies the Project confronted was the "English Only" or "English First" movement now active in many areas of the country.

Fueled by a backlash from the growing perception that America is rapidly becoming a multicultural and, in many areas, a multilingual society, several states have formally adopted legislation declaring English as their "official" language, undercutting public funding of educational programs serving students who speak little or no English.

A paper prepared by the National Immigration, Refugee & Citizenship Forum suggested the appeal of this movement results from a variety of sources—patriotism, fear of the consequences of bilingualism, visions of uncontrollable immigration, a misunderstanding of the movement's true agenda, chauvinism, and racism.

Without regard to the merits of the various supporting arguments, the consequences might well be played out in the public schools in ways even "English Only" proponents would not support—a denial of the opportunity to learn English.

The "English Only" movement has other perverse outcomes. Because it arises from attitudes that those who speak only English are somehow superior to those who speak other languages, it sends a clear message to newcomers that their languages and cultures are unwelcome and inferior—a point of view which ill-prepares this country for the realities of its domestic and international future. . . .

The Challenge of Immigrant Students

At public hearings in America's great gateway cities, and during interviews with scores of immigrant parents and their school-age children, the Immigrant Student Project heard many examples of how schools and school systems are struggling to provide for the unique and often urgent needs of recently arrived immigrant students.

Although the Project found many examples of promising school practices and school personnel who are committed to success for immigrant students, overwhelming evidence documented how the nation's public schools are failing to serve newcomers. These failures, so widespread and so graphically described, seem especially devastating because they contrast so starkly with the high hopes held by so many immigrant parents. A Mexican mother from Chicago poignantly asked: "What better heritage do we poor leave to our children, if not education?". . .

Estimates of the number of limited English proficient [LEP] students in the nation's public schools range from 3.5 million to 5.5 million, based upon a definition which includes persons with a non-English language background whose ability to understand, speak, read, and write English is limited enough to deny them the chance to learn in classrooms where instruction is only in English. Immigrant students are a large and growing component of the LEP school population.

Hernan LaFontaine estimates that about two-thirds of LEP school-aged children are not receiving the language assistance they need to succeed in their studies. The problem promises to intensify as a 35% increase in LEP students is projected by the year 2000. . . .

Even when services are offered for LEP students, the quality is uneven. A discussion of bilingual education programs available to immigrant students follows. . . .

Bilingual Education

Generally, bilingual education services are intended to have two goals: to allow a child to achieve competence in English; and to provide transitional instruction in a student's native language to enable the child to meet grade promotion and graduation requirements.

Two-thirds of the estimated 3.5 million to 5.5 million LEP children now enrolled in public schools are not receiving the language assistance they need to succeed. The results are predictable:

> The courts have ruled favorably on instruction to respond to children's first language, but language barriers continue just the same and are almost overwhelming. Failure is the result, and is accepted all too easily. . . . *Vito Perrone, Carnegie Foundation for the Advancement of Teaching, Princeton, NJ.*

As noted earlier, immigrant parents interviewed by the Project expressed without exception the strong desire to have their children learn English; most wanted their children to retain their first language and culture, as well. The pressure of such expectations falls squarely on the student, as observed by LaFontaine:

> Limited English proficient children have a formidable task facing them as they enter school. If they are to succeed in school, they must overcome the obstacles caused by poverty and assignment to low-achieving schools, learn to deal successfully with an institution and individuals from a culture other than their own, master all the subjects taught in the regular school curriculum, and become completely proficient in a second language— English.

While the stories differ from place to place, the theme remains the same: school success is tragically undercut when children do not receive basic instruction in their own language, at least, until they can become fully proficient in academic English; and lifelong success is threatened if they are unable to learn English at all. . . .

Research and advocacy experience confirm that some schools consistently empower minority students, while others effectively "disable" them. Canadian researcher James Cummins is convinced that schools which empower minority students have teachers who have personally redefined their own relationships with minority children and their communities.

School success for these children may be strongly affected by three sets of interactions: between teachers and students; between schools and minority communities; and intergroup power relations within the broader society.

Within empowering schools:

• minority students' language and culture are an integral part of the school program;

• minority communities participate in the education of their children;

• teaching strategies motivate children to use language actively to generate knowledge; and

• assessment strategies do not assume the student is the cause of academic problems.

Empowering teachers see their task as adding a second language and culture to their students' experience, rather than replacing the primary language and culture with a new one. Such teachers don't necessarily instruct immigrant students in their first language, but they do communicate a clear message to these students that their primary language and culture are valued. . . .

Inadequate Programs

The Project found bilingual programs in common use in U.S. schools to range from very minimal English-as-a-Second-Language models—providing inadequate English acquisition instruction taught by monolingual, English-speaking teachers using English texts and materials—to high quality two-way bilingual programs enjoying enthusiastic support from students, educators and parents. There are far more of the former than the latter.

The project also found that many school districts offer no special services for limited English proficient students. While school districts, especially small and medium sized districts, argue that bilingual education is impractical, a U.S. Government Accounting Office report estimated that only 22% to 26% of LEP students are in schools where bilingual education is truly impractical due to very small numbers of children in a given language group.

> *"Bilingual education fails the very children it is meant to help."*

Bilingual Education Hurts Immigrants

Rosalie Pedalino Porter

Rosalie Pedalino Porter is head of English-as-a-second-language and bilingual programs for the Newton, Massachusetts public school system. She is the author of Forked Tongue: The Politics of Bilingual Education. *In the following viewpoint, she argues that most bilingual education programs segregate immigrant children into inferior classes, and retard the learning of English. She advocates programs such as those in her school system which emphasize English rather than the children's native language.*

As you read, consider the following questions:

1. What evidence does Porter cite to support her belief that bilingual education is not working?
2. According to the author, what are the two false premises of bilingual education?
3. What alternatives to bilingual education programs does Porter support?

Rosalie Pedalino Porter, "Bilingual Education Has Muted the Future for Minority Children," *The Washington Post National Weekly Edition*, April 30-May 6, 1990. Reprinted with permission.

In the name of "cultural sensitivity," we are systematically undereducating our language-minority children, severely reducing their opportunities for economic and social advancement. The politics of ethnicity—and in particular, pressure to continue the widely applied experiment called bilingual education, in which children are taught not in English but in their native language—has distorted public education policy and limited the search for alternatives.

In the 22 years since bilingual education began, the number of languages represented in schoolrooms nationwide has grown to 153, and the programs have become the single most controversial area in public education. No wonder: They segregate limited-English children, provide them inferior schooling and often doom them to unskilled jobs as adults.

Evidence of Failure

Yet bilingual programs continue to increase, despite striking evidence of their failure:

• In November 1988, Con Edison, the public utility company of New York City, gave an English-language aptitude test to 7,000 applicants for entry-level jobs. Only 4,000 passed—and not one of those was a graduate of the city's bilingual education programs. Yet a coalition of ethnic activists recently succeeded in convincing the state Board of Regents to pass new regulations that will keep more limited-English children enrolled for more years in native-language classrooms.

• In Los Angeles, which has the largest enrollment of limited-English students in the country (142,000), a survey of teachers in 1988 revealed that they are opposed to bilingual education by a ratio of 78 percent to 22 percent. These results have been ignored and a bilingual master plan has been imposed on the Los Angeles schools that requires even more teaching in the native language.

• In New Jersey, the state Board of Education announced that limited-English students may take the test of basic skills required for high school graduation in any of 12 languages. The board didn't explain how a student who has passed math and science tests only in Arabic, for example, can possibly use that knowledge to get a job in our English-speaking society or to qualify for college entrance.

• The U.S. Department of Education—despite its own studies showing that bilingual education fails the very children it is meant to help—continues to direct the major portion of federal funding for language-minority children into these same bilingual programs.

Millions of children are affected, and their numbers are growing much faster than the rest of the school population.

Estimates range from 1.5 million to 7.5 million—from 5 percent to 20 percent of the total enrollment. The most recent survey by the department in May 1989 reports that from 1985 to 1988, enrollment of limited-English students in kindergarten through 12th grade increased by 7.1 percent while total school enrollment nationwide declined by 1.3 percent. Five states reported that as many as 22.5 percent of all their schoolchildren are not able to use the English language well enough to benefit from regular classroom teaching in English.

The Bilingual Education Act

The Bilingual Education Act of 1968 was designed to remove language barriers to learning. Access to an equal education was the primary goal and early mastery of English was seen as the key to such access. The act mandated three years of study under a new initiative called bilingual education, which was expected to help students learn English faster, develop self-esteem and master subjects for grade-promotion and high school graduation. These presumed benefits were entirely hypothetical; there was no evidence that such results would actually occur.

Dick Hafer. Reprinted by permission of AICF, Box 525, Monterey, VA 24465.

Bilingual advocacy groups soon began to exert pressure at the state level for public schools to provide support for maintaining students' native cultures as well. In some instances, the original program title was changed to "bilingual/bicultural education." Often schools were urged to hire only teachers of the same ethnic background as the students. Instructors from the Dominican

Republic, it was argued, could not "relate" to Puerto Rican students. There were repeated efforts to amend state laws to keep students in bilingual classes beyond the three years originally mandated.

In many cases, political pressure changed what was to have been a temporary, "transitional" program into a permanent vehicle for developing students' native language and culture at the expense of English-language learning and integration into mainstream classrooms. "The most significant thing about bilingual education is not that it promotes bilingualism," says Stanford University bilingual advocate Kenji Hakuta, "but rather that it gives some measure of official public status to the political struggle of language minorities, primarily Hispanics."

The two basic premises of bilingual education are that it will make minority children equally literate in two languages while at the same time preserving their cultural identity. Neither is the case.

For two decades, federal- and state-funded bilingual education programs throughout the country have failed to prepare language-minority children for high school graduation, much less for jobs or higher education. Moreover, they have conspicuously failed to reduce the extraordinarily high dropout rate for Latino students—between 40 and 50 percent nationwide, compared with 25 percent for African-Americans and 14 percent for non-Hispanic whites, according to the National Association for Bilingual Education.

Bilingualism in Practice

As a classroom teacher of fifth- and sixth-grade Hispanic students in Springfield, Mass., I found that most of these children had not just arrived from another country but had lived on the U.S. mainland most of their lives. Yet after five or six years in bilingual classrooms, they were able neither to do math or reading at the proper grade level in Spanish nor to master the English-language skills they needed. My experience was representative of the conditions in other school districts. A study of the Boston public schools' bilingual program completed in 1986, for example, revealed that more than 500 Hispanic students who had been in bilingual classrooms since kindergarten were not able, on entering seventh grade, to take classes in English.

When students are taught in Spanish a substantial part of each day, Spanish is the language they will know well, not English. This is not surprising. Educators call it the "time on task" concept—the proven link between the amount of time spent studying anything and the degree of success in learning it.

Two multi-year research projects conducted for the Department of Education in school districts with large Hispanic populations confirm this common sense principle. In Dade County, Fla., and El Paso, Tex., language-minority students were divided into two groups: One was taught entirely in Spanish; the other received all instruction in an English-language "immersion" program. Each study showed the same result. Both student groups attained the same levels in math, science and social studies. But the immersion students were far ahead in English speaking, reading and writing skills. Furthermore, in both cases researchers found no evidence of greater self-esteem on the part of the students taught in their native language.

Alienating Immigrants

By promoting native-language instruction above all possible approaches, we have created an artificial teacher shortage. In our attempts to cope with this "shortage", we have brought into the classroom unqualified teachers operating under "emergency certification" for lack of a college degree or other professional requirements. We have gone on a mad binge of hiring teachers recruited in another country, such as Spain or Mexico, or in the Commonwealth of Puerto Rico, where New York City has opened a permanent mission to lure teachers to its schools. To these foreigners, ignorant of our country's values and traditions, we have delegated the job of leading immigrant children out of their alienage and into the family of American citizens. How better could one possibly plan for the permanent alienation of these youngsters from the mainstream than to lock them up all day with strangers? How better could one arrange to permanently implant another language and culture into the heart of America?

Gerda Bikales, *Imprimis*, October 1989.

Across the nation, classroom teachers have learned firsthand how unsuccessful bilingual programs are. But they rarely speak out for fear of being labeled "racist." Now, however, even supporters of bilingual programs are realizing that linguistically separate education of minority students for most of the school day is difficult to reconcile with our commitment to integrate schools along racial lines.

Hinders Integration

Indeed, such programs can provoke ethnic discord. As early as 1977, Alfredo Mathew Jr., a pioneer in bilingual education, warned that "while bilingualism, from a political point of view, is meant to foster the Puerto Rican/Hispanic identity and consequently encourages concentrations of Hispanics to stay together and not be integrated, one also has to be wary that it not become so insular and ingrown that it fosters a type of apartheid that will generate animosities with others, such as blacks, in the competition for scarce resources, and further alienate the Hispanic from the larger society."

Continued exclusive reliance on bilingual programs is also incompatible with another national goal—increased economic competitiveness. In the next 20 years, at least half the new workers entering the labor force will be minorities. U.S. companies depend upon well-educated workers; but many fear that the new work force will lack even basic skills. Young people are doubly at risk if they have neither the ability to communicate adequately in English nor the literacy and numeracy skills they need for good jobs. The ability of minority populations to use the language of the majority society is linked directly to their individual opportunity and thus, most basically, to social justice.

Certainly other factors besides language contribute to the failure of language-minority students, including poverty, family instability and overt discrimination. These students need more supervision and opportunity in their lives and more special help in their schooling if they are to overcome their disadvantages. They need early and intensive help not only in learning the language of the schools and society but in mastering the subject matter of math, science, history and information technology. No one argues that these students should be subjected to the old "sink or swim" policies of neglect that earlier ethnic groups experienced.

America's Diverse Culture

But neither should we confine them only to traditional bilingual education, given America's astonishing diversity of cultures. To propose that one program can successfully meet the needs of such disparate communities as Cambodians, Navajos, Vietnamese and Russians is either naive or willfully misleading. Spanish speakers alone comprise many distinct communities from more than three dozen countries in Central and South America, the Caribbean and Europe, with members in all economic and social levels. Their goals may be equally diverse.

A recently published national survey of Asian, Cuban, Mexican-American and Puerto Rican parents of limited-English students reveals their very different attitudes. Asians (whose numbers rose 70 percent during the 1980s) are the most likely to cite learning English as one of the three most important objectives of schooling and give a much lower priority to the teaching of the home language in school than the other three groups. Puerto Ricans and Mexican-Americans are more likely than

Asian or Cuban parents to want their children in native-language programs and to expect schools to teach the history and customs of their ancestors. Asian and Cuban parents tend to believe that this is the family's responsibility.

Clearly, we need to give parents and educators a range of alternatives—as well as the right to choose the most effective approaches for their communities and the power to assign public funding to support their choices.

One highly effective alternative has been promoted by Canada and Israel: second-language learning by the technique of "immersing" students in the new language as early as age 5. This method requires trained teachers and a special curriculum. Comparable "early immersion" programs in the United States are operating successfully in El Paso and Uvalde, Tex.; Arlington and Fairfax, Va.; Berkeley and San Diego, Calif.; Elizabeth, N.J., and Newton, Mass. They use new language teaching techniques that include early immersion in the English language. The aim of these programs is not primarily the strengthening of the student's native language but is instead pragmatic and double-barreled: Early and intensive English-language instruction together with strong emphasis on computation, analytical mathematics, biological and earth science, history and the study of different cultures.

Teach English

One of our most urgent social obligations of the '90s is to ensure that our language-minority children have educational opportunities equal to those of their English-speaking classmates. In addition to our fostering respect for each child's ethnic culture and language, limited-English children must be given the means and the motivation to complete a high school education and to prepare for productive work or for higher education and professions. Such motivation comes only from real achievement. That means putting aside the segregative and inadequate program of bilingual education and replacing it with a rich, content-filled education in English, the empowering language of our society.

"Making English our nation's official language
by law *will send the proper signal to newcomers
about the importance of learning English."*

Making English the Official Language Would Help Immigrants

S.I. Hayakawa

S.I. Hayakawa is a former U.S. senator from California and former president of San Francisco State University. He is the founder and honorary chairman of U.S. English, an organization that seeks to establish English as America's official language. In the following viewpoint, he argues that a single language is a vital part of what makes America a unified nation. Hayakawa states that the refusal of some immigrants to learn English retards their progress in adapting to the U.S., and advocates laws requiring all immigrants who wish to become U.S. citizens to learn English.

As you read, consider the following questions:

1. What problems does Hayakawa see with making the U.S. a bilingual nation?
2. Why does the author believe official recognition of English is necessary?
3. According to the author, why are bilingual voting ballots racist?

S.I. Hayakawa, "Bilingualism in America: English Should Be the *Only* Language." Reprinted from *USA Today* magazine, July 1989. Copyright © 1989 by the Society for the Advancement of Education. Reprinted with permission.

During the dark days of World War II, Chinese immigrants in California wore badges proclaiming their original nationality so they would not be mistaken for Japanese. In fact, these two immigrant groups long had been at odds with each other. However, as new English-speaking generations came along, the Chinese and Japanese began to communicate with one another. They found they had much in common and began to socialize. Today, they get together and form Asian-American societies.

Such are the amicable results of sharing the English language. English unites us as Americans—immigrants and native-born alike. Communicating with each other in a single, common tongue encourages trust, while reducing racial hostility and bigotry.

My appreciation of English has led me to devote my retirement years to championing it. Several years ago, I helped to establish U.S. English, a Washington, D.C.-based public interest group that seeks an amendment to the U.S. Constitution declaring English our official language, regardless of what other languages we may use unofficially.

A Unifying Force

As an immigrant to this nation, I am keenly aware of the things that bind us as Americans and unite us as a single people. Foremost among these unifying forces is the common language we share. While it is certainly true that our love of freedom and devotion to democratic principles help to unite and give us a mutual purpose, it is English, our common language, that enables us to discuss our views and allows us to maintain a well-informed electorate, the cornerstone of democratic government.

Because we are a nation of immigrants, we do not share the characteristics of race, religion, ethnicity, or native language which form the common bonds of society in other countries. However, by agreeing to learn and use a single, universally spoken language, we have been able to forge a unified people from an incredibly diverse population.

Although our 200-year history should be enough to convince any skeptic of the powerful unifying effects of a common language, some still advocate the official recognition of other languages. They argue that a knowledge of English is not part of the formula for responsible citizenship in this country.

Some contemporary political leaders, like the former mayor of Miami, Maurice Ferre, maintain that "Language is not necessary to the system. Nowhere does our Constitution say that English is our language." He also told the *Tampa Tribune* that, "Within ten years there will not be a single word of English spoken [in Miami]—English is not Miami's official language

—[and] one day residents will have to learn Spanish or leave."

The U.S. Department of Education also reported that countless speakers at a conference on bilingual education "expounded at length on the need for and eventuality of, a multilingual, multicultural United States of America with a national language policy citing English and Spanish as the two 'legal languages.' "

Problems of Bilingualism

As a former resident of California, I am completely familiar with a system that uses two official languages, and I would not advise any nation to move in such a direction unless forced to do so. While it is true that India functions with 10 official languages, I haven't heard anyone suggest that it functions particularly well because of its multilingualism. In fact, most Indians will concede that the situation is a chaotic mess which has led to countless problems in the government's efforts to manage the nation's business. Out of necessity, English still is used extensively in India as a common language.

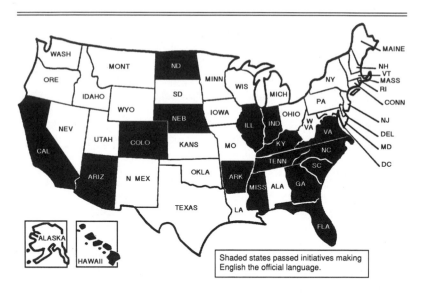

Shaded states passed initiatives making English the official language.

Human Events, January 14, 1989. Reprinted with permission.

Belgium is another clear example of the diverse effects of two officially recognized languages in the same nation. Linguistic differences between Dutch- and French-speaking citizens have resulted in chronic political instability. Consequently, in the aftermath of the most recent government collapse, legislators are working on a plan to turn over most of its powers and responsibilities to the various regions, a clear recognition of the diverse effects of linguistic separateness.

There are other problems. Bilingualism is a costly and confusing bureaucratic nightmare. The Canadian government has estimated its bilingual costs to be nearly $400,000,000 per year. It is almost certain that these expenses will increase as a result of a massive expansion of bilingual services approved by the Canadian Parliament in 1988. In the U.S., which has 10 times the population of Canada, the cost of similar bilingual services easily would be in the billions.

We first should consider how politically infeasible it is that our nation ever could recognize Spanish as a second official language without opening the floodgates for official recognition of the more than 100 languages spoken in this country. How long would it take, under such an arrangement, before the U.S. started to make India look like a model of efficiency?

Can English Survive?

Even if we can agree that multilingualism would be a mistake, some would suggest that official recognition of English is not needed. After all, our nation has existed for over 200 years without this, and English as our common language has continued to flourish.

I could agree with this sentiment had government continued to adhere to its time-honored practice of operating in English and encouraging newcomers to learn the language. However, this is not the case. Over the last few decades, government has been edging slowly towards policies that place other languages on a par with English.

In reaction to the cultural consciousness movement of the 1960's and 1970's, government has been increasingly reluctant to press immigrants to learn the English language, lest it be accused of "cultural imperialism." Rather than insisting that it is the immigrant's duty to learn the language of this country, the government has acted instead as if it has a duty to accommodate an immigrant in his native language.

Bilingual Education

A prime example of this can be found in the continuing debate over Federal and state policies relating to bilingual education. At times, these have come dangerously close to making the main goal of this program the maintenance of the immigrant child's native language, rather than the early acquisition of English.

As a former U.S. senator from California, where we spend more on bilingual education programs than any other state, I am very familiar with both the rhetoric and reality that lie behind the current debate on bilingual education. My experience has convinced me that many of these programs are shortchanging immigrant children in their quest to learn English.

To set the record straight from the start, I do not oppose bilingual education *if it is truly bilingual*. Employing a child's native language to teach him (or her) English is entirely appropriate. What is not appropriate is continuing to use the children of Hispanic and other immigrant groups as guinea pigs in an unproven program that fails to teach English efficiently and perpetuates their dependency on their native language.

The Role of English

As a nation, we must reassert our desire to retain the role of English by declaring English our official language. As a nation of immigrants, made up of people from all corners of the globe, we share no common race, religion, or ethnic background. One important bond that we do share, however, is a common language.

Our history has taught us that if government holds fast to our tradition of English as the official language of the United States, then newcomers to our nation will respond to this incentive and learn our common language. If, however, we continue to duplicate every government document, brochure, or booklet in a multitude of languages, and grant further official recognition to an immigrant's native tongue, we may be destroying the incentives necessary to bring people quickly into the mainstream of American society.

Stanley Diamond, *Chronicles*, March 1989.

Under the dominant method of bilingual education used throughout this country, non-English-speaking students are taught all academic subjects such as math, science, and history exclusively in their native language. English is taught as a separate subject. The problem with this method is that there is no objective way to measure whether a child has learned enough English to be placed in classes where academic instruction is entirely in English. As a result, some children have been kept in native language classes for six years.

Some bilingual education advocates, who are more concerned with maintaining the child's use of their native language, may not see any problem with such a situation. However, those who feel that the most important goal of this program is to get children functioning quickly in English appropriately are alarmed. . . .

If this method of bilingual education is not the answer, are we forced to return to the old, discredited, sink-or-swim approach? No, we are not, since, as shown in Berkeley and other school districts, there are a number of alternative methods that have been proven effective, while avoiding the problems of all-native-language instruction.

Sheltered English and English as a Second Language (ESL) are just two programs that have helped to get children quickly proficient in English. Yet, political recognition of the viability of alternate methods has been slow in coming. In 1988, we witnessed the first crack in the monolithic hold that native language instruction has had on bilingual education funds at the Federal level. In its reauthorization of Federal bilingual education, Congress voted to increase the percentage of funds available for alternate methods from four to 25% of the total. This is a great breakthrough, but we should not be satisfied until 100% of the funds are available for any program that effectively and quickly can get children functioning in English, regardless of the amount of native language instruction it uses.

My goal as a student of language and a former educator is to see all students succeed academically, no matter what language is spoken in their homes. I want to see immigrant students finish their high school education and be able to compete for college scholarships. To help achieve this goal, instruction in English should start as early as possible. Students should be moved into English mainstream classes in one or, at the very most, two years. They should not continue to be segregated year after year from their English-speaking peers.

Bilingual Ballots

Another highly visible shift in Federal policy that I feel demonstrates quite clearly the eroding support of government for our common language is the requirement for bilingual voting ballots. Little evidence ever has been presented to show the need for ballots in other languages. Even prominent Hispanic organizations acknowledge that more than 90% of native-born Hispanics currently are fluent in English and more than half of that population is English monolingual.

Furthermore, if the proponents of bilingual ballots are correct when they claim that the absence of native language ballots prevents non-English-speaking citizens from exercising their right to vote, then current requirements are clearly unfair because they provide assistance to certain groups of voters while ignoring others. Under current Federal law, native language ballots are required only for certain groups: those speaking Spanish, Asian, or Native American languages. European or African immigrants are not provided ballots in their native language, even in jurisdictions covered by the Voting Rights Act.

As sensitive as Americans have been to racism, especially since the days of the Civil Rights Movement, no one seems to have noticed the profound racism expressed in the amendment that created the "bilingual ballot." Brown people, like Mexicans and Puerto Ricans; red people, like American Indians; and yellow people, like the Japanese and Chinese, are assumed not to be smart enough to learn English. No provision is made, however, for non-English-speaking French-Canadians in Maine or Vermont, or Yiddish-speaking Hasidic Jews in Brooklyn, who are white and thus presumed to be able to learn English without difficulty.

Voters in San Francisco encountered ballots in Spanish and Chinese for the first time in the elections of 1980, much to their surprise, since authorizing legislation had been passed by Congress with almost no debate, roll-call vote, or public discussion. Naturalized Americans, who had taken the trouble to learn English to become citizens, were especially angry and remain so. While native language ballots may be a convenience to some voters, the use of English ballots does not deprive citizens of their right to vote. Under current voting law, non-English-speaking voters are permitted to bring a friend or family member to the polls to assist them in casting their ballots. Absentee ballots could provide another method that would allow a voter to receive this help at home.

Congress should be looking for other methods to create greater access to the ballot box for the currently small number of citizens who cannot understand an English ballot, without resorting to the expense of requiring ballots in foreign languages. We cannot continue to overlook the message we are sending to immigrants about the connection between English language ability and citizenship when we print ballots in other languages. The ballot is the primary symbol of civic duty. When we tell immigrants that they should learn English—yet offer them full voting participation in their native language—I fear our actions will speak louder than our words.

Preserving English

If we are to prevent the expansion of policies such as these, moving us further along the multilingual path, we need to make a strong statement that our political leaders will understand. We must let them know that we do not choose to reside in a "Tower of Babel." Making English our nation's official language *by law* will send the proper signal to newcomers about the importance of learning English and provide the necessary guidance to legislators to preserve our traditional policy of a common language.

"Our energies need to be directed at language policies that empower all citizens rather than punish some."

Making English the Official Language Would Hurt Immigrants

Arturo Madrid

Arturo Madrid is the founding president of the Tomas Rivera Center, an institute for policy studies on Hispanic issues. He previously was a professor and administrator at the University of Minnesota in Minneapolis. In the following viewpoint, he argues that the U.S. is not in danger of being divided by language, and that making English the official language would be unfair to immigrants. Madrid writes that the U.S. should encourage people to learn more than one language.

As you read, consider the following questions:

1. What has united the American people throughout history, according to Madrid?
2. What evidence does Madrid cite to support his belief that the U.S. is not in danger of becoming divided by language?
3. In the author's opinion, what is the real education crisis facing the U.S.?

Arturo Madrid, "Official English: A False Policy Issue," *The Annals of the American Academy of Political and Social Science,* volume 508, March 1990, pages 63-65, © 1990 by The American Academy of Political and Social Science. Reprinted by permission of Sage Publications, Inc.

Making English the official language of the United States is a false policy issue. The principal argument of its proponents, namely, that the use of languages other than English fragments American society and debilitates the nation, is spurious at best. Moreover, there is little basis to their claim that the use of English is declining and that its status is threatened. Rather than promoting the mastery and use of English, the advocates of English-only policy seek instead to impose an official language of state on the American population. Rather than encouraging civic assimilation and participation, they would limit the benefits of citizenship to English speakers.

The English-only movement taps into and is informed by deeply rooted fears: fear of persons who are different from the majority population and fear of change. Change is threatening and results in protectionist behavior. The economic change American society has been undergoing over the past two decades has resulted in the resurgence of economic protectionism. Demographic protectionism has characterized American immigration policy throughout history and became acute during the 1980s. The movement to give English official status is a manifestation of linguistic protectionism and is inseparable from the dark and exclusionary underside of demographic protectionism. Not surprisingly, it manifests xenophobic and nativist tendencies.

Examining History

There is no historical basis for the thesis that English, or language itself, holds this society together. On the contrary, the attempts to impose English on the American population have served historically to divide the nation. Language policy has been an instrument of control, used to exclude certain groups from participating fully in America's institutions as well as to deny them the rights and benefits that accrue to members of this nation. The most pernicious historical example of this was the de jure and de facto denial of English-language literacy to American Indians as well as to the population of African and Mexican origins. So-called literacy tests were used to keep non-whites from voting until the 1963 Voting Rights Act. The most outrageous current example is the absence of a national policy to teach English to non-English speakers.

Contrary to popular belief, American society never enjoyed a golden age in which we all spoke English; we never were all one linguistically. The history of the United States is one of bi- and multi-lingualism. At the time of the Declaration of Independence, for example, a significant proportion of the population spoke German. The founders of the American nation wisely chose not to single out English as the national or official

Danziger for *The Christian Science Monitor*, © 1986 by TCSPS.

language. While cognizant of the need for a common language, they did not propose that English officially displace other languages. For the most part they pursued the goals of maintaining the use of languages other than English and of enabling those who did not speak English to learn it. No mention of language choice, for instance, is made in the Declaration of Independence or in the United States Constitution. Far more important as forces to unify the nation were individual rights, freedoms, and protections; governmental and societal tolerance for cultural, linguistic, and religious diversity; democratic representation; and unfettered commerce.

How should we judge the supposed threat of societal fragmentation and linguistic anarchy? The answer lies in facts rather than perceptions. Despite the propaganda of those who promote English-only policies, English is the language of state and the common language of the U.S. population. In the absence of up-to-the-minute, comprehensive national data, all concerned parties must perforce turn to the U.S. census, which documents that 98 percent of American residents in 1980 felt they spoke English "well" or "very well." Even in California, the most culturally and linguistically heterogeneous state, 94 percent of the population spoke English. Those who did not were overwhelmingly 25 years old and over. The Department of Education estimates that less than 3 percent of America's school-age population has limited proficiency in English. English is the language of America's children, whether native-born or immigrant. According to data of the Immigration and Naturalization Service, the newest immigrants have even higher levels of education than the native population, and local, regional, and national surveys record that they give highest priority to learning English. These facts do not support the charges of social and linguistic fragmentation.

None of this is to say that the growth in the number of non-English speakers does not warrant attention. Certainly the ability to cope with the increasing complexity of contemporary society requires the entire population to have increasingly high language skills. Surprisingly, however, there is no federal legislation mandating the teaching of English to non-English speakers, much less programs or appropriations to do so. The state and local programs that do exist are oversubscribed and poorly funded. Support for federal legislation and appropriations has not been forthcoming from the English-only advocates, and in at least one instance, the English Literacy Act, they refused to support it. The proponents of English-only policy would rather raise the shibboleth of bilingual education and the supposed threat it represents to the American way of life. The debate thus focuses on the means and loses sight of its ultimate goal: literacy.

Literacy

The real policy issue facing the United States is literacy. What the United States needs and lacks is a highly literate population, a population that can cope with accelerating change in all realms of our national life. We currently have over 25 million illiterates in the United States, the overwhelming majority of whom speak only English. Not surprisingly, no national policy requires Americans to be literate. The national programs that promote literacy are, for the most part, privately—and inadequately—funded as well as voluntary in nature. There is, more-over, precious little recognition of the fact that persons who are literate in one language are more able and more likely to become literate in English than illiterates, whatever language the latter speak.

There can be such a thing as a sane national language policy. It would give primacy to literacy; it would advocate and make possible the learning of English by all citizens; it would recognize and promote the value of multilingualism. A literate and multilingual population is not an unreasonable national goal. Certainly, it is fast becoming a necessary condition for maintaining America's socioeconomic and political status internationally.

Immigrants Learn English

There is no evidence to suggest that non-English speakers, both immigrant and native-born, are refusing to learn English. A May 1988 study on language shift among Hispanics in the United States by Calvin Veltman, professor of urban studies at the University of Quebec at Montreal, states that after 15 years, some 75 percent of all Hispanic immigrants speak English on a regular daily basis. Seven out of 10 children of Hispanic parents become English speaking for all practical purposes, and their children—the third generation—have English as their mother tongue.

Martha Jimenez, *ABA Journal,* December 1, 1988.

More important, however, the U.S. population will never again be what it was at midcentury. Americans and American institutions must come to terms with the demographic changes that have taken place since then. One of the principal strengths of American society has been its tradition of struggle against discrimination, exclusivity, and xenophobia. What makes the United States so attractive to people the world over are the protections and opportunities it offers. What makes us a great nation is the power and the creativity of our demographic diversity. If the unity and strength of American society are at issue, then our energies need to be directed at language policies that empower all citizens rather than punish some. Instead of succumbing to the rhetoric of those who equate patriotism with speaking English and strength with demographic homogeneity, let us insist on the primacy of literacy, on the power of our diversity, and on the participation of all our citizens in the institutions of our society.

"Today's immigrants, like their predecessors, will become tomorrow's accepted Americans."

Third World Immigrants Are Adapting to the U.S.

National Council of La Raza

National Council of La Raza is one of the largest national Hispanic organizations. It provides policy analysis, lobbying, and public information programs on behalf of Americans of Hispanic descent. In the following viewpoint, it argues that while Americans have long held fears of immigrants refusing to become part of mainstream society, such fears are unfounded. The Council argues that today's immigrants, including those from Mexico and other Third World countries, have been successful in adapting to the U.S. and are highly patriotic. It states that fears of bilingualism and separatism are often based on racism.

As you read, consider the following questions:

1. What two themes have dominated immigration debates in the U.S., according to the Council?
2. What do the authors believe about the American melting pot?
3. Why does the Council say fears of Hispanic separatism are unfounded?

National Council of La Raza, *Beyond Ellis Island: Hispanics—Immigrants and Americans,* 1986. Excerpted with permission.

Americans have always been ambivalent about immigration, cherishing their immigrant heritage while at the same time fearing new immigration. According to sociologist Charles Keely of the Population Council:

> On the one hand, the country has historically been a place of refuge, a place of new beginnings, accepting and even recruiting new settlers to build the nation and its economy. On the other hand, the theme of protectionism has found recurrent expression in the capacity of the culture and economy to absorb newcomers, in the desire to limit labor market competition and assure minimal health standards, and even in nativism and racist theories. The history of immigration policy is a dialectic of these two themes of acceptance and protection.

These two themes have dominated immigration policy debates from the birth of the nation. With rare exceptions, however, major changes in immigration policy have resulted when protectionism is in the ascendancy. Public opinion polls dating back to the late 1800s confirm that the protectionist or restrictionist view has almost always commanded a majority of popular opinion. . . .

Fear and Mistrust

Much of the protectionism in American attitudes toward immigration is based on fear of "different" ethnic and nationality groups—people the public believes may not become "real Americans." While a part of this fear and mistrust stems from active racism and nativism, much of it is rooted in ignorance and a lack of historical perspective. The descendants of most of the feared immigrants of the nineteenth century have become the respected mainstream Americans of today. More than a century ago, Germans were a culturally distinct, and therefore a threatening, immigrant group; today, more than one-fifth of all Americans claim some German ancestry.

The process of acculturation was probably never as rapid as it appears to us in retrospect; it has usually taken several generations. However, today's mass media increase immigrant visibility and therefore may create unwarranted concerns. A century ago, the arrival of immigrants from east Europe was evident primarily in the cities where they settled. Today, the evening news makes Americans in every part of our nation aware of new Indochinese immigrants in California or Cubans in Florida. The short-term visibility of new immigrants with their distinctive language and culture can make native Americans uneasy, but over the long term, the effects of acculturation and time make these immigrants and their children and grandchildren less identifiable and more familiar. We do not notice them because they have become a part of American society.

The experience of history and the evidence of recent research both indicate that today's immigrants, like their predecessors, will become tomorrow's accepted Americans.

The Melting Pot Myth

Immigrants become a part of American society by a process of acculturation. Typically, they do not totally assimilate; they do not lose their culture entirely and become part of a homogeneous existing culture in their new country. In fact, there is no homogeneous American culture. The melting pot was always part myth; if it existed, it would probably be incredibly boring, compared to the vibrancy and variety of American society. When differing cultures come into long-term contact, changes occur in both; the dominant culture changes least, but the acculturation process requires some adaptation by everyone. What results is a changing, developing society that adopts the strengths of its varied ethnic components.

Making Americans

Migration from . . . the Third World as much as the First and Second ones replenishes our work force; absent jobs, people would not come, or would come and go home (as many do). Ours is not a declining population, like that of Europe. But unlike the Europeans, we can make Americans of the dark-skinned as much as the light-skinned people, Muslims as much as Anglicans, Hindus as much as Jews. A German professor once said to me, speaking of the Turkish immigrants in Germany, "But they can never really become Germans like us. They are not even Christian." I: "Yes, so the Jews found out too." But for us, there is nothing un-American about Muslim faith, and the Turk as much as the Italian or the Pole or the Norwegian or the Brazilian or the Mexican will in due course find a home and a welcome here. That is how it has always been. Our system—our social order—being what it is, that is how it always will be.

Jacob Neusner, *Chronicles*, July 1990.

Each major immigrant group over the past two centuries has contributed to, and enriched, American culture. The value of immigration was recognized even earlier, by the framers of our democracy. As James Madison noted during the Constitutional Convention: "That part of America which has encouraged them [immigrants] the most has advanced most rapidly in population, agriculture, and the arts."

Our pluralistic society has been identified in recent years as a salad bowl or a stew; it was more eloquently described by Horace Kallen and John Dewey as an orchestra, in which the different instruments play in harmony. From music to food to crafts, the United States is a patchwork of unique ethnic components which complement each other. Kallen and Dewey also note that the hyphen sometimes used in ethnic American designations—Mexican-American, Italian-American—connects; it need not separate.

Alexis de Tocqueville considered Americans unique in their ability to set aside their individualism when necessary for the greater good; for example, when a neighbor's barn burned down, the neighbors helped to build another. He considered Americans more able to tolerate and accept differences and less xenophobic than other peoples, attributing this to their recognition that because they were all members of different ethnic groups they themselves could be targets; he viewed this recognition as "self-interest rightly understood."

Diversity and Unity

The motto of the United States, *E pluribus unum* ("from many, one"), reflects the American confidence that diversity can strengthen unity. In spite of tremendous ethnic and racial variation—or perhaps because of it—Americans are an identifiable people not because of how they look, but because of the political values they share. To "become American" is not to lose all ethnic heritage, but adopt and share certain basic beliefs. Lawrence Fuchs, former executive director of the Select Commission on Immigration and Refugee Policy, made this point:

> The genius of the American system has been that loyalty to the United States is compatible with other ties of affection—regional, local, religious, and ethnic. The ties which bind Americans are the ideals of individual freedom and equality of opportunity, regardless of ethnicity or other social characteristics.

These beliefs have been adopted and treasured by immigrants and their children for more than 200 years, regardless of their native language or place of birth.

Fears of Today

Most Americans accept these concepts of acculturation and recognize that ours has always been a nation of immigrants. Our veneration for the Statue of Liberty reflects pride in our pluralism and our immigrant heritage. Yet many Americans also fear that today's immigrants will be different from those who have come before them, that they will not become a part of American culture.

One stated cause for concern is the relatively small number of nationality groups which currently make up most of the recent immigrant population. Recent immigrants and refugees are predominantly Hispanic (Mexican, Cuban, and Salvadoran) and Asian (Filipino, Chinese, Vietnamese, Cambodian, and Laotian). Yet historically, immigration during any single year or decade has always been dominated by just a few nationality groups. Starting in 1821, and for the next four decades, at least 35% of new immigrants to the United States were Irish. From the 1830s through the 1880s, Germans constituted at least 25% of all immigrants. Mexicans today constitute about 13 to 14% of legal immigrants and perhaps 50% of undocumented entrants; even if the largest estimates are used, Mexicans probably constitute less than 25% of total immigrants today. The actual proportion of immigrants is far lower if we exclude the large number of Mexican entrants who do not plan to stay in the United States permanently.

Commitment to the U.S.

Many people fail to see that the immigrants who come to America today, whether Asian or Hispanic, are predisposed to the American way of life. Immigrants come to America from other nations because they are dissatisfied with where they have lived. Those coming from Mexico, for example, have no inclination to go back because they have seen the fallacies and failures of other systems—economically, politically and in terms of personal freedom and upward mobility. Therefore, the commitment they are making to the United States is total.

Henry Cisneros, *New Perspectives Quarterly*, Summer 1988.

Another cause for fear has been the seemingly large number of immigrants in recent years. In fact, there are proportionately fewer foreign-born people in the United States now than during almost any earlier period in our history. Between 1860 and 1920, for example, the foreign-born never dropped below 13% of the total population. In 1980, the figure was 6.2%. In a 1908 survey of 37 U.S. cities, a U.S. Senate immigration commission found that 60 nationalities were represented in the school population and that 58% of all students had fathers born outside the United States. Even if Latin American immigration, legal and illegal, were to double for the next 60 years, Hispanics would still constitute only 18% of the population at the end of that time (they now constitute at least 7.2%). Notes Fuchs: "Only those who lack confidence in the acculturation power of American society could give a second thought to the idea that the number of foreign entries in recent years by itself constitutes a threat to American unity."

Concerns about acculturation frequently show themselves in

public worries about whether new immigrants will learn English. Too often, this translates into a fear of bilingualism. In fact, having Americans who can speak two or more languages is not a threat; even poorly educated people in many countries speak at least two languages, as do educated persons in nearly all European countries. The legitimate concern is not whether people speak their native language, but whether they learn English. Historically, immigrants have tended to learn some English but speak their native language better, and their children have typically been bilingual. Their grandchildren, however, have almost always been English-dominant, and the native language has largely disappeared by the fourth generation. A study of the French-speaking community in the United States indicates that language shifts may be occurring even more rapidly—that children of immigrants generally are English-dominant and use French only occasionally. The research also indicates that this language shift occurs more quickly in the United States than in other countries. Many experts concerned with world economic interdependence believe that such loss of language represents a serious waste of national resources, but it has been—and remains—the norm.

Hispanic Acculturation

Available information indicates that Hispanics follow the same acculturation process as other immigrants. Several studies have concluded that by the third generation, the vast majority of Hispanic-Americans are English-dominant. Surveys in San Antonio and Los Angeles found that 89% of Mexican-American citizens were bilingual or spoke only English; for those 18 to 25 years of age the figure was 94%. A study by the Rand Corporation found that 90% of the Mexican-American children of immigrants in California were proficient in English, and more than half of their children were monolingual English speakers. The study concluded that "the transition to English begins almost immediately and proceeds very rapidly."

This fact, however, is not always obvious, because there is significant new immigration; in communities with large Hispanic populations, new arrivals whose primary language is Spanish are much in evidence. As with earlier immigrant groups, the children and grandchildren of immigrants, speaking English, are far less visible. In addition, there is considerable movement between the United States and Puerto Rico and Latin America, which tends to encourage language mainte-nance. Puerto Ricans, who move freely between the island and the mainland, are educated in Spanish on the island and in English on the mainland, and many Mexican-Americans retain family ties south of the border because of the proximity of their homeland. For earlier immigrants, especially before the advent of air travel and international long-distance telephone systems, continued contact with their native country was far less likely.

Recent immigrants also face real obstacles in their quest to learn English. Only a minority of limited-English-proficient children receive special language services in school. Adult literacy programs have been severely reduced because of federal budget cuts, and almost no existing programs are geared to limited-English-proficient adults. There are far too few English as a second language programs for adult immigrants, and the result is that hundreds of thousands of new immigrants who want to learn English find it difficult to do so.

Separatist Fears

An often unspoken but very real public fear is that, rather than acculturating, Hispanic immigrants, especially Mexicans, will pursue a goal of separatism, perhaps seeking to reunite the southwestern states with Mexico. Parallels with Quebec are often drawn, but most expert observers believe that the two situations are totally dissimilar. In fact, no national Hispanic organization or leader supports such separatism, and Hispanic groups are unanimous in their advocacy of additional opportunities to learn English. People of Mexican origin do not constitute anything approaching a majority of the population in any state except New Mexico (36%), and they are increasingly dispersed. Nor do Mexican-Americans face anything approaching the religious, linguistic, political, or historical differences which separate English-speaking from French-speaking Canadians. Throughout the United States, Hispanic leaders seek increased opportunities for Hispanics to join the economic mainstream. . . .

Bilingual ballots are also sometimes attacked as preventing acculturation. In fact, available evidence indicates that one of the best ways of "Americanizing" immigrants is by helping them to participate in the political process. Bilingual ballots and assistance not only help native-born Americans who had limited educational opportunities but also encourage new citizens who are not fully English-proficient to become involved. One of the requirements of naturalization is some capacity in English, but for many older immigrants, extra help is needed at the ballot box. Such participation helps show new Americans that representative democracy is a reality, not just an ideal, in the United States.

Sometimes, other Americans express concern that Hispanics don't seem to become part of the mainstream quickly enough. This typically occurs not as a result of Hispanic preferences but because of a legacy of discrimination. Hispanics face special obstacles to acculturation, primarily because most are recognizable minorities who may encounter discrimination in housing, education, employment, and other areas of life. They must overcome the effects of limited opportunities which have kept both native-born and immigrant Hispanics concentrated in certain neighborhoods and denied them full political and economic access. Making Hispanics part of the mainstream requires eliminating discrimination and encouraging full Hispanic participation in American society.

Given such opportunities, "the behavior of the children and grandchildren of Hispanic-ethnic immigrants . . . tends to veer sharply toward middle-class norms," according to studies reported by the Select Commission on Immigration and Refugee Policy.

Proof of Americanism

Perhaps the best proof of loyalty and Americanism on the part of Hispanics can be found in the stated beliefs and actions of Hispanic-Americans. All available attitude surveys show an exceptionally high level of patriotism among Hispanic-Americans, and this is reflected in their behavior. Puerto Ricans have consistently been overrepresented as members of our Armed Forces. As Henry Ramos has noted in his history of the American G.I. Forum, a national Hispanic veterans group, Hispanics were overrepresented on military casualty lists in World War II, Korea, and Vietnam. Seventeen Mexican-Americans received the Congressional Medal of Honor for action in World War II and Korea; this represents the highest proportion of Medal winners for any identifiable ethnic group, a distinction that continued in Vietnam. During World War II, not a single Spanish-surnamed soldier was reported to have deserted or was ever charged with cowardice or treason. Like the 442nd Regional Combat Team, made up of Japanese-Americans, the predominantly Mexican-American 36th Combat Divisions of Texas distinguished themselves in World War II; the 36th had the highest casualty rate of any division. . . .

Keep the Torch Lit

More than 200 years of experience show that this nation can best meet the challenges of the twenty-first century by continuing its tradition as a nation of refuge, providing opportunities to individuals and families willing to risk the physical dangers and psychological stresses of immigration. The lessons of history tell us that the nation as a whole will benefit by keeping the torch lit, as a symbol to the world of America's unique heritage and ideals.

"There is no evidence that the European tradition can or will be transmitted to immigrants of African, Asian and Hispanic origin."

Third World Immigrants Cannot Adapt to the U.S.

Robert N. Hopkins

In the following viewpoint, Robert N. Hopkins argues that the problem of helping immigrants adapt to the U.S. is accentuated by the growing numbers of immigrants from the Third World. Hopkins argues that many of these immigrants from Asia, Africa, and Latin America come from cultures very different from American culture, and that these immigrants threaten to divide U.S. society. Hopkins is a demographer and contributing editor to *Conservative Review*, a journal of opinion published by the Council for Social and Economic Studies in Washington, D.C.

As you read, consider the following questions:

1. What ideal of American culture has guided immigration policy in the past, according to Hopkins?
2. What does the author find threatening about the present wave of immigrants?
3. Why is Hopkins pessimistic about the future of the U.S.?

Robert N. Hopkins, "Can the United States Assimilate the Wave of New Immigrants?" *Conservative Review*, April 1990. Reprinted with permission.

The problem of assimilating immigrant peoples into the United States culture and society has had a varied history, depending largely on who the immigrant peoples were and what the dominant culture of America was at that time.

When the majority population of the United States was still British by origin, the ideal of "Anglo-conformity" was the standard. This demanded, in the words of Milton M. Gordon, in his book *Assimilation in American Life: The Role of Race, Religion and National Origins*, the "renunciation of the immigrant's ancestral culture in favor of the behavior and values of the Anglo-Saxon core group."

Assimilation in the Past

Although early America had almost as many settlers of German, Dutch and French descent as of Anglo-Saxon origin, the concurrent values and ethnic similarities shared by all West, Northwest and North European immigrants ensured that collaboration and harmony was attained with little if any friction. Indeed, there was a generally widespread acceptance of the English language and of the Anglo-Saxon character of the common law legal system and Constitution of the United States.

This attitude prevailed until the closing decade of the nineteenth century, when the immigration of numbers of immigrants from southern, central and eastern European countries stimulated people to begin to think consciously about a process of assimilation which they called the "melting pot." Because the immigrants were almost all of European origin, America did partially become a melting pot, but with the essential persistence of the "Old American" culture as the basis of "Americanism."

With this change of philosophy it has become popular to assume that the future of American society involves the preservation of distinctive immigrant cultures within a broadly overriding concept of American citizenship, and with only a steadily increasing integration of the immigrants into the American economic and political scene. The possibility that the immigrants might go so far as wishing to retain their own language was, at first, seldom considered as a serious question of any significance.

While America had acquired a small immigrant community of Asians, imported mainly as laborers in the nineteenth century, these were regarded with a tolerant nature as a rather amusing and quaint anachronism. The large black community, which had been a part of the fabric of America since colonial days, and the surviving American Indian element, were both likewise generally accepted as subgroups essentially subordinate to the truly "American" population of European provenance. In short, America was still a nation, albeit one with several relatively small, accepted, but definitely subordinate minorities.

Numerous Problems

The argument that we need not worry about the assimilation of massive migrant groups ignores our actual experiences with immigration over the past decade. In fact, there have been numerous and profound problems in cities where recent large movements have settled. There has been as recent and threatening history of cultural clash and conflict, a record of widening community rifts, a new splintering of our society that results directly from large and continuing immigration—legal and illegal.

I'm not going to dwell on these incidents, but here are just a few examples: Vietnamese shrimpers have fought with Texas fishermen who accused them of overfishing. Vietnamese refugees in San Francisco have trapped squirrels in public parks for food and have encouraged their very young children to work as peddlers on the city's streets. Gangs of blacks and Hispanics have fought one another in Denver. Lawrence, Massachusetts, has been racked by firebombings, looting, and fighting between those of Hispanic and of French-Canadian descent. Many more examples could be cited from every large city and from many small towns.

Richard D. Lamm and Gary Imhoff, *The Fragmenting of America*, 1985.

The way in which America thinks it can absorb new immigrant minorities while still remaining a nation is important, since prevailing beliefs about assimilation may be more significant in determining public policy concerning immigration than the reality of assimilation. In daily life, moreover, relations between the "Old Americans" and the new Third World immigrants may be significantly affected by the ideal of assimilation which they do or do not hold in common; an ideal which may be perceived as inspiring, or threatening, depending upon the status of the individuals involved. Finally, the extent to which the "Old Americans" and the immigrants are able to identify with the nation—their implicit answer to the question whether they think of themselves and of others as being a part of "our nation"—is significantly influenced by the concept of assimilation and of national identity that they hold.

Assuming that elites do exist in a nation, and that these elites may or may not share the same views as the larger majority population, it becomes necessary also to ask whether the elite which dominates the political scene holds the same view on the question of how to absorb large immigrant minorities into the "American" culture, or indeed, whether such minorities should be absorbed at all. It is worth mentioning here that demands for "English only" in education have been attacked as "racist". This is nonsense, since a real racist would obviously prefer other stocks to remain separated by linguistic barriers, rather than risk the possibility of their children interbreeding with the original European stock.

Attempts to Restrict Immigration

During the 1920's the concept of Anglo-Saxon culture as constituting the root of American culture and of European stock as constituting the root base of the American ethnic type was still sufficiently strong among both the elite and the majority of the population of "Old Americans," to ensure a common desire to restrict immigration largely to people of European origin.

But the Anglo-Saxon cultural tradition and white America ideal has in recent decades found neither sufficient spokesmen in the governing elite and media nor sufficient grass roots support to constitute an effective mass movement. What feelings many of them had on this matter have been more recently weakened by the phenomenon of "neo-conservative" propagandists who continually portray every issue solely in economic terms, as though no other human goals or values existed. Although it could be argued that the elements of the "national" concept were still implicit in the Walter-McCarran Immigration Act of 1952, which reaffirmed the principle of quotas based on country of origin, the spirit of this ideal had died by the time John F. Kennedy, in 1963, came to publish his book, *A Nation of Immigrants*. This treatise expressed quite contrary views which were to become official policy with the Immigration Act of 1965 and all subsequent immigrant legislation—which effectively reversed the former policy of discrimination in favor of European immigrants to discrimination in favor of Third World immigrants. The official target now seems to be the reshaping of the American population into a miniature replica of the entire world.

Simply, the Kennedy viewpoint argued that America was traditionally a nation of immigrants, and that the "Old Americans" who had founded America, fought for its independence, given it its language, constitution and legal system, was no more "American" than any other immigrant group. The concept of the melting pot, with a subsidiary concession to the cultural pluralism view, has subsequently prevailed.

But the belief in the melting pot theory has come to be questioned as a result of the arrival of increasing numbers of non-European immigrants. Instead, the theory of America as a land of "cultural pluralism" has caught the official imagination—the idea of America as a multi-cultural and multi-racial microcosm of the entire world.

Since the legislation presently governing immigration gives preference not to the Northwest European countries that established the United States, but to the surplus populations of the overcrowded and teeming Third World—which are also entering the country in large numbers illegally, only to be given the legal right to remain and become American citizens after they have effected illegal entry successfully (not a difficult thing to do) and have managed to evade the law for a further period of time, again successfully. It is quite clear that it is no longer realistic to assume that this vast and growing number of immigrants, who also prove to be more prolific in child-bearing than the native white American population, are likely to comply with the cultural ideal of conformity to "Old American" ideals and institutions.

Becoming an American

It should be obvious that the process of becoming American is not an empty one. The "salad" model of American society, in which distinct ethnic and racial groups are assumed to live side by side, unaffected and unchanged by each other, is simply nonsense. People who feel "American" share some commonalities. Certainly, there are people who live in America who do not share these commonalities—and they feel like outsiders. Increasingly, the political power of more than fifteen million Hispanics is being used not to support assimilation but to advance "ethnic pride" in belonging to a different culture. The multiplication of outsiders is not a model for a viable society, and we should discourage it.

Richard D. Lamm and Gary Imhoff, *The Immigration Time Bomb*, 1985.

This has become particularly obvious in areas which have been heavily settled by Hispanics, where even the Spanish language has taken root, and political pressures by the immigrants have ensured that they receive permission to operate radio and T.V. stations dedicated to their own language and culture. Interestingly, this has sometimes caused tension amongst resident minorities, particularly the black minority, when a decision had to be made whether a new T.V. station should be allocated to the black minority or to the Hispanic minority.

Indeed, recent legislation has affirmed the right of illegal immigrants who have been permitted to stay in the U.S. under the amnesty provisions to benefit from Affirmative Action programs, which is thus unfair to the American blacks and American Indians who were originally targeted to benefit from such programs in light of past disadvantages.

Surprisingly, one aspect of the "Old American" conformity concept does linger on as a phantom "residue," much like the whiff of scent which remains in a long-emptied bottle. Although realistically it seems apparent that this is currently a politically unrealizable ideal, the notion that the new immigrants will be absorbed into the historic Anglo-Saxon culture is allowed to survive as a perennial source of solace whenever anyone dares to suggest that future immigration might challenge the national premise of *e pluribus unum*.

America's Political Heritage

This notion assures those who believe in it that, even if the "Old American" core group continues to dwindle in numbers and power to the point of becoming marginal, the political heritage of the Founding Fathers will survive. According to the most optimistic exponents of this belief, the republic will endure even if the descendants of its founders go into extinction, because it is based on an imperishable tradition going back to William Blackstone, John Locke, Magna Carta and Anglo-Saxon common law. Some even argue that these values will be better defended by Third World immigrants than by the "Old American" members of the nation which created that heritage.

This last "residue" of belief in the ability of the "Old American" institutions to survive simply because of their innate superiority would be simply an innocuous illusion were there not indications that official public policy is in fact moving in a direction directly contrary to those traditions. Today the government deliberately gives no recognition to race or ethnicity, except to advance the interests of minority ethnic and racial groups, which are thereby encouraged to maintain their own identity and to avoid being absorbed into the "Old American" tradition so readily accepted by most earlier immigrants of European origin.

But the reality is that there is no evidence that the European tradition can or will be transmitted to immigrants of African, Asian and Hispanic origin, or to any other of the millions of Third World immigrants who are now entering the country at an increasing rate.

Indeed, the social comforts of being among 'people of one's own kind,' and the political advantages of ethnic unity and ability to form pressure groups become significant forces now that the philosophy of cultural pluralism has gained broad acceptance in ruling circles.

As evidence that the new ethnic pluralism is becoming official public policy, author Gordon cites "recently introduced measures such as government-mandated affirmative action procedures in employment, education, and stipulated public programs, and court-ordered busing of school children across neighborhood district lines to effect racial integration. . . . As is widely known, the federal government has experienced difficulties implementing such measures with its present population. It is certainly not unreasonable, therefore, to expect that the present problems will only be exacerbated with the incorporation—one cannot call it assimilation—of masses of Third World immigrants."

The Melting Pot Process

There are optimists who still believe that the melting pot process will lead to the assimilation of today's immigrants into the "Old American" way of life—with all that means in respect of liberty, justice, democracy, and cultural tradition. They hope for an end result that will congeal in favor of the survival of the traditionally prized political and legal heritage of freedom and rational democracy.

Forecasting, it is to be admitted, is a hazardous enterprise, but major anomalies can be expected as the United States becomes the host country to truly massive numbers of Third World immigrants.

Asia, for example, has an enduring heritage of not simply feudalism, but of that Oriental Despotism, masterfully analyzed in Karl Wittfogel's thus named book, which has shown a capacity to overwhelm liberalizing Western tendencies. Japan, supposedly a parliamentary democracy, has given evidence—not limited to the widely-publicized statements of Prime Minister Nakasone—of being one of the most ethnocentric nations in the world. China remains a one-party state. The parliamentary democracy of India may not survive internecine warfare among the subcontinent's linguistic and religious power blocs. The future of democracy in the Philippines is very uncertain. The massacres in Cambodia are indistinguishable in enormity from the depredations of Tamerlane.

Latin America, with few exceptions, reveals a history of rotating authoritarian rule with failing democratic government, in which *el caudillo* follows *el golpe de estado*, and vice versa, in a succession without end. Mexico experienced a long period of what in effect has been corrupt one-party rule. The one notable exception to this pattern, Costa Rica, is virtually a European country, and possibly may not endure much longer. Democracy is, if anything, in even more disarray in Africa. The one African nation with any history of democratic forms, Liberia, fell to a military dictatorship several years ago which is now threatened by another military insurrection.

After even a cursory survey of the Third World, anyone can see that only a foolish ethnocentrism can account for the fond belief of many Americans that their political heritage—imperfectly received in the past by immigrants from nations having cultures closely related to that of the nation's founders—will in the future transform and overwhelm all that is alien. Such a universal constant cannot anywhere be found in the records of political history.

a critical thinking activity

Understanding Words in Context

Readers occasionally come across words which they do not recognize. And frequently, because they do not know a word or words, they will not fully understand the passage being read. Obviously, the reader can look up an unfamiliar word in a dictionary. By carefully examining the word in the context in which it is used, however, the word's meaning can often be determined. A careful reader may find clues to the meaning of the word in surrounding words, ideas, and attitudes.

Below are sentences adapted from the viewpoints in this chapter. In each excerpt one word is printed in italicized capital letters. Try to determine the meaning of each word by reading the excerpt. Under each excerpt you will find four definitions for the italicized word. Choose the one that is closest to your understanding of the word.

Finally, use a dictionary to see how well you have understood the words in context. It will be helpful to discuss with others the clues which helped you decide on each word's meaning.

1. Typically, immigrants do not entirely lose their diverse cultural attributes; they do not become part of a *HOMOGENEOUS* existing culture in their new country.

    HOMOGENEOUS means:

    a) uniform   c) yogurt
    b) varying   d) happy

2. People from southern and eastern Europe who immigrated to the U.S. at the turn of the century eventually adapted and fit into their new country. This process of *ASSIMILATION* has been more difficult for recent refugees.

    ASSIMILATION means:

    a) deportation   c) teaching
    b) blending in   d) cooking

3. Communicating with each other in a single, common language encourages trust and reduces racial hostility. Such are the *AMICABLE* results of sharing the English language.

AMICABLE means:

a) unfortunate   c) silent
b) neighborly   d) test

4. Bilingual education in its present form is education's greatest *MISNOMER*. Instead of teaching two languages, it tries to transform an immigrant speaking only his or her native tongue into an Americanized student who speaks only English.

MISNOMER means:

a) false label   c) danger
b) success   d) contribution

5. To believe that one program can successfully meet the needs of such *DISPARATE* communities as Cambodians, Navaho Indians, and Russians is naive.

DISPARATE means:

a) similar   c) intelligent
b) immigrant   d) different

6. The use of languages other than English fragments American society and *DEBILITATES* the nation.

DEBILITATES means:

a) weakens   c) helps
b) multiplies   d) teaches

7. Few countries are as open to foreign people or ideas as the U.S. One of the principal strengths of American society has been its tradition of struggle against discrimination and *XENOPHOBIA*.

XENOPHOBIA means:

a) fear of snakes   c) fear of foreign things
b) fear of distances   d) fear of failure

8. The founders of the American nation wisely chose not to make English the national language. While *COGNIZANT* of the need for a common language, they did not propose that English officially displace other languages.

COGNIZANT means:

a) ignorant   c) boasting
b) insulting   d) aware

Periodical Bibliography

The following articles have been selected to supplement the diverse views presented in this chapter.

William Broyles Jr.   "Promise of America," *U.S. News & World Report,* July 7, 1986.

Robert C. Christopher   "Refilling the Reservoir," *The World & I,* May 1989.

Howard G. Chua-Eoan   "Strangers in Paradise," *Time,* April 9, 1990.

Yolanda T. De Mola   "The Language of Power," *America,* April 22, 1989.

Stanley Diamond   "Making English Our National Language," *Chronicles,* March 1989.

James Fallows   "Viva Bilingualism," *The New Republic,* November 24, 1986.

Joshua Fischman   "A Journey of Hearts and Minds," *Psychology Today,* July 1986.

Mark R. Halton   "Legislating Assimilation: The English-Only Movement," *The Christian Century,* November 29, 1989.

William A. Henry III   "Beyond the Melting Pot," *Time,* April 9, 1990.

Leon Howell   "Speaking American," *Christianity and Crisis,* March 2, 1987.

Gary Imhoff and Gerda Bikales   "The Battle over Preserving the English Language," *USA Today,* January 1987.

Thomas Kleven   "Cultural Bias and the Issue of Bilingual Education," *Social Policy,* Summer 1988.

Andrew Lam   "Why We Eat Dogs," *Mother Jones,* July/August 1990.

Eva Pomice   "The Ties That Bind—and Enrich," *U.S. News & World Report,* April 25, 1988.

Al Santoli   "Asylum and Assimilation in America," *The World & I,* May 1989.

Walter G. Secada   "Research, Politics, and Bilingual Education," *The Annals of the American Academy of Political and Social Science,* March 1990.

Peter Skerry   "Borders and Quotas: Immigration and the Affirmative-Action State," *The Public Interest,* Summer 1989.

Abigail M. Thernstrom   "Bilingual Miseducation," *Commentary,* February 1990.

Lawrence A. Uzzell   "Bilingual Education: Immigrants Know Better," *The Wall Street Journal,* September 8, 1987.

Chronology of Immigration

1598	Spanish immigrants settle in what is now Texas and New Mexico.
1607	The first permanent English settlement is established in Jamestown, Virginia.
1619	The first shipment of African slaves arrives in Virginia.
1634	The first Jewish immigrants arrive in New Amsterdam (now New York).
1683	The first German settlers arrive in Pennsylvania.
1751	Benjamin Franklin worries about German immigrants, and writes, "This Pennsylvania will in a few years become a German colony; instead of learning our language, we must learn theirs, or live as in a foreign country."
1776	One of the reasons given in the Declaration of Independence for the colonists' secession from Great Britain is that the British king has obstructed "the laws for naturalization of foreigners, refusing to pass others to encourage their immigration hither."
1790	The first U.S. census counts 3,227,000 Americans, of which 75 percent are of British origin. Population density is 4.5 persons per square mile. Congress passes first naturalization law requiring for citizenship a two-year residence in the U.S. and the renunciation of all former allegiances.
1798	Alien and Sedition Acts give President John Adams arbitrary power to seize and expel resident aliens suspected of subversive activities. Laws expire after two years and are not renewed.
1812	The War of 1812 brings immigration to a complete halt as hostilities prevent transportation across the Atlantic.
1819	Approximately 125,000 immigrants have entered the U.S. since the Revolutionary War. Congress enacts legislation to count the number of immigrants entering the U.S.
1820-1880	The first great wave of immigration to the U.S. Over ten million immigrants arrive, with northwest Europeans predominating. Many settle in the rural Midwest.
1845-1849	The Irish potato famine causes over 1.6 million Irish to migrate to the U.S. by 1854.
1846-1848	Mexico loses two-fifths of its territory to the U.S. in the Mexican-American War. U.S. gains what are now parts of California, Arizona, New Mexico, and Texas.
1848	First immigrants from China arrive in California. In addition, upheaval in Germany brings political refugees to the U.S.
1854	The Know-Nothing movement wins sweeping victories in Congress and in state legislative elections. An

amalgam of political parties and secret societies, the Know-Nothings object to the increasing numbers of Roman Catholic immigrants from Ireland and other countries. They call for limits on immigration and a twenty-one-year period before immigrants can become voting citizens. The Know-Nothing movement ceases to be a national force by 1860.

1855	Castle Garden, a central immigration depot in New York City, opens.
1870	Japanese workers first arrive in California, joining the over 123,000 Chinese already living there. Racial tensions grow between Asians and other Californians.
1875	Supreme Court rules in *Henderson v. New York* that only Congress, not the states, has the power to make laws restricting immigration. The first federal restrictions on immigration bar prostitutes and convicts.
1880-1920	The second wave of immigration to the U.S. Over 23.5 million immigrants arrive, predominately from southern and eastern Europe. Many settle in cities and become factory workers.
1882	The Chinese Exclusion Act prohibits all Chinese immigration into the U.S. It is the first U.S. law barring immigration because of race or nationality.
1886	The Statue of Liberty is dedicated.
1891	Ellis Island in New York City becomes main reception center for immigrants from Europe. Congress creates the office of superintendent of immigration within the Treasury Department, the precursor of the present Immigration and Naturalization Service (INS).
1894	The Immigration Restriction League is founded. The private organization argues that the increasing numbers of immigrants from outside of northern Europe are a threat to the U.S. It becomes a leading advocate of restrictive immigration laws.
1897	President Grover Cleveland vetoes literacy test for immigrants, arguing that immigration restrictions are not needed.
1903	Congress passes laws to exclude polygamists and political radicals from immigrating.
1907	Immigration peaks at 1.3 million. U.S. negotiates with Japan to stop Japanese immigration. Congress establishes Dillingham Immigration Commission to study immigration; its 1911 report favors restricting immigration.
1906	Congress makes knowledge of English a requirement for citizenship.
1913	The California legislature passes laws barring Japanese immigrants from owning farmland in the state.
1914-1918	World War I interrupts mass migration to the U.S.
1917	Literacy tests as a condition of immigration are finally passed into law over President Woodrow Wilson's veto. The ban on Chinese immigrants is extended to all Asian countries.

1919	Many Americans panic, believing that the nation is threatened by a communist menace, two years after the Russian Revolution succeeds. Thousands of immigrants are seized and hundreds deported for their anarchist or communist beliefs.
1920-1950	The third wave of immigration to the U.S. Restrictive immigration laws and the Great Depression are two factors that limit the number of immigrants to 5.5 million.
1921	The first law creating broad restrictions on immigration is enacted. The highly discriminatory law severely limits the number of immigrants allowed from southern and eastern Europe, Asia, Africa, and Latin America.
1923	The Supreme Court strikes down laws passed after World War I that banned the teaching of German and its use in public meetings. The Court rules that the "protection of the Constitution extends to all, to those who speak other languages as well as to those born with English on their tongue."
1924	The Nationality Origins Law (Johnson-Reed Act) sets temporary annual quotas at 2 percent of each nationality's U.S. population as determined in the 1890 census. Its effect is to sharply limit immigration from all places outside of northern Europe.
1929	The stock market crash marks the beginning of the Great Depression. National origins quotas are set to the 1920 census and made permanent.
1929-1934	As unemployment grows during the Great Depression, people complain about Mexicans taking jobs from U.S. workers. To combat illegal immigration from Mexico, more than 400,000 persons are deported to Mexico without due process, including U.S. citizens of Mexican descent.
1939	Congress defeats a refugee bill that would have allowed twenty thousand children fleeing Nazi Germany to enter the U.S.
1941	The American port of Pearl Harbor is bombed in a surprise Japanese attack. The U.S. declares war on Japan.
1942	Japanese-Americans are held in detention camps, victims of prejudice and fears of sabotage and espionage.
1942-1964	*Bracero* program is established between Mexico and U.S. Mexico supplies *braceros*, or temporary agricultural workers, for American farms. The agreement ends in 1964 because of high U.S. unemployment. Many *braceros* stay in the U.S.
1943	The Chinese Exclusion Act is repealed.
1946	The War Brides Act provides for the admission of foreign-born wives of American servicemen.
1948	The Displaced Persons Act establishes U.S. policy of admitting war refugees and enables 400,000 refugees to enter the U.S.

1950-present	The fourth wave of immigration to the U.S. Between 1950 and 1980 immigration almost doubles from the previous thirty years to almost ten million. About half of U.S. immigrants come from the Western Hemisphere.
1952	The McCarran-Walter Immigration Bill passes over President Harry Truman's veto. It relaxes some restrictions on Asian immigration, but reaffirms the national origins quotas found in the 1924 Act.
1953	The Refugee Relief Act admits 200,000 refugees, who are not counted against national origins quotas.
1953-1955	Operation Wetback deports 2.2 million Mexicans, including unknown numbers of Hispanic U.S. citizens.
1954	Ellis Island closes because of expense and lack of use.
1965	The Immigration Act of 1965 removes the national origins quotas system. It establishes a ceiling of 270,000 immigrants per year, with no more than 20,000 from any one country. It creates a system of preferences, with highest priority given to family reunification. The law greatly increases immigration from Asian and Latin American countries.
1968	The Bilingual Education Act provides federal funding for bilingual education programs for students whose native language is not English.
1974	The Supreme Court rules in *Lau v. Nichols* that children who do not know English are entitled to special treatment to ensure equal educational opportunity. The ruling spurs the development of bilingual education programs.
1975	The end of the Vietnam War begins a flow of Asian refugees to the U.S. Over 900,000 refugees from Indochina arrive in the U.S. by 1990.
1977	Jimmy Carter is the first president to propose granting amnesty to illegal immigrants who are long-time residents of the U.S.
1978	Congress establishes an annual limit for legal immigration of 290,000 (not including refugees).
1980	Congress lowers the limit of annual U.S. immigration to 270,000. It passes the Refugee Act establishing criteria and procedures for admitting refugees.
1982	The Supreme Court in *Plyler v. Doe* rules that the Fourteenth Amendment of the U.S. Constitution grants children of illegal immigrants the right to attend public schools.
September 1985	Secretary of Education William Bennett calls bilingual education a failure. He urges funding of alternatives to bilingual programs.
July 1986	The centennial celebration of the Statue of Liberty features a celebration of American immigration. California, in a referendum vote, declares English its official language.
October 1986	After years of debate, Congress passes the Immigration Reform and Control Act (IRCA). The Act offers

amnesty to illegal immigrants who have lived in the U.S. prior to 1982, establishes criminal sanctions against employers who hire illegal immigrants, and authorizes a temporary guest worker program that admits farm workers.

May 1988	Deadline for applying for amnesty under IRCA passes. Approximately 1.8 million illegal immigrants apply for temporary resident status.
November 1988	Arizona, Colorado, and Florida voters pass ballot initiatives making English the official language of their states.
March 1989	New Mexico becomes the first state to reject an initiative declaring English its official language.
July 1989	Congress debates reforms of U.S. immigration law. Some members of Congress propose that preferences be given to skilled immigrants who lack family connections in the U.S.
February 1990	The Immigration and Naturalization Service announces that it will stop deportation proceedings against spouses and children of illegal immigrants with amnesty.
March 1990	A study by the General Accounting Office finds that employer sanctions established by the 1986 IRCA cause "widespread discrimination" against people with "a foreign appearance or accent."

Organizations to Contact

The editors have compiled the following list of organizations that are concerned with the issues debated in this book. All of them have publications or information available for interested readers. The descriptions are derived from materials provided by the organizations. This list was compiled upon the date of publication. Names and phone numbers of organizations are subject to change.

American Civil Liberties Union (ACLU)
132 W. 43rd St.
New York, NY 10036
(212) 944-9800

The ACLU is a national organization that champions the rights found in the Declaration of Independence and the U.S. Constitution. The ACLU Immigrants' Rights Project works with refugees and immigrants facing deportation, and with immigrants in the workplace. It has published reports and position papers, and the book *The Rights of Aliens and Refugees* which details what freedoms immigrants and refugees have under the U.S. Constitution.

American Friends Service Committee (AFSC)
1501 Cherry St.
Philadelphia, PA 19102
(215) 241-7000

The AFSC is a Quaker organization that believes in the dignity and worth of every person. It lobbies against what it believes to be unfair immigration laws, especially sanctions criminalizing the employment of illegal immigrants. It publishes *Friends Journal* and has published *Employer Sanctions,* a pamphlet.

The American Immigration Control Foundation (AICF)
PO Box 525
Monterey, VA 24465
(703) 468-2022

The Foundation is an independent research and educational organization that believes uncontrolled immigration is not in the interest of most Americans. It calls for an end to illegal immigration and stricter controls on legal immigration. The Foundation publishes a monthly newsletter *Border Watch,* and a series of reports and monographs including *Illegal Immigration: Job Displacement and Social Costs.*

American Immigration Institute (AII)
1625 K St. NW, Room 380
Washington, DC 20006
(202) 363-4240

The Institute is a public information organization which publishes and distributes research and analysis on immigration. It believes that immigration is good for the U.S. and opposes restrictive immigration laws. The Institute publishes a monthly newsletter, *Focus on Immigration,* as well as monographs and reports on U.S. immigration policy.

American Immigration Lawyers Association (AILA)
1000 16th St. NW, Suite 604
Washington, DC 20036
(202) 331-0046

AILA is a professional association of lawyers specializing in the field of immigration and nationality law. It publishes the *AILA Immigration Journal,* and compiles and distributes a continuously updated bibliography of government and private documents on immigration laws and regulations.

Americans for Immigration Control (AIC)
717 Second St. NE, Suite 307
Washington, DC 20002
(202) 543-3719

AIC is a lobbying organization which works for reforms that would reduce U.S. immigration. It calls for increased funding for the U.S. Border Patrol to prevent illegal immigration. It also supports sanctions against employers who hire illegal immigrants and opposes amnesty for illegal immigrants. AIC publishes *Immigration Watch,* a newsletter which appears eight times a year.

The Brookings Institution
1775 Massachusetts Ave. NW
Washington, DC 20036
(202) 797-6620

The Institution, founded in 1927, is a liberal research and education organization that publishes material on economics, government, and foreign policy. It has published analyses of immigration issues in its quarterly journal *Brookings Review* and in various books and reports.

Center for Public Policy
University of Denver
2301 S. Gaylord St.
Denver, CO 80208
(303) 871-2468

The Center is a research institute that analyzes problems facing American society. It has published books and position papers which argue that too many immigrants strain America's resources and threaten America's cultural unity. The Center advocates restrictions on immigration. Its publications include *America in Decline?* and *Brave New World of Public Policy.*

El Rescate
2675 W. Olympic Blvd.
Los Angeles, CA 90006
(213) 387-3284

El Rescate provides free legal and social services to Central American refugees. It is involved in federal litigation to uphold the constitutional rights of refugees and illegal immigrants, and compiles and distributes articles and information in this field. One paper is titled *Day Laborers and Street Vendors in Los Angeles: Survival Strategies of Immigrant Workers.*

Federation for American Immigration Reform (FAIR)
1666 Connecticut Ave. NW, Suite 400
Washington, DC 20009
(202) 328-7004

FAIR works to stop illegal immigration and to limit legal immigration. It believes the increasing influx of immigrants causes higher unemployment and taxes social services. FAIR has published many reports and position papers, including *Rethinking Immigration Policy* and *Ten Steps to Securing America's Borders.*

The Foundation for Economic Education, Inc. (FEE)
Irvington-on-Hudson, NY 10533
(914) 591-7230

The Foundation publishes information and research in support of capitalism, free trade, and limited government. It occasionally publishes articles opposing government restrictions on immigration in its monthly magazine *The Freeman*.

The Heritage Foundation
214 Massachusetts Ave. NE
Washington, DC 20002
(202) 546-4400

The Foundation is a conservative public policy research institute. It has published position papers and articles supportive of immigration in its *Backgrounder* series and in its journal *Policy Review*.

National Association for Bilingual Education (NABE)
Union Center Plaza
810 First St. NE, Third Floor
Washington, DC 20002-4205
(202) 289-8173

NABE is a professional association of educators, policymakers, parents and others interested in bilingual education. It publishes *NABE NEWS*, a newsletter with information on the latest legislative and research developments in bilingual education, and the *NABE JOURNAL*.

National Center for Immigrants' Rights (NCIR)
1636 W. Eighth St., Suite 215
Los Angeles, CA 90017
(213) 487-2531

NCIR serves as a national clearinghouse on immigration and refugee issues for church and community organizations. It acts as an advocate for the legal rights of immigrants in the U.S. NCIR publishes a directory of agencies that assist immigrants, and immigration law manuals.

National Clearinghouse on Bilingual Education (NCBE)
1118 22nd St. NW
Washington, DC 20037
(800) 321-6223

NCBE is a government-funded information service which compiles and disseminates information on the educational needs of students who have limited proficiency in the English language. It produces a bimonthly newsletter and other publications, and provides toll-free reference services.

National Coalition of Advocates for Students (NCAS)
100 Boylston St., Suite 737
Boston, MA 02116-4610
(617) 357-8507

NCAS is a national network of child advocacy organizations that work on public school issues. Through its Immigrant Student Program it works to ensure that immigrants are given sufficient and appropriate education. The Coalition has published two book-length reports: *New Voices* and *Immigrant Students: Their Legal Right of Access to Public Schools*.

National Council of La Raza (NCLR)
810 First St. NW, Suite 300
Washington, DC 20002
(202) 289-1380

NCLR is a national Hispanic organization which seeks to improve opportunities for Americans of Hispanic descent. It conducts research on many issues including immigration, and opposes restrictive immigration laws. The Council publishes and distributes much of its research, analysis and government testimony. Its publications include *Beyond Ellis Island: Hispanics—Immigrants and Americans*.

The National Network for Immigrant and Refugee Rights
310 Eighth St., Suite 307
Oakland, CA 94607
(415) 465-1984

The Network includes community, church, labor, and legal groups committed to the cause of equal rights for all immigrants. These groups work to end discrimination and unfair treatment of refugees and illegal immigrants. The Network aims to strengthen and coordinate national educational efforts among immigration advocates around the country. The Network publishes a monthly newsletter *Network News*.

Negative Population Growth, Inc. (NPG)
16 E. 42nd St., Suite 1042
New York, NY 10017
(212) 599-2020

NPG is an organization which believes world population must be reduced. It believes the U.S. is already overpopulated, and calls for the end to illegal immigration and an annual cap on legal immigration of 100,000 people. This would achieve "zero net migration" and prevent U.S. population growth, it argues. NPG publishes position papers and a monthly newsletter. A recent paper is titled *Immigration and the U.S. Energy Shortage*.

Refugee Policy Group (RPG)
1424 16th St. NW, Suite 401
Washington, DC 20036
(202) 387-3015

Refugee Policy Group is an independent center for policy analysis and research on international and domestic refugee issues. It works to improve the treatment of refugees worldwide. It publishes *RPG Review*, a monthly newsletter, as well as reports and policy papers including *Emigration, Immigration and Changing East-West Relations*.

Refugee Women in Development (RefWID)
810 First St. NE, Suite 300
Washington, DC 20002
(202) 289-1104

Refugee Women in Development is a national nonprofit organization that seeks to help refugee women achieve economic independence while maintaining their culture and identity. It has published two manuals: *Understanding Family Violence Within U.S. Refugee Communities* and *The Production and Marketing of Ethnic Handicrafts in the U.S.*

Rockford Institute
934 N. Main St.
Rockford, IL 61103-7061
(815) 964-5053

The Institute is a conservative research center that studies capitalism, religion, and liberty. It has published several articles questioning America's immigration policy in its monthly magazine *Chronicles*.

The U.S. Committee for Refugees (USCR)
1025 Vermont Ave. NW
Washington, DC 20005
(202) 347-3507

USCR is the public information program of the American Council for Nationalities Service. It was established in 1958 to inform the public about world refugee issues and to encourage the American people to help ensure protection for the world's refugees. It publishes an annual *World Refugee Survey* as well as numerous reports and issue papers on world refugees and U.S. policies.

U.S. English
818 Connecticut Ave. NW, Suite 200
Washington, DC 20006
(202) 833-0100

U.S. English is a national organization whose purpose is to promote and defend the use of English in the United States. It supports a Constitutional Amendment making English America's official language, and to ensure that all residents who do not know English have the opportunity to learn. It publishes a newsletter and a series of monographs. Titles include *A Kind of Discordant Harmony: Issues in Assimilation* and *One Nation . . . Indivisible?*

Bibliography of Books

Mary Antin — *They Who Knock at Our Gates.* Boston: Houghton Mifflin, 1914.

Frank D. Bean, Jurgen Schmandt, and Sidney Weintraub — *Mexican and Central American Population and U.S. Immigration Policy.* Austin: University of Texas Press, 1989.

Frank D. Bean, Georges Vernez, and Charles B. Keely — *Opening and Closing the Doors.* Lanham, MD: University Press of America, 1989.

William J. Bennett — *Our Children and Our Country.* New York: Simon & Schuster, 1988.

Theodore Blegen, ed. — *Land of Their Choice: The Immigrants Write Home.* Minneapolis: University of Minnesota Press, 1955.

George J. Borjas — *Friends or Strangers: The Impact of Immigration on the U.S. Economy.* New York: Basic Books, 1990.

Patrick Burns — *To Import a Poverty Class.* Washington, DC: Federation for American Immigration Reform, 1988.

David Carliner et al. — *The Rights of Aliens and Refugees,* 2d ed. Carbondale: Southern Illinois University Press, 1990.

Robert C. Christopher — *Crashing the Gates.* New York: Simon & Schuster, 1989.

Henry Steele Commager, ed. — *Immigration and American History.* Minneapolis: University of Minnesota Press, 1961.

Ted Conover — *Coyotes: A Journey Through the Secret World of America's Illegal Aliens.* New York: Vintage Books, 1987.

Wayne A. Cornelius — *Legalizing the Flow of Temporary Migrant Workers from Mexico.* La Jolla, CA: Center for U.S.-Mexican Studies, 1981.

Wayne A. Cornelius, ed. — *The Changing Role of Mexican Labor in the U.S. Economy.* La Jolla, CA: Center for U.S.-Mexican Studies, 1989.

John Crewdson — *The Tarnished Door.* New York: Times Books, 1983.

Paul R. Ehrlich and Anne H. Ehrlich — *The Population Explosion.* New York: Simon & Schuster, 1990.

Robert Ernst — *Immigrant Life in New York City, 1825-1863.* New York: King's Crown Press, 1949.

James Fallows — *More Like Us.* Boston: Houghton Mifflin, 1989.

Raul A. Fernandez — *The Mexican-American Border Region.* Notre Dame, IN: University of Notre Dame Press, 1989.

Finbarre Fitzpatrick — *The Open Door.* Philadelphia: Multilingual Matters, 1987.

Nathan Glazer, ed. — *Clamor at the Gates.* San Francisco: ICS Press, 1985.

Madison Grant — *The Passing of a Great Race.* New York: Charles Scribner's Sons, 1916.

Madison Grant and Charles Stewart Davidson, eds. — *The Alien in Our Midst.* New York: The Galto Publishing Co., 1930.

David W. Haines, ed.	*Refugees as Immigrants.* Totowa, NJ: Rowman & Littlefield Publishers, 1989.
Yamato Ichihashi	*Japanese in the United States.* Stanford, CA: Stanford University Press, 1932.
Gary Imhoff, ed.	*Learning in Two Languages.* New Brunswick, NJ: Transaction Publishers, 1990.
Shirley Jenkins, ed.	*Ethnic Associations and the Welfare State.* New York: Columbia University Press, 1988.
Leif Jensen	*The New Immigration.* Westport, CT: Greenwood Press, 1989.
John F. Kennedy	*A Nation of Immigrants.* New York: Harper & Row, 1964.
Carol Kismaric	*Forced Out: The Agony of Refugees in Our Time.* New York: Random House, 1989.
Joel Kotkin and Yoriko Kishimoto	*The Third Century: America's Resurgence in the Asian Era.* New York: Crown Books, 1988.
Stephen Krashen and Douglas Biber	*On Course: Bilingual Education's Success in California.* Sacramento: California Association for Bilingual Education, 1988.
Richard D. Lamm et al.	*Hard Choices.* Denver: The Center for Public Policy and Contemporary Issues, 1989.
Richard D. Lamm and Gary Imhoff	*The Immigration Time Bomb.* New York: E.P. Dutton, 1985.
Lester D. Langley	*Mexamerica.* New York: Crown Books, 1988.
Michael C. LeMay	*From Open Door to Dutch Door.* New York: Praeger, 1987.
Stanley Lieberson Mary C. Waters	*From Many Strands: Ethnic and Racial Groups in* and *Contemporary America.* New York: Russell Sage Foundation, 1988.
Amado M. Padilla et al., eds.	*Bilingual Education.* Newbury Park, CA: Sage Publications, 1990.
Rosalie Pedalino Porter	*Forked Tongue: The Politics of Bilingual Education.* New York: Basic Books, 1990.
Alejandro Portes and Ruben G. Rumbaut	*Immigrant America: A Portrait.* Berkeley: University of California Press, 1990.
Robert B. Reich	*Tales of a New America.* New York: Times Books, 1987.
David M. Reimers	*Still the Golden Door: The Third World Comes to America.* New York: Columbia University Press, 1985.
Peter Roberts	*The New Immigration.* New York: Macmillan, 1912.
Mike Rose	*Lives on the Boundary.* New York: The Free Press, 1989.
Julian Samora	*Los Mojados: The Wetback Story.* Notre Dame, IN: University of Notre Dame Press, 1971.
Al Santoli	*New Americans: An Oral History.* New York: Viking, 1989.
Arthur M. Schlesinger	*Paths to the Present.* New York: Macmillan, 1949.
Peter M. Schuck and Rogers M. Smith	*Citizenship Without Consent.* New Haven, CT: Yale University Press, 1985.

Maxine Seller, ed.   *Immigrant Women.* Philadelphia: Temple University Press, 1981.

Julian L. Simon   *The Economic Consequences of Immigration.* Cambridge, MA: Basil Blackwell, 1989.

Julian L. Simon   *Population Matters.* New Brunswick, NJ: Transaction Publications, 1989.

Richard Mayo Smith   *Emigration and Immigration.* New York: Charles Scribner's Sons, 1890.

Palmer Stacy and Wayne Lutton   *The Immigration Time Bomb,* rev. ed. Monterey, VA: The American Immigration Control Foundation, 1988.

Lothrop Stoddard   *The Rising Tide of Color.* New York: Charles Scribner's Sons, 1920.

Roger Waldinger et al.   *Ethnic Entrepreneurs.* Newbury Park, CA: Sage Publications, 1990.

Frank Julian Warne   *The Immigrant Invasion.* New York: Dodd, Mead, and Company, 1913.

Louis Winnick   *New People in Old Neighborhoods.* New York: Russell Sage Foundation, 1990.

Daniel Wolf   *Undocumented Aliens and Crime.* La Jolla, CA: Center for U.S.-Mexican Studies, 1988.

Norman L. Zucker and Naomi Flink Zucker   *The Guarded Gate: The Reality of American Refugee Policy.* New York: Harcourt Brace Jovanovich, 1987.

Index

Abbey, Edward, 69, 171
Acle, Luis, Jr., 125
Adams, James Truslow, 61
Africa, 70, 240
Aid to Families with Dependent
  Children, 116, 162
American Friends Service
  Committee, 192-193
American Indians, 174, 222, 239
  bilingual ballots for, 219, 220
  in schools, 203, 212
Antin, Mary, 43
Asay, Chuck, 139
Asia
  immigrants from, 235
    contributions of, 142
    in schools, 201, 202, 203
    knowledge of English, 212, 213
    restrictions on, 52, 56, 122
    statistics on, 70, 77
    political traditions in, 240
Australia, 123, 128

Bailey, W.B., 44
Bandow, Douglas, 141
Behar, Richard, 180
Bikales, Gerda, 145, 211
bilingual education. See education
  bilingual
Bilingual Education Act (1968), 209
bilingualism
  benefits of, 231
  dangers of, 216
    myth of, 224, 225
  in Canada, 71, 217
  blacks, 235, 238, 239
Block, Herb, 49
boat people, 131, 138, 139
Bock, Alan W., 176
Border Patrol. See Immigration and
  Naturalization Service
Border Watch, 94
Brookes, Warren T., 84
Bush, George, 167

California
  farm workers, 183
  illegal immigrants, 160, 161
    cost of welfare for, 162
    crimes committed by, 163-164
    improve economy, 179
    prejudices against, 98-99
  language policy, 118, 216, 224

refugees in, 144
schools
  bilingual education in, 208, 216
  immigrant population in, 200-201,
    202, 231
Camacho de Schmidt, Aurora, 188
Cambodia, 202, 212
Canada, 71
  education programs, 213
  immigration policy, 123, 128, 187
Carter, Jimmy, 91, 159
Castillo, Leonel J., 159
Center for Immigrants' Rights, 192
Central America
  1986 immigration law's effect on,
    191-192
  refugees from, 148, 168, 193
Chapman, Leonard, 158, 159
China, 94-95, 201
Chiswick, Barry R., 121
Church World Services, 142
Cisneros, Henry, 230
Colombia, 94
Commons, John R., 34
communism, 60, 118
  and refugee policy, 138, 140, 141
crime
  against immigrants, 98
  illegal immigrants cause, 90-95,
    163-164
    con, 96-99
  in ghettos, 119
Cuban immigrants
  are criminals, 91-92
  attitudes toward learning English,
    212-213
  benefits of, 142
  Mariel boatlift of, 91, 93, 162
Cuello, Jose, 167

Danziger, Jeff, 223
Davis, Garrett, 25
Diamond, Stanley, 218
drug trade, 89, 93, 94, 95, 164
Duncan, Marion Moncure, 54

education, 123
  adult, 232
  bilingual
    discourages learning English,
      210-211, 216-218
      con, 205, 206
    funding for, 219

helps immigrants, 199-206
   con, 207-213
costs of
   for illegal immigrants, 162
   for refugees, 151
immersion programs
   are successful, 211, 213
   con, 203
immigration's effect on, 111-112
of immigrant children
   as successful, 82, 128
   statistics on, 200, 209
employer sanctions
   are beneficial, 182, 187
   are harmful, 188-193
   enforcement of, 186-187, 191
   public opinion on, 185-186
English as a Second Language
   programs, 206, 219
English language
   knowledge of
   needed for democracy, 215
      con, 222-224
   needed for job success, 118, 212,
      219
   learning to speak
   difficulties in, 202-203
   immigrants are reluctant to, 210,
      211
   myth of, 225, 231-232
   programs needed in, 224-225, 232
   should be America's official
      language, 214-220
      con, 204, 221-225
   see also education, bilingual
environment
   immigration threatens, 86, 87,
      172-175
      con, 21, 82, 115-116
   improvements in, 116
Europe
   birthrates in, 43
   Eastern, 93, 138, 227, 235
   refugees from, 140-141
   persecution of Jews in, 150, 181
   political oppression in, 35-36
   population in 1800s, 26-27

Fallows, James, 74
family ties
   as criteria for admitting immigrants
   abuses of, 72, 125, 172
   reasons against, 123, 125, 147
   reasons for, 129-136
   definition of, 132-133
Federation for American
   Immigration Reform, 184, 185
Ferrone, Vito, 205

Fleming, Thomas, 66
Francis, Samuel T., 68
Franklin, Benjamin, 117
Fuchs, Lawrence, 229, 230

gangs, 93, 94, 95, 99, 236
Garner, Bill, 173
Germany
   immigrants from, 222, 227
   are taking over U.S. land, 30
   contributions of, 22, 24
   statistics on, 76, 230
   Jewish refugees from, 146, 150, 181
   population of, 27
   racial prejudice in, 228
Geyer, Georgie Anne, 163
González, Justo L., 78
Goodrich, Samuel Griswold, 21
Gordon, Milton M., 235, 240
Grant, Madison, 35
Great Britain, 84, 139-140

Hacker, Myra C., 56
Hafer, Dick, 92, 107, 209
Haiti, 70, 76, 91, 93
Hamill, Pete, 165
Hardin, Garrett, 85, 115
Hayakawa, S.I., 214
health care, 112, 116, 162, 163
Helton, Arthur C., 129
Higham, John, 75
Hill, Martin, 169
Hispanic immigrants
   are patriotic, 233
   bilingual ballots for, 219-220
   bilingual education's impact on,
      210, 211, 212
   do not learn English
   as harmful, 210, 212-213
   as threatening, 238
      con, 76-77, 169
   myth of, 225, 231-232
   participate in drug trade, 94
   prejudices against, 169-170, 230,
      232, 233
   school population of, 201, 202
   drop-out rate, 203, 210
   statistics on, 76
Historical Society of Missouri, 33
Hmong people, 202, 203
Hopkins, Robert N., 234
Human Events, 216

illegal immigration, 164, 239
   causes crime, 90-95, 163-164
      con, 96-99
   employer sanctions can reduce,
      182-187

259

con, 188-193
is a crisis, 157-164
con, 83, 165-170
provides needed labor, 167, 168-169,
179
should be legalized, 176-181
should be stopped, 171-175
is impossible, 166-167, 170
statistics on, 158, 159, 168, 169
Imhoff, Gary, 67, 70, 236, 238
immigrants
are dregs of other societies, 27, 28,
91
con, 40, 44, 179
are intelligent, 21, 23, 81, 82, 120
con, 26
are patriotic, 181, 233
assimilation of
family members help, 133-134,
135, 136
private groups help, 45
attitudes toward, 48, 83
birth rates of, 238
contributions of, 21-22, 42, 51
criteria for admitting
ability to speak English, 126, 217
family ties, 53, 122, 129-136
abuses of, 72, 125, 172
con, 123, 125, 147
humanitarian reasons, 122
work skills, 53, 72, 121-128
depress wages, 29, 32, 34, 37, 59-60
con, 42, 116-117
hate crimes against, 98-99
improve economy, 44, 75, 179
con, 34, 89
prejudices against, 169, 170
are ignorant, 40, 44, 52, 99, 222,
227
are justified, 73, 240
should be welcomed, 17-24, 46, 120,
177
con, 25-30, 35
support American institutions, 23
con, 26, 27, 57
immigration
economic effects of
as beneficial, 20-21, 44, 80-84,
179-180
as harmful, 34, 85-89, 109-110,
172-173
creates jobs, 81, 116-117
con, 88-89, 108
depletes welfare, 111, 112
con, 81
promotes inequality, 38
con, 42
from Europe, 35

is dangerous, 26, 30, 37
con, 40, 46
national origins quotas' effect on,
50
restrictions on, 36-37, 45
from Third World
must be restricted, 71-72
threatens American culture, 66-73,
174, 175, 239-240
con, 74-79, 117-118, 228
harms the environment, 86, 87,
172-175
con, 21, 82, 115-116
is a right, 18, 193
con, 59, 160
rate of, 67, 84, 131
as low, 82, 114, 117, 141, 181, 230
should be reduced to zero, 86, 89,
174
restrictions on
are needed, 31-38, 105-112
con, 39-46, 43, 79, 113-120
are racist, 83-84
from Asia, 52, 56, 122
prevent population explosion, 59
protect American culture, 56-57
threatens U.S., 37-38, 175
con, 75, 120
Immigration Act (1965), 122, 126, 237
Immigration and Nationality Act
(1952), 51, 72, 237
enactment of, 55-56
preference categories created by,
130
protects U.S. from communism, 60
Immigration and Naturalization
Service, 131, 224
Border Patrol, 93, 97, 161, 166, 189
is underfunded, 94, 158, 160, 185
statistics on illegal immigration,
158, 159, 163
are exaggerated, 83, 169
Immigration Reform and Control
Act (1986), 123, 159, 181
amnesty provision, 189
employer sanctions provision
enforcement of, 186-187, 191
improves working conditions,
183-185
con, 191, 192
is effective, 182-187
con, 188-193
India
immigration from, 70
language policy of, 216, 240
Irish immigrants, 140
contributions of, 20, 21
poverty of, 27, 178

statistics on, 230
Italian immigrants, 134

Jamaica, 70, 95
Jasper, William F., 157, 186
Jefferson, Thomas, 28, 70
Jews
  persecution of, 146, 150, 181
  Soviet, 138, 142-143
Jiminez, Martha, 225
Johnson, Albert, 37
Keely, Charles, 227
Kennedy, John F., 45, 59, 237
Kennedy, Ted, 72
Kennedy-Simpson bill, 83-84
Kotowitz, Victor, 159
Kwoh, Stewart, 133

LaFontaine, Hernan, 205
Lamm, Richard D., 67, 70, 89, 105,
  115, 147, 236, 238
Lane, Chuck, 76
language
  difficulty of learning, 202-203
  policy
    should promote English, 214-220
    should promote multilingualism,
      224-225
  see also education; English language
Laos, 202, 203
Latin America, 175
  culture of, 174, 240
  immigrants from, 77, 189
Lazarus, Emma, 52, 177
Lewis, Sinclair, 52
Lincoln, Abraham, 61
literacy, 224-225, 232
literacy tests, 222
Lutton, Wayne, 90, 109, 149, 151

Madison, James, 48, 228
Madrid, Arturo, 221
manifest destiny, 170
Margulies, 178
Martínez, Roberto, 96
Mathew, Alfredo, Jr., 211-212
Medicare, 116
melting pot, 228, 235, 237-238, 240
Mexico, 70
  border with U.S., 166-167, 170
  crime along, 97-98
  must be patrolled more heavily,
    158, 160, 161
  drug trafficking from, 93, 164
  immigrants from
    attitudes of, 230
    criminal acts of, 93, 94
    hate crimes against, 98-99

provide needed labor, 167, 168-169
stereotypes of, 169, 232
poverty in, 97, 168, 179, 192, 193
migrant workers, 99
Moore, Stephen, 117, 137
Moore v. City of East Cleveland,
  131-132
Morris, Charles R., 109-110
Murray, Allen, 184

National Coalition of Advocates for
  Students, 199
National Council of La Raza, 226
national origins quotas law, 122
  enactment of, 48, 79
  is discriminatory, 50-51, 52
    con, 58
  should be abolished, 47-53
    con, 54-61, 72
Native American National Council,
  27
Negative Population Growth Inc., 87
Neusner, Jacob, 228
New York City
  bilingual education programs in,
    208
  crime rate in, 91-93
  immigrant population in, 201-202
Nguyen-Huynh, Mai, 201
Nichols, Thomas L., 17
Nieto, Sonia, 203
nursing, 88, 123

O'Sullivan, Lumina, 203

Panunzio, Constantine, 45
Papandreas, John, 51
Pett, Joel, 98
Philippines, 201, 202
Pilgrims, 160
population, 111
  decline in U.S., 114
  growth of, 107, 172-173, 175
Porter, Rosalie Pedalino, 207
poverty, 89, 124
  immigrants worsen, 108, 112
    con, 117, 119, 179
Puerto Rico, 201, 203, 210, 211,
  212-213, 220

races, 73
  clashes between, 29, 78
  mingling of
    is beneficial, 19-20
    is harmful, 77
Reagan, Ronald, 150, 161, 189
Refugee Assistance Act (1980),
  143-144

261

refugees
  after World War II, 146, 149, 150
  boat people, 131, 138, 139
  cost of welfare for, 143-144, 151
  criteria for admission, 122, 149
  political, 140, 148, 149-150
  U.S. should accept more, 137-144
    con, 71, 145-151
Richman, Louis S., 123
Roberts, Peter, 39, 41
Rodriguez, J. Michael, 161
schools
  fail to serve immigrant children,
    204-205, 206, 213
  population in
    of immigrants, 200-201, 230
    of limited English proficient (LEP)
      students, 204-205, 209
  should mainstream minority
    children, 211, 213
  should offer bilingual programs,
    199-206
    con, 207-213, 216-218
Select Commission on Immigration
  and Refugee Policy, 134-135, 229,
  233
Simon, Julian L., 80, 116, 119, 142,
  180
Simpson-Mazzoli law, 67, 83
Simpson-Rodino Act, 168
slavery, 28, 29-30
Social Security
  immigrants contribute to, 81, 83,
    116, 180
  immigrants drain, 149, 163
Soviet Union, 138, 142-143
Stacy, Palmer, 90, 109, 149, 151
Statue of Liberty, 52, 68, 229
Stein, Daniel A., 182
sweatshops, 185

Taylor, 115
Thatcher, Margaret, 84
Third World
  immigrants from
    adapt to U.S., 226-233
      con, 234-241
    birth rates of, 238
    in schools, 202-203
    threaten American culture, 66-73,
      162-163, 174, 175
      con, 74-79, 117-118, 228
    political trends in, 240
  refugees from, 147
Tocqueville, Alexis de, 229
Trevor, John B., Jr., 58
Truman, Harry, 52

unemployment
  among refugees, 142, 143
  immigrants cause, 89, 108
    con, 81, 116-117, 179
  rate of, 87, 118
United Nations High Commissioner
  for Refugees, 130-131, 150, 151
United States
  budget deficit, 106
  Census Bureau, 82, 114
  culture of, 69, 177
    as diverse, 225, 227, 229
      con, 238
    Third World immigrants threaten,
      66-73, 174, 175, 239-240
      con, 76, 78, 117-118, 228
  Declaration of Independence, 222,
    223
  demands that U.S. accept
    immigrants, 18, 43, 51
      con, 56
  demographics, 200, 225, 230
  Department of Education, 208,
    210-211, 216, 223
  Drug Enforcement Administration,
    93
  General Accounting Office, 83-84,
    184-185, 191, 206
  illiteracy in, 224-225, 232
  industrial development of, 170
    immigrants helped, 20-21, 42, 44,
      45
      con, 34, 36
  Office of Refugee Resettlement, 143
  population of, 174
    aging of, 83
    in 1790, 160
  Universal Declaration of Human
    Rights, 130
  U.S. English, 215

Vietnam, 138, 139, 140, 142, 150,
  178, 236
Vinson, John, 175
voting ballots
  should be bilingual, 232
  should be in English only, 219-220
Voting Rights Act (1963), 222

Walter-McCarran Act. See
  Immigration and Nationality Act
  (1952)
Warne, Frank Julian, 31
Washington, George, 28, 48, 53
Wattenberg, Ben J., 82, 113
welfare, 124, 180
  harms refugees, 138-139, 142,
    143-144

immigrants deplete, 111, 112, 149,
    151, 161, 163
  con, 81, 116
Western Journal, 19
Whelpley, Samuel, 29
Wilkinson, Signe, 190
Williams, William, 37

Zinsmeister, Karl, 82, 113